AF527913

Sectarianism, Politics and Development

Sectarianism, Politics and Development

Edited by
Uday Mehta
Ram Puniyani

RAWAT PUBLICATIONS
Jaipur • New Delhi • Bangalore • Hyderabad • Guwahati

ISBN 978-81-316-0523-3

© Contributors, 2012

No part of this book may be reproduced or transmitted in any form or by any means, electronic or mechanical, including photocopying, recording or by any information storage and retrieval system, without permission in writing from the publishers.

Published by
Prem Rawat for **Rawat Publications**
Satyam Apts, Sector 3, Jawahar Nagar, Jaipur 302 004 (India)
Phone: 0141 265 1748 / 7006 Fax: 0141 265 1748
E-mail: info@rawatbooks.com
Website: www.rawatbooks.com

New Delhi Office
4858/24, Ansari Road, Daryaganj, New Delhi 110 002
Phone: 011 2326 3290

Also at *Bangalore, Hyderabad* and *Guwahati*

Typeset by Rawat Computers, Jaipur
Printed at Chaman Enterprises, New Delhi

Contents

Section IV: State of Human Rights

Contributors

Sarbani Banerjee Belur completed her Master's degree in Sociology and in Demography. Her Ph.D. in Population Studies from the University of Groningen, The Netherlands was titled "Higher Education and the Reproductive Life Course: A Cross-Cultural Study of Women in Karnataka and the Netherlands". She has worked in IGIDR, Mumbai on UN State Human Development Indicators. She has also taught sociology courses at IIT, Bombay as a guest lecturer.

Kiran Desai is an Associate Professor at Centre for Social Studies, Surat. His main areas of research interest have been working class, communal relations, informal sector, society-literature interface and urbanization. He is a member of editorial board of *Arthat,* a Gujarati journal published by Centre for Social Stuides, Surat and a co-author of *Rural Migrant Labour in Gujarat, The Pardi Annakhed Satyagraha: Adivasi Assertion for Rights* and *Child Labour in Diamond Industry.*

Lancy Lobo is a doctorate in sociology from Delhi School of Economics, Delhi. He is now the Director, Centre for Culture and Development, Vadodara. Earlier, he also served as Director, Centre for Social Studies, Surat. He has conducted extensive studies on dalits, tribals, OBCs and minorities in rural and urban Gujarat. He has authored seven books and many articles in professional and other journals. He was an International Fellow at the Woodstock Centre, Georgetown University, Washington, D.C. during 1999–2000.

Harsh Mander, eminent social worker and writer, is the founder of the campaigns such as Aman Biradari, for secularism, peace and justice; Nyayagrah, for legal justice and reconciliation for the survivors of communal violence; and Dil Se, for street children and homeless people. He is member of the National Advisory Council, and also Special Commissioner to the Supreme Court of India in the Right to Food case, and Director, Centre for Equity Studies. He worked formerly in the Indian Administrative Service in Madhya Pradesh and Chhatisgarh for almost two decades. He writes columns for dailies like *The Hindu* and *Hindustan Times*, and his books include *Unheard Voices: Stories of Forgotten Lives* and *Fear and Forgiveness: The Aftermath of Massacre* (Penguin India). He was awarded the Rajiv Gandhi National Sadbhavana Award for peace work, and the M.A. Thomas National Human Rights Award 2002.

Anand Mazgaonkar is an activist with the Paryavaran Suraksha Samiti and National Alliance of People's Movements (NAPM) in Gujarat. He started his work in a tribal village named Kantidra in Bharuch district. He is currently involved in struggles against in development-induced displacement and adivasi land rights.

Uday Mehta was Vice Principal and Head of Department of Sociology in the prestigious Mithibai College in Mumbai. He is a sociologist with broad interdisciplinary background. He received his SSA and Ph.D. from TISS and Mumbai University respectively. He has made immense contribution to the field of sociology through his various books, which include, *Agrarian Strategies in India, State Secularism and Religion: Western and Indian Experience* (edited with Asghar Ali Engineer), and *Modern Godmen in India.* He also contributed chapters in many volumes edited by eminent scholars. He is also involved in various social movements like housing rights and preservation of secular values in the country. He is currently undertaking research on the phenomenon of God men and religiosity in Indian society.

Arjun Patel is working as Associate Professor at Centre for Social Studies, Surat. His research interests are Marginal Communities, Displacement & Development. He has published four books in Gujarati: *Dali Identity, Caste in Changing Society: A Study of Koli Community* (with Kiran Desai), *Migrant Labour in Rural Gujarat,* and *National Policy Regarding Rehabilitation of the Displaced People* besides a number of Gujarati booklets and presented research papers at national and international seminars. Currently, he is working a manuscript on Dalits conflict in Gujarat.

Girish Patel is retired as Principal of Gujarat Law College, Ahmadabad. He is well known for his academic excellence and intellectual integrity. He is an eminent human rights law practitioner in Gujarat. He is deeply committed to the issues of human and democratic rights and for engaging constantly in the struggles to support the weaker sections of society.

Fr. Cedric Prakash S.J. is the Director of PRASHANT, the Jesuit Centre of Human Rights, Justice and Peace in Ahmedabad. He is the recipient of several awards, including the Kabir Puraskar by the President of India and the Knight of the Legion of Honour by the French Government, for his work in promoting communal harmony, justice and peace.

Ram Puniyani is former Professor IIT, Mumbai and has been working for promotion of plural, secular democratic values since 1992. He writes on these issues regularly, and also conducts workshops and delivers lectures on themes related to threat of fundamentalism, communalism, and terrorism. He is associated with Centre for Study of Society and Secularism, Anhad and All India Secular Forum. He has written several books, and is also the recipient of Maharashtra Foundation (Communal Harmony), 2002; Association for Communal Harmony, Star Award, 2003; Indira Gandhi National Integration Award, 2006; and National Communal Harmony Award, 2007.

Introduction

Last three decades of Indian Republic have seen the impact of globalization and a resurgence of identity politics. The social and political phenomena have been far-reaching and profound all around. The impact has been immense on the Indian society as a whole. Placed in the context of a world where globalization process saw a big upswing, India also had inner factors affecting the social changes. These global changes were in the form of a bipolar world getting transformed into a uni-polar world due to the decline of Soviet states and the unchallenged political hegemony of the United States. Parallel to this was the phenomenon of decline of United Nations and also the process of globalization becoming lopsided, being dominated by few powerful Western nations. There took place the rise of fundamentalism, very overtly in some Muslim countries, Iran, Afghanistan and Pakistan to name a few. Christian Right became more visible in some Western states. The power and leadership of United Nations started going to the backstage.

In India, this period, coincided with the rise of an affluent middle class, which on one hand was the biggest beneficiary of the economic reforms and on the other it started clinging to the politics of identity, as that had the inherent politics of putting a brake on the process of social transformation and also the complicated mechanism to give vent to the sections of the society becoming deprived due to the process of globalization and the rise of an economic system which was resulting in the deprivation of large sections and all-round rise of the small affluent sections of the society. The closure of mass production factories and consequent loss of jobs of the large sections of workers resulted in the marginalization of vast labour force. In this background, the massive changes took place in Gujarat too at social, economic and political levels. The outcome of these was to some extent the coming up of violence at regular repetitive intervals. This violence first manifested in anti-Dalit riots in the 1980, followed by anti-OBC violence in 1985 and post-Babri Masjid demolition violence in some cities of Gujarat. The peak of this violence was the post-Godhra train burning violence which took the form of a pogrom and changed the face of Gujarat for good. After this, Gujarat was transformed much farther, with the erosion of democratic norms assuming structural form and the minorities, Dalits and Adivasis started becoming marginalized more than before.

The 2002 carnage had the strongest impact on the psyche of the people of Gujarat. This carnage witnessed the new phenomenon of social engineering which revealed the social processes which had been undertaken by political forces in a very subtle manner, such as the process of cultural manipulation and co-option of section of marginalized in the political scheme of the status quo. The politics of hate operates through co-option of Dalits and Adivasis to attack the religious minorities, thus killing two birds with a single stone. It used one section of the marginalized to intimidate and suppress other section.

After the carnage, on the one hand, the minorities were relegated to secondary place in the society, no rehabilitation, no legal justice and the intensification of the process of excluding them from social, economic and political life of the state, on the other, the economic processes, lop-sided development, was given a big boost, a sort of free run to the big industrialists in the state. Gujarat did emerge as a phenomenon of sorts, where the earlier social and economic phenomena became more structured and much more accessible for the big business and more congenial for the upper section of middle classes. This drew the attention of all towards the 'phenomenon' of Gujarat. The practitioners of religion-based politics started looking up at the state as a role model of development, and religious minorities had to live in terrible situation. The big business eulogized the state leadership and the marginalized dreaded the state of affairs prevalent there. The divide between 'shining India' on one side and 'whining India' on the other, was visible in a most glaring fashion.

This forms the background of this compilation of essays contributed by social activists and scholars who have been engaging with different issues in Gujarat. This is a broad canvas, which the book covers through these contributions.

Uday Mehta in his background essay elaborates most of the factors which have contributed to the developments in Gujarat in recent times. He takes up from the historical roots of conservatism in the state. There has been an absence of radical reform movements in the state and this becomes more obvious when compared to the neighbouring Maharashtra. The Bhakti tradition remained weak and the likes of Narsi Mehta were few with limited impact on the society. Many such saints could not go far in their critiquing the hold of dominant sections in the name of religion. Later even with the introduction of industries, etc., the hold of Communist, radical labour movement was insignificant; the arena was dominated by the industrialists. Instead of trade unions we see the Majoor-Mahjan, a collaborative endeavour of owners and workers. In such organizations, the conservatism is the norm. In agriculture, there has been no radical programme. In the absence of radical, progressive ideological milieu, the conservative RSS ideology had an easy spread in the state. The political alliance of KHAM (Kshatriya, Harijan, Adivasi and Muslim) could not become a deeper alliance at social level so it could not last the reaction from upper castes, who imposed their politics soon enough. The caste equations shifted in favour of the social bonding of Patidar, Bania and Brahmin. In this background, the anti-Muslim propaganda flourished, and the series of Rath Yatras and the politics around issues such as Ram Temple consolidated the upper caste-class political alliance, which is at the root of the communal politics leading to communal violence. The massive land acquisitions and displacements led to a distorted urbanization and large sections of deprived thronging to cities in abominable conditions. The civic space came to be dominated by the conservative mindset full of hate for the minorities. This scenario was strengthened by the role of God men and modern Gurus who have been spreading the message of status quo and moving back to feudal social relations in the garb of 'our traditions and religion'. Ahmedabad city had its own contribution to the issue. It has been segregated along class/caste lines since ages. This came to be polarized round religion in later times and more so after the carnage of 2002. The role of print and visual media further ensured the shrinking of liberal space in the society.

In 'Hindutva and Human Rights: A Case of Gujarat', Ram Puniyani gives a brief background of the Ram Temple movement and the bloodbath following that. Communal politics, which resurfaced in the decade of 1980, had deeper roots in the British period of Indian history. British pursued the policy of divide and rule, and declining sections of the society, landlords, king, etc., resorted to the politics in the name of religion, Muslim and Hindu both, to preserves their privileges. The word 'Hindutva' was coined for the politics of elite sections of Hindus and it draws from identity of a section of Hindus. The communal politics gets expressed in the form of violence, which further polarizes the society. The Gujarat carnage was unleashed on the pretext of Godhra train burning imputed on Muslims. This theory was totally debunked by the Bannerjee Commission. The Citizens Tribunal which investigated Gujarat violence pointed out that there was state complicity in the carnage. And later, the state totally shirked away from its responsibility of rehabilitation, and giving justice to the victims of the violence. The overall situation has been created in Gujarat where minorities have to live in the state of fear and deprivation. They have been relegated to the status of second-class citizens.

Anand Mazgaonkar takes a stock of the ecological impact of crass industrialization of the state. In his essay, 'Gujarat: Screaming Fiction and Mute Facts' he points out that the reckless industrialization is resulting in severe damage to the environment in the state. The hype of industries is very glaring and far from the reality. The industrialization is being made easy to give the facilities to the industrialists to the extent that the interests of employment and state exchequer are being compromised for the profits of the big businessmen. The pollution of industries is causing a heavy damage to the coastline and marine life and drop in the fish catch. The creation of hazardous waste is huge and its disposal is not as per the norms of industrial safety. The creation of jobs is not anywhere in the priority line and there is rising unemployment in the state. At the same time, a clever state propaganda is creating an illusion about the industrialization, which is not fully true.

'Land Acquisition and Displacement in Gujarat, 1974–2004' by Lancy Lobo is the study of displacement from rural areas due to the industrialization going on without a holistic consideration of social factors. Most of the displaced people are tribal. The displacements have been due to water resource management, roads and industrialization. Those uprooted are not compensated and are left to fend for themselves. The land acquisition acts have been very unfair to the small landowners. The displacement is related to poverty and similar factors. It causes joblessness, homelessness, deprivations, marginalization and social fragmentation. These are the factors which lead to great social unrest. Lobo gives a graphic account of the struggles of the people to save their lands as a protracted response to the oppressive nature of state policies, and observes very aptly that women, Dalits and Adivasis are the major victims of displacement process.

Kiran Desai in 'A Kaleidoscopic Panorama of Agrarian Struggles in Gujarat' gives a comprehensive overview of the struggles around agrarian issues. He points out that there are diverse types of struggles in this area, such as those against British planters, landlords, forest bureaucracy and moneylenders. The major struggles have been related to land alienation and land reforms. In most cases of these revolts, land revenue, tenants' rights and their exploitation had remained the main issues for discontent. After the formation of Gujarat state, there was weak implementation of tenancy laws as rich upper castes were in the control of social scenario and in ruling Congress party. Later, the net result of encroachment of the law as well as forest department on the livelihood of the Adivasis and on their land is that they are left with small uneconomic landholdings which are not sufficient for subsistence of majority of them, who are then forced to migrate out as migrant labourers in semi-bonded conditions as cane harvesters and informal labourers in other rural and urban sectors. Mostly, the struggles did have an effect of betterment on the condition of peasants. In Gujarat, the major land struggles have been around the rights of tribals. Desai outlines the details of these struggles and concludes with outlining the impact of these on the social scenario of the state.

Arjun Patel in his 'Dalit Movements in Gujarat: From Imitation to Transformation' points out that there is a feeling around that there is no Dalit movement in Gujarat. This is contrary to the truth as the literature of Dalit movements has not been translated into English and other languages. Dalits have launched various movements all through against untouchability and other types of discrimination against them. There also have been movements for Sanskritization among some Dalit communities; still there is absence of full-fledged, comprehensive studies on the Dalit movements. Patel's article describes various facets of Dalit movements, and deals with them elaborately. He gives a graphic account of the sequence of different movements, impact of Ambedkar's initiatives and impact of Gandhi. Conversion to Buddhism was also one of the mechanisms to escape the oppression in Hindu fold. Similarly, Dalit Panther literature has also played an important role in the enhancement of Dalit movement. On the other side, there are counter-movements such as Swadhyay and Swaminarayan sect, which try to co-opt Dalits into the hegemonic fold of upper caste norms. Dalit literature is the expression of the anguish of Dalits and their longing for change. Phule-Ambedkar ideas had a great impact on the Dalit movement as such.

In 'Hindutva's Foot Soldiers: Dalits, Adivasis', Ram Puniyani points out that the carnage of 2002 was conducted through Dalits and Adivasis. The Hindutva movement, after the anti-Dalit riots of 1980 and anti-OBC violence of 1985, changed its strategy and started co-opting the Dalits/Adivasis in a bigger way. Their propaganda technique presented the Muslims and Christians as being outsiders, who are exploiting and harassing the Hindus. Along with this propagation there was also the use of religiosity to co-opt the Dalits and Adivasis. In the absence of strong Dalit movement, the Hindutva ideology occupied the space and made inroads among these sections of the society. So, during the carnage, the leadership was in the hands of Hindutva followers, while the execution was achieved through these deprived sections of the society. They were also mobilized for Kar Seva during the Babri demolition. The RSS had already worked on creating a rift between 'Hindu Adivasis' and 'Christian Adivasis', which was used to target the Christians later. The heavy propaganda against the minorities aided in targeting Muslims during the carnage.

Sarbani Banerjee Belur, in her article, 'Communal Violence and the Women in the Context of Gujarat' points out that communal politics also concerns with the patriarchal powers. It has always played a major role in determining the rights and limits of women's universe. In Gujarat, violence against women and their sexuality was treated as the symbol of culture, honour of the community and nation, as usually happens in communal violence. In Gujarat it was particularly noted that there is a dark sexual obsession about the allegedly ultra-virile Muslim male bodies and over-fertile Muslim female ones. In cases of communal violence, mass use of rape is the most widely used form of sexual violence inflicted upon women. In Gujarat, in particular, different forms of violation on female body were inflicted on the hapless Muslim women. The author points out the ghettoization resulting from communal violence restricts the lives of women. This further brings to surface the impact of such violence as a trauma to the psyche of surviving women, those living in ghettoes. The chapter also highlights the proposed communal violence bill and its focus on violence against women.

In 'Gujarat Minorities: A Struggle for Justice', Fr. Cedric Prakash outlines the steps taken by human rights/minority rights groups for getting justice to the minorities. The author recalls the work and conclusions of People's Tribunal. In its findings and recommendations, the tribunal set up by Citizens for Justice and Peace clearly indicts the Government of Gujarat and holds it responsible for the unfettered violence, murder, arson and looting that took place in Gujarat that year. This violence (though not an 'action-reaction' syndrome) was undertaken on the pretext of the burning of the S6 compartment of the Sabarmati Express at Godhra in eastern Gujarat, and resulted in the death of 59 people. The whole Muslim community was targeted and subjected to abominable violence in the aftermath of this train burning. This chapter discusses different facets of Gujarat carnage, the violence, the post-violence ghettoization, the manipulation of judiciary, the manipulation of educational institutions and the Freedom of Religions Act among other issues.

Harsh Mander in 'Some Paths to Forgiveness: Religious Conflict and Shared Living in India' focuses more on post-violence situation related to rebuilding the trust among communities. As gujarat has been witnessing violence on regular basis, due to such tragic and hopeless situation of recurrence of the trauma of loss and suffering in violent communal upheavals, no enduring peaceful future can be built easily. The ideas of forgiveness and reconciliation that this essay explores are a response to the sporadic but repeated hostilities and this perceived certainty of recurrence. The imperative of reconciliation after conflict is that in its absence, hate is retained and nurtured, with stereotypes, myths, selective memory and lies about the demonized 'other', and passed on as a dubious legacy from generation to generation. Mander makes a pertinent conclusion that, "it is only when the crimes of the past are acknowledged, and atonement made with public expressions of genuine remorse, when the state, the perpetrator and survivor all join hands to rebuild broken lives, and when justice is done and seen to have been done, is it possible for those who suffer to forgive, to heal, to trust and possibly to even love again".

Girish Patel, in his long essay, 'Hinduized Globalization and Human Rights in Gujarat', takes a broad sweep at the processes which have resulted in the events which took place in Gujarat. He sees the phenomenon in Gujarat as an outcome of globalization and Hindutvization. According to him, Gujarat is one of the advanced states where poor and backward abound. He gives a detailed trajectory of the process of development and the social movements which took place in Gujarat. He also outlines the different mechanisms adopted by Hindutva movement to infiltrate into the state, and the consequent and parallel violation of human rights. He opines that the constitutional institutions and human rights have suffered big erosion, leaving behind only a skeleton. Patel points out that Narendra Modi uses the entire government machinery and public money to project one side of Gujarat as number one state in India, the model of development for the entire nation, pushing back more than 60 per cent of the population of the state as invisible and voiceless humanity. He feels the need to bring forth the real truth of vibrant Gujarat, the other Gujarat; the real Gujarat hidden behind the glitz and glamour of globalization.

Thus, the themes taken up in the volume cover the entire gamut of issues and will be a valuable resource to the scholars and activists grappling to understand and engage with the issues in Gujarat. It also gives a linear understanding of the stages through which Gujarat has landed up in the present impasse.

Section I
Backdrop

[illegible] of [illegible] at [illegible] the proposed project is likely to [illegible] the lives of some 50,000 people in the region. As the local Member of Legislature (MLA), Mr Kanubhai Kalsaria, who is from the ruling BJP and who is leading the agitation against the proposed plant, informed the *Indian Express* (February 21, 2010), the acquired land also includes a water body spread over 100 hectares and two dams are coming up in the area which would provide irrigation facilities to the lakh of fertile land. Obviously, people of this sub-region have been protesting over this project for quite some time which has [illegible]

[illegible] attacked by a gang of ruffians and security personnel of the company and both were [illegible] the ruling party's MLA attending Gujarat Vidhansabha and raised the issue.

To conclude, the nature and issues pertaining to agrarian problems have changed over a period of time and the characteristics of the response of the affected peasants to them, hence, would also require careful observation. With reference to post-independent India, of the five major prototypes of agrarian struggles that David Hardiman has typified, mainly two: struggle against the landlords and against the state and its agencies, mainly forest department, have largely been witnessed in the post-independent era, if the case of Gujarat is taken into consideration. In most of the cases, the struggle contains three actors: peasants waging battle for their land-related rights against alliance of the state and the capital that may be in the form of landlords (as in most cases) or as seen in recent times in the form of large industrial groups. However, each case needs to be examined carefully with regard to the

1 Gujarat
Historical Backdrop and a Brief Appraisal of the Recent Trends in Gujarat Polity and Society

Uday Mehta

There is no dearth of studies that seek to explain why and how the Sangh Parivar could succeed in making deep inroads in the social, cultural, administrative, judicial, economic and political set-up in Gujarat, extending its influence from urban to rural and tribal areas, and in provoking a series of violent anti-Dalit/OBC, especially anti-minorities, disturbances culminating in the ghastly post-Godhra genocide in 2002. The present chapter is an attempt to briefly analyse the emerging trends in Gujarat's society and polity in regional and national perspectives. For the purpose of understanding the recent socio-political and economic scenario, it is imperative to keep in view the historical backdrop of Gujarat society.

Gujarat has witnessed a reformist, revivalist trend in social, cultural and religious spheres of civic society right from the medieval period. Along with the liberal, humanist trend represented by Narsingh Mehta, Akho and Dalpatram, we find the revivalist current manifested among Dayaram, Govardhanram Tripathy and others. Narmad, who advocated social reform in casteist Gujarat society, succumbed to the pressure of the dominant conservative upper-caste lobby and retracted from his earlier position.

Contrast with Maharashtra

In sharp contrast to Gujarat, Maharashtra, for instance, witnessed a radically different situation right from the medieval period. During the medieval period, Maharashtra saw the emergence of several eminent saints such as Tukaram, Eknath and others who came from lower castes, but exercised profound influence in the religious and social spheres. The Varakari sect, which still has a strong presence in the Maharashtrian society, is the outcome of the impact of the teachings of these medieval saints, especially Tukaram. Apart from this, Sufi saints also exercised significant influence in medieval Maharashtra and one could notice their influence even on Hindu saints such as Eknath and others. As a matter of fact, unlike Gujarat, Maharashtra witnessed a combined impact of Sufi saints and Bhakti traditions in promoting communal harmony and liberal ethos in the society.

OBC and Dalit movements also played significant roles in contesting the hold of the upper castes in Maharashtra during the 19th century. Maharashtra has a rich tradition of the Dalit along with Muslim Marathi writers. There were also a number of progressive and radical literary figures of great eminence who dominated the Marathi literary scene during the freedom struggle. The state also has a history of a powerful working class movement and heroic leadership subscribing to communist and socialist ideology. Maharashtra also experienced powerful Dalit and OBC movements as initiated and led by pioneers such as Dr Ambedkar and Jotiba Phule. Dr Ambedkar's sound and scholarly critique of Hinduism is so refreshing even now and he strived till the end to offer strong ideological, cultural and social resistance to the dominance of Hinduism in the Indian society. Similarly, Phule's exposure of Brahmin philosophy, its upper caste and anti-women bias even in modern context, sound so appealing and quite inspiring to young as well as all radical sections of the Indian society.

Similarly, the strong influence of the radical currents in freedom struggle and even in post-independence period cannot be overstressed. Communist current became evident even in 1920s and Communist Party had a significant influence in trade union and peasant struggle since early period. Socialist influence within the Indian National Congress became quite evident in the 30s. Apart from communist and socialist presence, there were also other small but militant independent radical parties and groups in Maharashtra that remained strong for a long time in its politics. Even within Congress, radical influence was quite evident as some of its old veteran leaders were influenced by Royist ideology.

Dalit Movement in Gujarat

Unfortunately, Gujarat has no history of any powerful OBC or Dalit movement though Dalit Panther movement emerged in response to the Dalit Panthers in Maharashtra. But, as compared to Maharashtra, the movement differed both in terms of emphasis and interpretations. In Gujarat, the speared of the movement is very restricted though it was not split up in different fractions like in Maharashtra. Further, the dominant Mahar caste which spearheaded the movement in Maharashtra has a martial tradition and because of that it remained more militant and acquired more power and much greater recognition. In Gujarat, there is no such caste which can compare itself with the Mahars, hence its leadership was not as effective as in Maharashtra. Most of the members of the movement in Gujarat were young and also government servants. The Panthers in the movement Gujarat subscribed to the philosophy of non-violence. The Gujarat Dalit Panthers also extended support to Congress (I). Expressing their differences with the communists, the Panther leaders maintain that they do not believe in class war but in varna war.

Since the leaders of the Dalit Panthers are mainly from Ahmedabad, the articles in their magazine 'Panther' also reflect their disagreement with the working of various institutions and organizations of Ahmedabad. One such organization used to be the Textile Labour Association (TLA), a labour organization started by Ansuyaben Sarabhai, with the active involvement of Gandhiji. The TLA has now become defunct with the rapid decline of textile industry in the city in the 80s. But earlier it used to be a very powerful and recognized organization of the textile workers in Ahmedabad. The Panther leaders always strongly felt that TLA was one more agency of exploitation as it worked in collaboration with the mill owners. Moreover, the TLA, according to them, has helped perpetuate caste differences in the mills. Another organization against which the Panthers have directed their criticism is the Gandhi Ashram. Panthers have 'exposed' the malpractices and malfunctioning of the Ashram by its organizers.

The Panthers attribute their lack of effective organization in Gujarat to not only the relatively greater influence of Gandhiji in Gujarat than in Maharashtra, but also to the less consciousness among the Gujarati-educated youth, their economic dependence on the higher castes and their inability to suffer further deprivations. On the other hand, the Panthers have many of its members as government servants and as such they cannot openly participate in the movements. There is no systematic effort to collect funds with the result that the movement depends on occasional donations from its active members and sympathizers.

Besides, the Panthers also call their movement non-political, but a movement which aims at increasing their members' participation in the power structure cannot for long remain non-political.

With regard to tribals, although they form a sizeable section of the Gujarat population, there is hardly any evidence of their independent, radical organization or struggle during pre- or post-independence period. Gandhian influence had been very strong and in south Gujarat especially Gandhian leaders, such as Jugatram Dave and subsequently Zinabhai Darji, eminent Congress (I) peasant leader, had acquired powerful hold over tribals. Attempts were also made to effectively involve tribals in satyagraha and anti-British struggle on the basis of programme of non-payment of tax to the British government which essentially served the cause of prosperous peasant proprietors. Similarly, ashrams and residential schools initiated by Thakkarbapa under the Gandhian influence succeeded in making deep inroads in tribal areas. The value system they projected was essentially based on upper caste, Brahminic culture. Like Dalit, Gandhian influence proved an effective deterrent in mobilizing tribals on their issues and also in the emergence of independent effective leadership. In the 80s and 90s, attempts were made by some radical section of some splintered Maoist groups to organize tribals, especially in south Gujarat, but in the absence of effective strategy and local support could not make any headway. The Communist Party of India – Marxist (CPM) had small tribal pockets in some areas in Gujarat – Broach district. But, instead of retaining or extending their hold over these pockets, their influence has diminished over last three-four decades.

Other Backward Classes: Uneven Spread

Though OBCs constitute as much as 40 per cent of the Gujarat's population, they are fragmented into clusters of castes and sub-castes which are highly heterogeneous, having no link with each other. The freedom movement hardly made any impact on them. As an overwhelming majority of these communities were small and backward, also recruited from erstwhile nomadic tribes, there was little scope for any political or social movement. Some of the traditional occupations of OBCs could able to transform into modern occupations in a new bourgeois society, such as tailors, cobblers, barbers, carpenters, etc., while others lost their significance. In the absence of any effective organization, some of the sections among OBCs such as lower Rajputs, their rank as such being so low, work as agricultural labour or have very small holdings or if they have bigger holdings, they are usually located in such dry and unproductive regions as Panchmahals. Though this lower category forms over 24 per cent of the Gujarat's population, it has hardly any effective voice in the Gujarat society and polity. They have been mobilized in the past by upper caste rich Rajputs who otherwise hardly form just 1 per cent of the population. This upper caste prosperous Rajputs formed their caste organization as Gujarat Rajput Sabha and mobilized this lower category also in order to make effective representation of their claim in the Gujarat electoral politics. By using this lower category as their vote bank, they succeeded to a considerable extent in getting representation first in Congress, subsequently also in Swatantra Party and in turn in BJP. Thus, some sections of OBCs have been manipulated by their upper caste leaders for subserving their political and economic interests. Likewise, Kolis who form lower rung of Patidar Patel were utilized by prosperous section of Patidars, also known as Leava Patidars, for their vested interests. Thus, some sections of OBCs were exploited by their upper caste counterparts for their narrow interests. Obliviously, such factors succeeded in preventing the growth of any organized OBC movement in Gujarat as was the case in South India in the early 20s and 30s under the effective leadership of Periyar and Justice Party, that he founded in the 20s. In North India also, OBCs, as Yadavas, Kurmis and others with their sizeable strength could built up a strong, militant organization and make deep dent in the polity and society in North India.

Similarly, even in labour movement, Gandhi's approach to industrial relations deserves serious consideration. Ahmedabad actually became a model of his philosophy of labour-employer relation based on the principles of class harmony and class reconciliation in place of the Marxist perspective of class conflict and class struggle. Gandhi's concept of trusteeship implies submission of labour, and under the INTUC leadership labour became a docile force. The same approach was extended to agricultural and sugarcane workers in south Gujarat where most of those recruited from the tribal areas were exploited as bonded labour, known as 'Hali', for decades.

Similarly, the peasant movement during the pre-independence period was dominated by rich Patidar farmers under the leadership of Vallabhbhai Patel. It never adopted any radical programme promoting the demands of agricultural labour and poor kisans, and always stood for peaceful agitation. Thus, the Gandhian influence on trade unions, kisans and Adivasis curbed the growth of any radical organization or militant struggles in Gujarat.

Limitations of Left Movement

Under the circumstances, it is not surprising to find that the left movement has remained very weak, barring socialists who emerged as a small challenge to the Congress leadership, especially in Saurashtra, where they developed strong influence in some towns such as Mahuva and Savarkundla. But this proved to be a short-lived phenomenon. With the merger of the Socialist Party under the Ashok Mehta's leadership in the Congress, this influence also withered away. Communists never posed any serious threat to the Congress or the BJP. In the entire electoral history of Gujarat, Communist Party could only twice win assembly seats in the 60s.

In the absence of any politico-socio-economic radical movement, as Girish Patel aptly argues, creating almost a political ideological vacuum, the Hindutva forces under the leadership of the BJP, VHP and RSS found on open field for their unhindered propaganda and indoctrination, and did succeed in penetrating these communities substantially. Instead of Marx, Ram became a rallying point.[1]

These peculiar features of the social history of Gujarat obstructed the growth of the left, progressive or radical movement of the oppressed in the state. As against this peculiar background, there were other factors which facilitated the growth of the Sangh Parivar in Gujarat. We shall briefly narrate some of these features which helped in promoting its hold over the state and civic society. Gandhiji's upholding of Varnashramdharma and the caste structure promoted the influence of Hinduism, which indirectly helped the Sangh Parivar in promoting advocacy of its concepts of the Hindutva and the Hindu Rashtra. Apart from this, the extensive influence of both Jainism and the Swaminarayana sect among Patidars and NRIs, with their fad for vegetarianism and anti-Muslim bias, respectively, have proved fruitful in extending the hold of the Sangh Parivar in the Gujarat society.

Even in the political sphere, the conservative, rightist leadership dominated the Congress since its inception. Sardar Patel, Morarjee Desai and their disciples had decisive voice in shaping the policy and programmes of the party since its formation in the state. Not surprisingly, the first major challenge to the Congress came from the further right, reactionary feudal and pro-industrial lobby for free enterprise and against the state intervention in economy. The political formation, designated as the Swatantra Party, posed a serious challenge to the Congress. In the 1960s and in the 1962 and 1967 elections, the party came quite close to capturing power in the state assembly. Some of the important leaders of this party who came from princely Rajput families and the Patidar caste switched their support to the BJP and were instrumental in consolidating the hold of the Sangh Parivar in Gujarat.

KHAM Policy

Keeping in view the existing socio-economic structure of Gujarat, Madhav Singh Solanki, then Chief Minister of the Congress (I) in the 80s, extended the KHAM policy, consisting of the alliance of Kshatriyas, Harijans, Adivasis and Muslims, together constituting around two-third of Gujarat's population. This advocacy could prove effective for some time, but as Girishbhai Patel rightly points out, as it remained merely an expedient combination of four castes or communities without any broad ideological framework, it would be fragile, opportunistic, ad hoc and would not transcend caste or religious loyalties. The alliance was a double-edged sword – it could lead to a radical movement or it might entrench caste and community loyalties and identities. As a matter of fact, exclusion of higher castes/classes from political power and threat to their hegemony alienated them and forced them to fight back. This actually happened after 1980. This first SC/ST anti-reservation agitation by the higher intermediate castes – Patels, Brahmins, Baniyas – against the reservation policy for admission to institutions of higher education and in promotion, erupted violently and resulted in open riots between the two. This prevented, to some extent, the upward mobility of Dalits and Adivasis belonging to better economic strata, and forced them to go back to their poor brethren. When an attempt was made for increasing reservation of OBCs from 10 per cent to 27 per cent, it led to the second anti-reservation agitation in 1983 and 1985 wherein more than 39 per cent of OBCs were brought into conflict with the privileged classes. The agitation was so violent and the hostility (between higher castes, OBCs and Dalits) so intense, coupled with strong vested interests of the builders lobby dominated by Patels and led by ex-Chief Minister Chimanbhai Patel and the BJP, that Rajiv Gandhi with his elitist background opted for appeasement of the dominant sections of Hindu, particularly the middle class. He advised Solanki to resign as Chief Minister and installed Amar Singh Chaudhari, the Adivasi leader, instead. The KHAM experiment was over, leaving behind only dangerous caste conflict and bitterness. The Congress (I) lost its moorings. Chimanbhai with his Janata Party/KMPP represented some sections of Patels and builders, while the BJP, being roped in, spread its nets, particularly among Dalits, OBCs and subsequently Adivasis – the politically rootless communities which can easily fall prey to temptations of higher mobility through sanskritization and higher political participation through opportunism. The Muslims, confused by the Hindu caste conflicts and losing faith also, could not join the BJP. Slowly and gradually, Gujarat politics and society moved towards its final goal – Hinduism.[2]

Apart from the above factors, the erstwhile Jan Sangh and RSS policy of indulging in anti-Muslim propaganda and fomenting communal disturbance in the state also played significant roles in extending the Parivar's influence in Gujarat. The anti-Muslim bias, prevalent among the upper-caste Hindus, especially among the Rajputs, Brahmins and Banias, facilitated this process. Local party functionaries fuelled these sentiments through speeches, circulation of rumours and attachment of charged symbols to localized conflict between the two communities. According to official figures, there were as many as 2,938 instances of communal violence between 1960 and 1969 in Gujarat. Some of them were major riots in Saurashtra and Kutchha. The Indo-Pakistan war in 1965 further aggravated tensions and provided fertile ground for rumour mongers. Anti-Pakistan sentiments could often be transformed into hatred against local Muslims. In 1968, the RSS organized a rally attended by 1,615 volunteers from different districts of Gujarat. M.S. Golwalkar, while addressing the rally, stressed that only Hindus were secular. They had tolerated all sorts of suffering at the hands of various 'others'. He pleaded for the making of a 'Hindu Rashtra', a concept on which there had already been extensive discussions in the press in Gujarat. The major thrust of the debate was that Muslims had destroyed Hindu culture and now enjoyed special favours in the country. Further, Hindu Rashtra was identified with Indian nationalism. Some religious leaders and the Jan Sangh formed the Hindu Dharma Raksha Samiti (Committee to Defend the Hindu Religion) in Ahmedabad in 1968, which played a very important role in fomenting anti-Muslim feelings in the city before the 1969 communal riots. The tension between the two communities culminated on a large scale. Communal riots in September–October 1969 spread to several cities. The Jan Sangh and RSS workers were actively involved in spreading unrest either by provoking the people, or taking initiative in leading mobs, or simply by providing money or material to the rioters. The Congress, which was in power, not only failed to control the riots, but its leaders also shared a good deal of the Hindu communal outlook. Not surprisingly, they also participated directly or indirectly in the strife, and were instrumental in helping the Jan Sangh to expand its support base in urban areas.[3]

The tension between Hindus and Muslims, as Ghanshyam Shah argues was at a high emotional peak in the late 1980s on the issue of the Ram Janambhoomi. In 1989, the Sangh Parivar organized the Ram Shila Pujan, a campaign aiming at collecting and consecrating foundation bricks for the future temple in Ayodhya. Religious sentiments were fanned by recitals of bhajans, slogans, legends, myths, movies and rituals.[4]

L.K. Advani started his dramatic Rath Yatra from Somnath in Saurashtra in September 1990, and several mini-Rath Yatras were organized by the BJP to spread the message of Ayodhya. Trishuls, saffron flags and caps, stickers inscribing slogans such as, "Say with pride that I am a Hindu" and also swearing by Ram that the temple would be constructed at the same place appeared in the cities and towns, and captured the public imagination for Hindu unity and nationalism. During the Rath Yatra, communal riots occurred at 26 places, killing 99 persons between 1st September and 20th November 1990. Repeated communal clashes, high-pitched campaigns for Hindutva and the issue of the construction of Ram Mandir of Ayodhya helped the BJP a great deal in the 1991 Lok Sabha elections.

Anti-Labour Practices

Gujarat is also notorious for its anti-labour practices, violation of all labour protective and security legislations. Surat is a classic case, like Bhiwandi in Mumbai. Small-scale units dominate industrial activity in Surat. Workers employed in these small units find it very difficult to organize them. Owners of units ignore labour laws with impunity and workers have little legal protection and security for their jobs.

Main employers of migrant labour are industries such as art silk and powerlooms, dyeing mills and diamond industry. Workers work 12 to 14 hours a day. Women employed in spinning and warping units are paid much less than men. Complaints of sexual exploitation are quite common. Child labour is also employed in different departments of art silk industry. Workers are often even beaten up by employers for a small mistake.

Workers can be thrown out at will without being paid any compensation. They have no proof of their employment. Even a single day's absence by a worker, due to sickness or any other emergency, can lead to abrupt termination of services. Severe working conditions requires only young workers. Employers do not permit any union activities.

Migrant workers live in miserable living conditions. They constitute more than half the population of Surat city. Living conditions are so horrible that most of them only keep their belongings in houses, and live and sleep outside.

As pointed out by Irfan Engineer, the growth of industries in Surat has been haphazard. With mostly unlicensed and unregistered units, labour laws are rarely unheard of and workers are paid on the basis of production. All means are employed to squeeze out maximum labour power of the workers by paying extremely low wages. There is no security of work.[5]

The lumpen entrepreneurs of the city want quick returns by any means – fair or foul. In search of super profits, they do large-scale evasion of octroi, excise and sales tax. This is so common that hardly anybody bothers about it. There are organized gangs with sufficient muscle power and powerful connections to help in evasion of octroi for a price. These gangs earn lakhs of rupees daily from octroi evasion alone. The super profits of lumpen entrepreneurs further thrive on thefts of electricity.

The lumpenized capital thus needs organized muscle power and criminals for its immoral and unregulated growth. The crime rate in Surat not surprisingly is very high. Of late, the city had begun to attract attention of Dawood Ibrahim and even Latif gang from Ahmedabad is known for its hold over the city through its liquor distribution networks, despite prohibition. There are other gangs also, notorious for dacoity and thefts. In Surat, extortion, blackmailing, protection money rackets, thefts, rapes, eve-teasing, tracking the agitating workers in exploitative informal and unorganized sector, liquor trade and organized evasion of octroi/sales tax are common activities yielding high returns.

The growing power of criminals in politics is also influencing the leaderships of parties such as the Congress and the BJP. The old leadership, which was not dependent on criminals, is being pushed out. They are being replaced with the new breed of politicians with direct and strong link with criminals. The Congress and BJP both have strong underworld connections. Guns and arms are readily available in Surat. Fake license rackets in which several politicians, criminals and builders were involved have come to light.

Surat is no exception. Gujarat has acquired distinction for brutal exploitation of labour, violation of human rights, atrocities on Dalits, intolerance of dissents and persecution of minorities. Sometime back, the Sangh Parivar organized attacks on Christian institutions in tribal areas.

Thus, the roots of the present genocide of Muslims, execution of the fascist pogrom by VHP and Bajrang Dal should be traced in what A.R. Desai terms 'expanding governmental lawlessness'. Upendra Baxi actually elaborates this very significant aspect of Indian reality, which is far more relevant in the case of the government in Gujarat. He distinguishes governmental lawlessness from the state's weak commitments to the rule of values in the following manner. The state's weak commitment to the rule of values (for the substantive justice values) is one aspect of the problem. The latter may well be called government lawlessness. Governmental lawlessness thus implies non-adherence to duties imposed by law by government in general or any agency of the government.

Governmental Lawlessness

As A.R. Desai argues on the basis of his studies of development that is taking place in India, that government lawlessness has acquired such bizarre proportions that it is increasingly become difficult for ordinary citizens to exercise even their limited rights which are given to them by law.[6]

Thus, the violation of democratic rights on a massive scale and active connivance of the state in evasion of its own laws have created conditions quite conducive for launching the fascist pogrom of the Sangh Parivar. Hence, the success of the Sangh Parivar in building up an atmosphere of communal hatred, and its ability to trap sections of the Gujarat society in its spread of canard against minorities and other liberal secular strata of the society have to be viewed in the context of the active involvement of the state apparatus and numerous cultural and social institutions sponsored by the state in such pursuit.

Horizons for upward mobility, and a compulsive consumerism, keeps transcending its own limits. The very pressure of growth is disturbingly destabilizing; the brave new world of global opportunities creates anomic and existential uncertainties.

The more reckless the concrete materials, fact of competition and fragmentation, the greater, perhaps, is the need for an image of shared anchorage and a theory of collectivity, for disciplined commitment to a system of values that would never, however, challenge the basic material interests and aspirations of these classes. New cults have therefore flourished and God men are created, while the RSS *shakhas*, which had worked primarily among urban trader groups since the 1920s, remained highly relevant with their disciplined solidarity, system of samskaras. But more perhaps, as so partly suggested, came to be needed. The relatively quiet *shakhas* with their long-term character-building perspective had probably reached a plateau by the 1970s. Militant rhetoric found little outlet in action, and there seemed small hope of dramatic political success. The BJP electoral performance reached its nadir in 1984. The cadres of Hindutva needed a new activist programme; the social groups from which they came could not be entirely satisfied with Jai Mata Di, Vaishno Devi or God man. They were still too individualized, unable to convey a sense of intense solidarity and collectivity life. Organized Hindutva was able at this conjuncture to effectively insert the new, aggressive, Ram-centred communalism, which raised solidarity to a new, intense emotional level through its inherent militancy. One of its major departures compared, say, to God men cults is the continuous invocation of a threatening 'other' with whom an endless war has been joined through the campaign for Ram Janambhoomi; far beyond Ayodhya looms Mathura, Benaras and the vista of around 3,000 temples still to be regained. The Muslim 'other', despite the propaganda about its threatening presence, is in real life a minority grossly under-represented in the bureaucratic, military, professional and business elites, while Hindutva can rely on complicity from many elements in the state apparatus. The court judgments about Ayodhya in 1949 and 1946, the PAC involvement in innumerable Uttar Pradesh riots, the role of the television serial *Ramayan*, and the prominence of ex-army men and retired civil servants in BJP today are just some illustrations of these crucial linkages.

Tapan Basu et al., conclude that the conjunction of the 1980s crystallized into today's powerful wave, not automatically, but because an ideological formation had emerged already overtried to trace. This formation, again, is far from being free of contradiction and inadequacies, and opportunities still remain for effective secular-democratic intervention to block the thrust towards Hindu Rashtra.[7]

What is true of the North Indian scenario is probably more relevant and applicable to the prevailing situation in Gujarat today. Economic development in Gujarat since the 1970s has proceeded along this line and it has witnessed a mushrooming growth of small capitalists, especially in the golden corridor (Ahmedabad, Vadodara, Surat, Mehsana, Anand and Navasari district) and traders, along with a new class of professionals who have emerged as strong supporter of the Sangh Parivar and the BJP.

Growing Economic Crisis

The impact of the deepening recessionary trend in the Indian economy and specially in Gujarat (where the earlier boom has disappeared) in vitiating the atmosphere of communal harmony cannot be overstressed. As Kinshuk Nag remarks, with the pressure on agriculture, both Ahmedabad and Vadodara have seen large-scale migration from rural areas in recent years. Vadodara, which was on par with cities like Pune and Bangalore in the early 1970s, is now a stagnating city. All the large central public sector units of companies such as Indian Oil and IPCL survive, but many of them are in bad shape. Ancillary units in nearby industrial estates are closing down. All this means that no new jobs have been created to absorb the migrants or even the new generation locals. After the decline of the textile industry, Ahmedabad, which was once called the Manchester of the East, has been left bereft of any substantial manufacturing activity.[8]

Apart from this gloomy scenario, the size of the organized industry like the diamond industry, polishing and powerlooms in the city is too small to absorb all the manpower available. Neither has retailing nor construction activities of any substantial size been spawned in Ahmedabad. All this has given rise to a class of young, unemployed persons in the two cities, full of energy and without any work to do. Many of these young persons have fallen prey to the ideology of hate by certain political formation and without any thought have participated in the dance of death seen on the streets of Ahmedabad and Vadodara recently.

Re-imagination of the State

Since the last several decades, as we could see from earlier discussion, social and political space in Gujarat has been gradually used by reactionary politics, allowing political mobilization only around the idioms of religion and caste. As aptly argued by Aseem Prakash, Congress tried to strategically mix both while the Sangh Parivar has embarked on its project of re-imaginating the state through weaving a matrix of the Hindu religion under the ideology of Hindutva. The re-imagination project entails restructuring the social domain – consolidating all social groups except the minorities for dominating electoral politics contribution to its objective in the material domain, allowing certain caste/class to own and control productive assets and sustain the existing hierarchy in social relationship through control of the state apparatus.[9]

Nearly 13 per cent of Gujarat's population, as we stated earlier, comprises Patidars or Patels. They initially constituted the social and political base for the Swatantra Party and then deserted it in favour of the Congress, and towards the end of 1980s switched their loyalty completely to BJP. Patels as a caste were originally cultivators. Their present prosperity has become possible largely because of the government's land reform programme, Green Revolution policies, state subsidy given to agriculture and resources of numerous cooperative societies. The surplus generated through agriculture allowed them to diversify in other trades and shift their economic base to fast-growing urban areas, while also keeping a close link with rural areas. Patels and Banias benefited tremendously by the state subsidy given to small-scale industries (SSIs) and become a powerful entrepreneurial class. Banias constitute only 3 per cent of the state population, but dominate in business and industry. Brahmins who occupy top position in educational institutions and dominate the profession of doctors, architects and engineers constitute 4 per cent of the state population. Recently, they have also moved into business. As indicated earlier, forward castes together constitute 26 per cent of population but occupy 75 per cent of the middle class and 95 per cent of rich class. Rajputs, with small exceptions, stand closer to backward classes in terms of their economic status.

These are the castes that have benefited the most from institutionalization of market-led growth. The prime aim of the material domain of the re-imagination project, as Prakash suggests, is to preserve the social and economic positions of these castes.

In this context, Takashi Shinoda's appraisal of the social composition of entrepreneurs with the help of their surnames across all the districts of Gujarat in nine SSIs deserves special consideration. Takashi notes that Brahmins and Banias, including Jains and Patidars, are found to be owners in all types of industries in all districts, though their concentration is highest in central Gujarat. Their presence is more pronounced in the units that are capital-intensive. Artisan castes, Muslims, Rajputs, followed by Dalits and Adivasis, have presence either in the types of industries with which they have some traditional linkages or in a industry that required a low amount of capital to enter and is labour-intensive. Shinoda also notes that agro-based and rural-based industries, as well as the construction industry, have also played a very important role in the entrepreneurial development of the Patidars.[10]

Dominant Castes in Gujarat

The other face of burgeoning entrepreneurial caste/class of Gujarat is represented by urban traders, that is, owners of modern showrooms, hotels, shopping malls, share brokerage, large and medium grocery shops, architectural firms, construction companies, trade in electronic goods, transport, jewellery shops, etc. Prakash, on the basis of his field work, suggests that the dominance of the Patidars and Banias is followed by Brahmins in the commercial and trading activities of Gujarat. His survey also reflects that Patidars, Banias and Brahmins largely control trade and commerce. Koli Patels, Panchals and Sonis coming from OBCs have only marginal presence in these activities. Patidars, Banias and Brahmins, though constituting only 20 per cent of the state population, today, rule the state.

As the same author argues that it is in the interest of political and economic elites, who mostly come from upper castes, to preserve the economic order and that they seek refuge in a social ideology that legitimizes the status quo. The Hindutva ideology in all its manifestation has never questioned caste and class inequality. The Hindutva envisaged social order and neo-liberalism both rely on the beliefs that one has to be satisfied with whatever endowment one originally had. The political manifestation of this logic is BJP and its social forms are RSS, VHP, Bajrang Dal and numerous other institutions and religious orders. This is probably the reason for the affinity of trading class with right-wing social land political formation. The majority of sampled traders were members of any one of the social collective representing the Sangh, particularly the VHP. Majority of Brahmin traders were found to be members of the RSS. The sampled small traders, for instance grocery shop owners, stationery merchants, milk dealers, etc., were found to be members of the Bajrang Dal. Nearly 70 per cent of them reported that the membership of the social collectives preceded their political choice of the party.

Individual traders are not only members of collectives represented by the Sangh, but at times are also important district- and states-level functionaries of these collectives. If these collectives and the political executives managing the state understand the society, politics and economics from the same vantage point – which is precisely the case in Gujarat – then, the strength of the former translates into the might of the latter and vice versa. Thus, state policies are efficient in spearheading the growth of commercial capital with the help of tax concessions and cost-related incentives, comprehensive infrastructural support and eliminating red-tapism and bottleneck. For such a growth, most of these initiatives have come after 1996.[11]

The beneficiaries of these policies are primarily the three dominant castes. State loans and subsidies are important for the growth of SSIs. Such enterprises owned by Dalits grew at nearly 4 per cent after 1992–93 but decline steeply in 1996–97.[12]

The BJP, not surprisingly, came to power with an absolute majority. State subsidy given to economic sectors such as industry, irrigation, power and agriculture is much higher compared to the social sector as education, health, water, welfare of Dalits and Adivasis, where it is reduced.[13]

During the course of field interviews conducted by Prakash, almost all traders hesitantly accepted that membership of the social collectivities representing the Sangh, along with their monetary contribution to their activities, permits proximity to the state power, which in turn allows them to speedily pursue their interest with the state government, deter frequent sale tax raids and demolition of business space beyond the legal limits.

Civil Society in Gujarat

Neera Chandhoke[14] in her excellent appraisal of the civil society with specific reference to Ahmedabad makes us to comprehend the vital influence of the civil society structure in promoting the hold of the Hindutva politics in Gujarat. Though appraisal is confined to Ahmedabad, it enables us to gain insight in process which enabled the Sangh Parivar to strike deeper roots in Gujarat.

The city it known, as the author brings out, for the frequency, the scale and the intensity of communal riots between Hindus and Muslims, even when the rest of the country and the state of Gujarat have not witnessed such riots. Consider the biography of communal riots in the city. The first communal riot occurred in 1941, and another took place on the eve of the partition of the country. In the major riot of 1969, 1,500 people were killed, 90 per cent of whom belonged to the Muslim community. Property worth ₹ 4 crore was destroyed. The next major riot took place in 1985, but minor riots occurred in 1971, 1972, 1973, 1977, 1980 and 1982. After a major riot in 1985, minor riots erupted in 1986, 1987 and 1989. Major riots took place in 1979, 1993, 1999 and 2000. In 2002, as it is now widely known, mobs belonging to the cadres of the Sangh Parivar and a motley collection of followers, administered what is best described as a 'near programme' of the Muslim inhabitants of Ahmedabad. The savage form it assumed in the city compared to other affected districts of Gujarat in terms of aggression against Muslims has hardly any parallel.

Civil society in democratic societies is expected to keep a watch on violations of democratic norms by the states through citizen activism, the making and circulation of informed public opinion, a free media and a multiplicity of social association.

As the author suggests, one cannot say that no civil society exists in Ahmedabad because at the turn of the 20th century, a number of associations of voluntary organizations in the city had initiated programmes of social reform, welfare, and housing. During the struggle against colonialism, and also against Indira Gandhi's authoritarian regime and the emergency imposed by her between 1975 and 1977, the city witnessed frantic political activity in defense of civil and political rights. Yet, it is also equally true that civil society organizations in the city can be held responsible for violent acts against the lower castes and the religious minority, and also for the creation of a segmented and divided city in general. It is also pertinent to note that neither Ahmedabad nor even Gujarat have witnessed any anti-caste movement that could challenge caste hierarchies, conservatism and pave the way for the consolidation of an egalitarian spirit in the city and the state.

Nevertheless, social and cultural conservatism cannot be held synonymous with blood lust. Thus, as Chandhoke suggests, there is a qualitative difference between the consolidation of hard communal prejudices in a society, and outbursts of inhuman communal violence. The translation of communal sentiments into violence demands a trigger. And, the construction of the trigger involves an entire host of distinct processes.

One cannot overstress the fact that Ahmedabad was the site of Gandhi's experiments with truth and non-violence. But these, it seems, were half-heartedly internalized in the collective psyche. In 1919, reports of Gandhiji's detention by the colonial government swept the city, and mob violence led to the jail, the telegraph office and the collector's office being set on fire. The Gandhian lesson of non-violence, it appeared, was soon forgotten. But, Gandhians, during this period, did register their protest against violence by organizing march through the streets and to restore normal situation. Unfortunately, no Gandhian has organized similar march through the streets during the most violent communal riots that have become a recurrent feature of the city. In 2008, when Muslims fleeing murderous mobs sought to seek shelter in the Sabarmati Ashram, which had been established by Gandhi as a project in inter-caste and inter-communal harmony, reportedly the Ashram inmates closed its doors in order to protect its property. The Jain community in the city is committed to the doctrine of non-violence, but this tradition has hardly acquired any root in the civil society. The community kept silence even in the face of tremendous brutality wreaked against the Muslim community.

Civil society in Ahmedabad, thus, has totally failed to realize its own project of bringing people together in shared project.

The residential structure in the city also distinctly brings out the limitations of the civil society in Ahmedabad and the potential for hostility among different sections of the city. As a matter of fact, there is a close correspondence between the unequal balance of power as articulated in the structure of manufacture, trade, commerce and labour and residential patterns of the main communities – the Hindus, the Jains and the Muslims-since the post-Mughal period. In 2002, Mahadavia (cited in Chandhoke, 2008) highlighted the segmental division of city structure in terms of levels of living, quality of housing and availability of basic services. The process of exclusion starts from the segmented city structure which was earlier segmented on the basis of class but now on the basis of religion. But segmented neighbourhood patterns on the basis of religion are not new to the city. For example, the 'puras' that once formed the seat of Mughal officers, declined after the fall of the Mughal empire. But, the 'puras' founded by the Hindu merchants extended the economic life of the main city into the suburbs. Within the walled city, residential, commercial and religious spaces were closely juxtaposed to each other. However, the residential pattern of the city was characterized by two kinds of housing clusters for the Hindus and for the Muslims. The Hindus lived in clusters known as the 'pol' and the Muslims in 'mohallas'. The word 'pol' is derived from the Sanskrit word 'pratoli' which means entrance to an enclosed area. This entrance or gate was generally known by the name of the community that inhabited the closed area. The 'pols' and 'mohallas' marked the clustering of the city population predominantly on religious lines, but the 'pols' themselves were organized largely on the basis of caste. Till the late 19th century, owners of the 'pol' would sell land within the area to people of their own caste. In 1872, there were 356 'pols' in Ahmedabad and some of them exist till today. Within the 'pols' were situated a quadrangle, a temple, a well and common toilets. To some extent, residential property in the 'pol' was held in common. The residents of the 'pol' maintained the area by collecting funds through fines, sale of house property and gifts.

In 1714, violence between Hindus and Muslims accelerated the move towards separate living. Communal violence was precipitated by the festival of Holi, which while earmarking the advent of spring involves the throwing of colour on each other. Najaf Haidar has narrated the origin of what is possibly the first communal riot in Ahmedabad. Though the riot was contained by the Muslim administration in two days, it seems to have intensified not only the trend of separate living, but also the construction of barricades in distinct clusters for purpose of defense. The 'pol' normally had one entrance, and this was cordoned off and locked. Hence, while the 'pol' and the 'mohalla' bred intense interaction within the community, within the walled city, these spatial forms pre-empted social interaction with the members of the other community, and thus generated distrust.

It is interesting to note that by the end of 1960s, three Ahmedabads had been established. The first Ahmedabad was the walled city in which the upper castes, Dalits and Muslims lived in their own clusters. The second Ahmedabad grew around the textile mills in the eastern periphery of the city in the early part of the 20th century. In these villages-turned industrial townships lived mainly Dalit and Muslim textile workers, who together formed two-thirds of the working population. Separated from the first two Ahmedabads was the third new city that grew across the river Sabarmati. But, here too, residential segregation was reproduced in a new form. In the western part of the city, housing societies bought land, sub-divided it and developed residential accommodation for individuals and families. But once housing societies were formed by caste and religious groups, it was relatively easy for them to cater to their own community and exclude people from other communities, and even other castes. In short, the exclusions of housing clusters in the old city were specially reproduced in the new city, with most housing societies determining who should or should not live there. Unlike classical theories of capitalism as so aptly brought out by Neera Chandhoke, according to which land becomes a mere commodity in capitalist societies, in Ahmedabad land was closely connected to religious and caste hierarchy.

Though the ghettoization process began in 1969, some Hindus and Muslims still continued to live in mixed neighbourhoods, though in discrete housing clusters separated by fence or a street. By the 1980s, the ghettoization process intensified and by the 1990s only a few mixed neighbourhoods remained. It was these mixed neighbourhoods that were systematically targeted in the violence of 2002. The victims of violence were herded into poorly funded and grossly inadequate relief camps mainly set up by Muslim religious organizations.

The Trigger Rise of the Sangh Parivar

Ahmedabad, as could be seen from our earlier perusal, has been constituted as a divided city: "the divide is articulated in the form of separate housing, fragmented polities, and segmented workplace and trade union polities".

Yet, as suggested by Neera, this is not the whole story. The fact that different communities in Ahmedabad reached out to each other only partially, at the most, explains the failure of the civil society to realize its historical mandate. This constitutive dimension still does not explain the periodic bloodletting that has taken place in Ahmedabad. The translation of prejudice, discrimination and hatred into acts of violence that target populations and seek destruction of property and livelihoods, requires a trigger. In Ahmedabad, this trigger was provided by the cadres of the religious right. "These cadres tapped social and cultural prejudices, excavated bigoted sentiments, made people remember historical wrongs, enunciated an ideology of Hindu supremacy, crafted a strategy to ensure the domination of Hindus, mobilized people, and identified appropriate moments for the inauguration of a riot, and the infliction of violence". In large parts of India, social groups have been able to live with each other, amid a high degree of intolerance and even social discrimination, without this breaking out in violence. Violence needs agents and purveyors of bloodshed. The Sangh Parivar in Ahmedabad, as well as in Gujarat, proved an ideal agent to transform the prejudices and animosities into a devastating communal carnage. Civil society, as argued by Neera Chandhoke, needs as a precondition a state that maintains a balance between communities and classes. When the state adopts a partisan agenda, the potential of civil society to battle, an undemocratic force is completely truncated.

Predominant Influence of Religious Sects, Gurus and God Men and Media

As we have indicated in our appraisal earlier, almost all over the country there is significant change in manifestation of religiosity, nature of institutionalization of religions, the mode of preaching, or religious practices, religious leaders and their style of functioning. In Gujarat, this could be seen on an extensive scale. As Ghanashyam Shah[15] suggests, traditionally loose and informal organizations of sects centred around one guru or family are slowly getting reoriented to institutional structures, opening to greater participation of devotees in day-to-day functioning. An organizational network with a line of command, and coordination among various units and office-bearers for recruitment, training and execution of various activities.

Oral, visual and printed media with modern sophisticated methods are being used for discourses and propagation of religious preachings. Apart from this, there is plethora of religious journals, pamphlets and booklets with regional newspapers giving extensive coverage to news related to religious activities. An often repeated and reinforced sentiment is that the present-day unhappiness in life is due to lack of devotion to religion. Though competition among various sects prevails, but a common message usually imported is pride in

Hindu religious traditions and importance of Hindus as custodian of Indian culture vis-à-vis the Muslims and Christians as aliens.

Traditional Bhajan-Kirtan sessions, recital of collective prayers and rituals have continued to be the pursuit of middle-aged and retired persons. In the past, especially among upper castes, Shaivites would hesitate to visit a Krishna temple, or devotees of Krishna would not ordinarily celebrate Ram Navami (Ram's birthday); such sectarian attitudes have now declined.

Social and religious reformers now are seen to be making conscious and well-organized efforts for building unity across sects within Hinduism. They condemn casteism and even untouchability as deformation and misinterpretation of the Hindu scriptures. Sachchidanand, one such 'radical' saints, stands for rejuvenation of Hinduism and nationalism. He has a sizeable audience from urban middle class, particularly professionals, freelance writers, journalists, teachers, etc. Colleges and universities invite him for lectures and he has been acclaimed as Narmad for his social reform and literary work. Pandurang Athavale, the architect of the Swadhyaya movement, which is largely popular among traditionally low castes such as fishermen, Kolis, Vagaries, tribals and Dalits, is also against the caste system. Swadhyaya lays stress on building up an 'intimate community' based on the equality and dignity of the individual. The deprived groups are made aware of the rich religious cultural legacy of our society, which is invariably reduced to Vedic heritage, euphemistically called Hindu culture. Swadhyaya combines religious activities with social reform and economic activities. Though, as Shah argues, Athavale does not talk about Rashtra, state and politics, his notion of traditional heritage seams to provide breeding ground for Hindu Rashtra ideology. He also received invitation from one university for convocation address.

Morari Bapu is one of the most popular Kathakars, for recital of Ramayana. He began public narration of Ramkatha in 1966 and has presented over 600 sessions, each one running upto eight to ten days. He advocates that the Ramayana was not meant for any particular varna. It was meant for Manav, all human beings, irrespective of sect or religion. It is a matter of faith for the devotees to listen to the Ramayana with devotion and follow its teachings. He says that the story of the Ramayana is well known, what is needed is to bring out its relevance in modern life. Without claiming to be a social reformer, he asserts that Ram Rajya can only be established when the Dalits get equal status with others. Morari Bapu's kathas attract a cross-section of society in several thousands, even at times in lakhs, both in urban and rural areas. Social and political elite too attend the kathas and compete with each other to get blessings from Morari Bapu. The rich patronise these programmes. Collections from the kathas, which often run into several lakhs of rupees, are used for charitable activities such as relief to drought, flood and fire victims, construction of temples, hospitals and school buildings. One of the leading universities of the state also organized Ramkatha programme for collection of funds and the then vice-chancellor who enjoyed an international reputation for his scholarship attended the function as a *bhakta,* i.e., devotee. Such programmes not only legitimize what Morari Bapu preaches but also add to his status.

Unity among the Hindus is the main concern of the Vishwa Hindu Parishad (VHP) also. The theme is repeatedly found in *Vishwa Hindu Samachar,* the organ of the VHP, used to be edited by late K.K. Shastry, an ex-president of the Gujarat Sahitya Parishad, who received the title of Vidya Vachaspati, i.e., a pre-eminent learned person. The journal used to often exhort that all Hindus should unite against Vidharmis (people of other religions, obviously a reference to Muslims). Outmoded feudal values still prevail in our villages which have kept the caste pollution intact and has thus resulted in friction within the Hindu fold – Savarna Hindus should now become alert and not widen the gap between the castes and compromise with Dalits, and should not continue to remain selfish. The orthodox schools of Hinduism, as Shah argues, either remain indifferent to such views or passively agree with them as an inevitable necessity in modern times if the religion is to survive. This, however, hardly alters their practices. Atrocities against the Dalits by upper-caste Hindus have not declined in any way. Thus contradictions prevail: casteism and inter-caste conflict continue in practice, but overt caste differences in the matter of rituals and customs decline. Casteism is being delegitimized even by those who adhere to it in their day-to-day interpersonal relationships.

Unlike orthodox believers, as the same author suggests, the reformers emphasize the political dimension of religion. They are the champions of nationalism, albeit Hindu nationalism and dominance of the majority in political and cultural spheres. For the protection, assertion and development of Hindu nationalism, the issue of unity among Hindus is emphasized time and again. Though the orthodox and reformers do not see eye to eye on the matter of caste purity and maintenance of the caste system, both share a common platform on the issue of Hindu nationalism. The VHP, RSS, Hindu Milan Mandir or Bharat Seva Sangh, which more or less function as frontier organizations of the BJP, neither consider religion a personal matter nor believe in dissociating religion from politics. Though these groups plead for Hindu unity and oppose differences on the basis of caste, they do not harp on the issue of caste, or untouchability, fearing that this would alienate the upper castes. Instead, they have, of late, intensified philanthropic and welfare activities among the low-caste Hindus and tribals to win them over. A number of spiritual leaders of different Hindu sects as well as Jain Munis have also joined the fray by expressing solidarity with Hindus and exhorting them to unite against the 'danger' facing Hinduism. They say that we attained geographical independence but not religious, spiritual and intellectual freedom. 'The present awakening for Hindutva is an inevitable consequence of a larger change – for rejuvenation of Hindu culture, the voters should vote for the BJP candidates', said Morari Bapu on the eve of the 1991 elections. Issuing an appeal to those who love their religion and love their nation, Bapu asked them to vote for those who are supporting the following issues of national importance: (1) construction of Ram Janambhoomi temple; (2) deletion of Act 370 which separates Kashmir from the rest of the country; and (3) ban on cow slaughter. Vote for only patriots – let martyrdom of those innocent Ram kar sevaks not go astray, he said. Such political overtones equating religion with nationalism became sharp during and before the elections. The anti-BJP political parties and activists found themselves lost, unable to cope with the propaganda of the BJP and other Hindu organizations. In fact, even these parties share the notion of Hindu nationalism, though they do not subscribe to its fanatic face.

We have so far made an attempt to examine multiple socio-economic and political factors, coupled with the extensive use of religious institutions and the role of the modern Gurus and God men, in consolidating and extending the hold of the Sangh Parivar and especially its political organ BJP in Gujarat in last several decades. We have also attempted to bring out how the absence of parallel left, progressive or any radical movement in terms of any strong political alternative as in some other parts of the country facilitated the rise and stronghold of the BJP and its associates in Gujarat. Apart from this, the conservative and weak leadership of the Congress in the earlier phase led by leaders such as Morarji Desai and subsequently Congress (I) leaders such as Madhav Singh Solanki, who opportunistically sought to provide alternative to upper caste, upper class dominated BJP by forming KHAM, a rival front composed of Kshatriya, Harijan, Adivasi and Muslims without any mobilization or movement of OBC and other weaker sections in the Gujarat society, contributed to the rise and consolidation of the BJP in Gujarat.

Unfortunately, when Congress (I) could come into power largely based on personal charisma of Indira Gandhi and her populist programme of Garibi Hatao, it destroyed the grass roots Congress organization and arbitrarily nominated leaders peeked up as per the whims and fancies of the high command. With the result that Congress (I) under the leadership of Solanki could not provide any effective alternative to BJP or Janata Dal as it had no grass roots organized support among the masses in Gujarat.

As a matter of fact, in late 90s BJP had started losing its hold on Gujarat. This had become evident in desertion of Shankar Singh Waghela and other OBC leaders from the BJP and as articulated in 2000 municipal and panchayat elections in Gujarat, BJP had suffered a massive defeat in its traditional stronghold and the Congress had registered significant victory replacing BJP in several municipal corporations and zilla parishad elections.

Emergence of Modi and 2002 carnage has proved again a turning point in BJP's retaining its dominance in the Gujarat society and polity. As a matter of fact, although Sangh Parivar's first organized attempt to establish the Hindu Rashtra seems to be successful in Gujarat, but in a paradoxical manner Modi substituting the party organization and also doing away with the influence of the RSS and its powerful associate like VHP has posed new challenges. Thus, the emergence of the Modi phenomenon in Gujarat deserves special consideration.

Attempts have been made to explain the Modi phenomenon and factors that could explain its success in Gujarat. It is not possible for us to examine all such endeavours. Keeping in mind the time and resources at our disposal, we confine our appraisal to some of the significant studies of the factors contributing to the success of the Modi phenomenon as being evident not only in 2002 elections but also in subsequent assembly and Lok Sabha elections in 2007 and 2009, respectively, in Gujarat.

Christophe Jaffrelot's appraisal of the meaning and implications of Modi's victory in 2007 assembly elections go a long way in explaining his unprecedented success in Gujarat. As he suggests, Narendra Modi represented a new kind of polities by playing on Gujarati nationalism and pride, by sustaining an anti-Muslim image and by building up a personality cult that appealed to both the urban middle class and the 'Gujarati' voter.

Modi initially projected himself as 'Vikas Purush' by focusing on the development issues and good governance, by publicizing his economic achievements. He obviously wanted to avoid any reference to 2002 carnage. It was only when Sonia Gandhi in her election campaign addressed him as a killer of mothers, wives and daughters of Gujarat, and also a barbarian, he shifted his focus, and accused the Congress government on being silent witness to acts of terror which claimed 5,614 in four years, whereas in Gujarat there was only one such death, and Sonia as a protector of merchants of death, Modi further communalized the campaign by taking pride in Sohrabuddin's encounter taking place on a Gujarat soil. This opportunity of shifting focus on communal agenda also enabled Modi to draw the support of RSS and other associates of the Sangh Parivar who otherwise had become lukewarm, and VHP leaders such as Pravin Togadia had openly started abusing Modi, his personality cult and not being of help to Hindus in anyway in Gujarat.

The Modi Phenomenon

The authoritarian and autocratic thrust in the Gujarat society and polity is much older than the dictatorial style of the functioning of Narendra Modi in Gujarat. Gujarat otherwise also is notorious for its violation of human rights, anti-labour, inhuman practices and brutal exploitation of labour, agricultural workers and small farmers since over two decades. Intolerance and ruthless suppression of any dissent from the official policy is accepted by all dominant institutions of the civil society, academic as well as literary and cultural circles as well as established NGOs and political parties as a normal phenomenon since the inception of the Gujarat state in early 60s. Humiliation and violent suppression of the activists, including Medha Patkar for opposing Sardar Sarover dam in Gujarat, is widely known and tolerated with tacit approval by all leading intellectuals and writers in Gujarat.

One should also not overlook the widely known fact that civil society in Gujarat has acquired a notorious reputation for Dalit atroc ities and gender oppression since ages. There are few parellels to such gross injustices and violence against untouchables and women. Gujarat could only be compared with Uttar Pradesh, Bihar or Haryana in this respect. Gujarat, especially Saurashtra, which forms an important part of the state, also gained prominence for women committing suicide as also for female infanticide. Gujarat is also one of the leading states where sex-determination tests are conducted extensively despite a legal ban on such tests.

While highlighting the factors contributing to success of Modi, Jaffrelot mentions two important aspects – one, an extreme personification of power and two, managerial style of governance.

In this high-tech campaign, Modi is equated with Gujarat and Gujarat with Modi. It is not surprising that Modi spent over 25,000 dollars a month on an American firm, specializing in the communication of public figure, which had also worked for the Nigerian dictator, Soni Abacha and such others, for reshaping his image. In his campaign he is projected as the only full-time CM in the country. Similarly, even well-established media carried almost every day Modi's biographical detail, about his childhood, his courage, his devotion to his parents, hardships and sufferings he underwent.

Apart from this, the use of internet, mobile phone and sms on a massive scale was another distinctive feature of his campaign.

Another aspect the same author highlighted is his managerial style of functioning – Modi as a corporate CEO. It is no wonder that this image of Modi has gone far and wide, and corporate world also is full of praise for his competence and style of functioning. Mukesh Ambani along with his brother Anil Ambani and even K.M. Birla have showered admiration for Modi, for his grand vision, amazing clarity, determination, as a great leader and a brilliant Chief Executive Officer of Gujarat.

It also should be noted that while the central leadership of the Congress, especially Sonia Gandhi, continued to be so critical of Modi for 2002 communal carnage and atrocities on minorities, Gujarat Congress leaders hardly mention this in their campaign. As a matter of fact, most of the Congress leaders as well as people who voted for them silently extended support to the Modi government during the 2002 carnage. They appeared to be not even soft secularist, but sharing communal hatred along with BJP followers.

Admiration and confidence of the leading magnets of the corporate world and some of them even visualizing the possibility and concurrence for Modi's devotion to the Prime Minister's position in India has a solid basis. Modi, indeed, believes in a market economy and has accelerated the retreat of the state. He has reduced the state spending on electricity by 9 per cent and reformed the Gujarat State Electricity Board. He also amended Industrial Dispute Act to make labour laws more flexible in the state's special economic zones.

Modi's policies, as suggested, are well in tune with the inclinations of the urban middle class which has developed because of the economic reforms. The social sector also has strong reservations about the state's intervention in the economy. This fact also becomes evident from the voting pattern in 2007 assembly elections. The following tables as provided by Jaffrelot also highlight this fact:

Table 1

Voting Pattern of Different Socio-Economic Groups (in 90)

Socio-economic Groups	*BJP*	*Congress*
Rich	62	28
Intermediary	50	35
Low	43	40
Poor	36	49
Very poor	36	50

Source: Indian Express, November 15, 2007, p. 4.

This group is also critical of the traditional political personnel who are viewed as not only ineffective but also corrupt – a liability which it seems is not affecting Modi. Such a political culture explains the rising anti-parliamentarianism of the urban middle class and its growing lack of interest in elections. The turnout is very low indeed in urban middle class residential areas. The alternative style of governance that this milieu is longing for borrows its main features from the corporate sector, the political system must deliver the same way, and no one really cares if it goes along with a dose of authoritarianism. This hidden face of political culture also lies in communalism.

The break-up in the following table also become evident in voting pattern by caste and religious community:

Table 2

Voting Patterns of Castes and Religious Communities

Castes/Religious Communities	*BJP*	*Congress*
Upper Castes		
Brahmin	64	20
Rajputs	50	37
Intermediate Castes		
Patidar	66	20
OBCs		
Koli	30	48
Mer	47	38
Other cultivating OBCs	46	35
Scheduled castes	30	56
Muslims	13	74

Source: As in Table 1.

Modi's Departure from BJP Politics

Jaffrelot further writes that Narendra Modi embodies a new style of politics in India. Generally speaking, the Sangh Parivar leaders are not supposed to develop such personality cult because for them organization comes first. Also, the RSS had to prevail in all strategic moves, right from the selection of the candidates for elections to policy of the party. Modi, although a staunch follower of Hindutva, tried to free himself from the RSS influence. He did not submit the list of candidates for the assembly election to Sangh high command and he was strongly criticized for his style of functioning and the policies adopted which some of the Parivar leaders openly criticized and stated that Parivar has not at all benefited from his rule. Even, the secretary general of the Akhil Bharatiya Vidyarathi Parishad (ABVP) accused Modi of killing 1, 00,000 cows and stated that Modi is not a protector of Hindu, but their destroyer (Indian Express, Ahmedabad edition, December 11, 2007).

This critique of Modi's style of functioning is also a manifestation of the Sangh Parivar's reservation about the BJP's style of functioning even at central level. BJP appears to be becoming less dependent on RSS for its functioning and winning election.

Jaffrelot concludes his observation on Modi's electoral victory in Gujarat assembly elections with remarks that Gujarat election results throw up new interrogation regarding not only Gujarat but the rest of India too. What kind of treatment will the Muslims meet in the state and what kind of justice and reconciliation now possible it. These questions acquire a new meaning in Gujarat, one of the most modern states, reinventing politics along lines of what the new middle class wants.[16]

Rise of Modi in the BJP

While analysing the electoral outcome of the Lok Sabha elections of 2009 in Gujarat, Nikita Sud[17] observes that there have been electoral ups and downs faced by the party over the years.

While referring to Narendra Modi's rise in the BJP, Sud refers to Modi's initial work in ABVP and his long association with RSS. He was appointed general secretary of the Gujarat unit of the BJP in 1987. He came into close contact with L.K. Advani on being made the chief organizer of the 1990 Ratha Yatra from Somanth to Ayodhya to popularize the cause of Ram Janambhoomi in Ayodhya. When the party faced rebellion in 1995, Modi was accused of skewing state politics and shifted to Delhi as the party's national secretary. In 1998, he was promoted to the post of general secretary (organization). He held the post till 2001 when the chief ministership of Gujarat beckoned. All this without ever having fought an election till then. The hovering presence of the RSS in Modi's career is clear from the site of his first electoral contest in 2001, Rajkot, the city with the highest number of RSS *shakhas* in India. While several BJP workers refused to campaign for him in light of the unceremonious way in which he had replaced their leader and fellow Rajkotian Keshubhai Patel, the RSS more than made up and ensured his election, but by an unspectacular margin of 14,000 votes.

A man who entered politics through the organizational and strategic backdoor gained some notice on being made Chief Minister of the important state. The event that catapulted him into national and international spotlight however was the mass violence of 2002. The Chief Minister himself made incendiary speeches not befitting the leader of a state, and members of his cabinet monitored and directed the course of the violence in their constituencies.

The man described by India's Supreme Court as a 'modern-day Nero' has been able to behave with impunity, ignoring accusations presiding over the most horrific carnage of religious minorities in post-independence India. The reason he has been able to do so, apart from his own personality described by party colleagues and rivals alike as 'autocratic' and 'egoistical', is that he believes he has the mandate to rule. While the English language media and liberals he derisively describes as 'pseudo-secularists' may be critical, Modi appears secure in the support of 'five crore people of Gujarat'. Gujarat obviously implies Hindu Gujaratis.

While contemporary Gujarat's politics and the continuing popularity of a man as Sud suggests, who has been trashed by the media, national and international tribunals alike, is a puzzle to many, it can be ventured that Modi is a product of his time. His political success is a combination of the following: (a) The economics of neo-liberal reform and the accompanying growth spurt that preceded his takeover of power. Despite his tall claims, Modi has created Gujarat's growth story. After all, the state has welcomed liberalization and facilitated the market with infrastructure and flexible rules well before 2001, (b) The politics of Hindutva mobilization that dates to the mid-1980s in

Gujarat. Initiated as a counter to the democratic upsurge of the Kshatriya-Harijan- Adivasi-Muslim (KHAM) combine and a proposed reservation policy for OBCs the politics of Hindu religious as opposed to the Ram Janambhoomi movement from the late 1980s. Gujarat's multiple yatras in the wake of the destruction of the Babri Masjid produced a large number of kar sevaks for this event and indeed have been a portent of the BJP's rising electoral fortunes in other parts of the country. Modi, the much touted Hindu Hriday Samrat, has ridden the high of this Hindutva wave, wrenching every ounce of capital from it in 2002 and through his brand of jingoistic politics that has developed in the aftermath of that event. (c) The global tide of spin: the prominence of politicians from Tony Blair to Modi can be attributed to a modern-day convergence of politics, entertainment and advertising. Here, symbols and style become as important as the policy message. Modi has been able to claim authorship of Gujarat's growth and Hindutva trajectory before a believing electorate and a national party desperate for idols in the post-Vajpayee, Advani-Ram Janambhoomi age. That the contributions of history, political economy, the larger government apparatus and the state party unit have been left out of this tale is a testament to the power of the spin machine propping up the 'number one Chief Minister of India' as much as it is to state craft.

Gujarat: A Skewed Development Model

While examining the outcome of the 2009 Lok Sabha elections in Gujarat, Nikita Sud argues that the BJP reached its vote share pinnacle of 50.40 per cent in the Lok Sabha elections of 1991 and almost repeated the feat with 49.90 per cent in the assembly elections of 2002. The Ram Janamboomi movement and the violence of 2002 are clearly the context for this. The party has lost seats as well as vote share in the assembly and parliament post 2002. It may have added one Lok Sabha seat to its 2004 tally of 14 in 2009, but this still is its lowest score since 1989. The much hyped 'five crore Gujaratis' never offered a universal mandate to the BJP and they are beginning to withdraw this even further. The same author explains this setback in terms of a skewed development model in the state. As she points out, first, Gujarat has followed a skewed development model and the disparities this has brought are more apparent today than ever before. In 1983–84, the primary sector employed 63.80 per cent of the workforce and contributed to 38.70 per cent of the Net State Domestic Product (NSDP). Due to policy focus on the secondary and tertiary sectors in the post-liberalization era, the share of the primary sector in the NSDP had fallen to 17.30 per cent by 2004–05, but it continued to employ a significant 46 per cent of the workforce. Gujarat faces not just widening inter-sectoral disparities, but also inter-regional ones. In 1993–94, the co-efficient of variation in the incidence of poverty in the geographical sub-regions of Gujarat was 0.225 in rural areas and 0.157 in cities and towns. By 1994–2000, this had risen to 0.258 for rural Gujarat and 0.245 for urban areas.

Also, Gujarati's record of human development is poor, in sharp contrast to its growth rate. As a combined measure of health, education and income, Gujarat's human development index (HDI) measured to 0.360 and ranked fourth among Indian states in 1981. By 1991, its HDI had improved to 0.431, but other states had taken over and it ranked sixth. In 2001, HDI stood at 0.479 and Gujarat still stood behind Kerala, Punjab, Tamil Nadu, Maharashtra and Haryana. Taking infant mortality as a measure of health and therefore human development, Gujarat's infant mortality rate (IMR) remained unchanged at 64 deaths per thousand between 1991–93 and 1996–98. This is far from Kerala where IMR in 1996–98 was 15. IMR was 62 in 2008, the same as Bihar. It was 54 by 2005. While there are improvement over previous years they fall into perspective, when one notes that in 2005, Gujarat ranked 25 among Indian states and union territories in terms of IMR.

Sud concludes her observation with the remark that 2009 elections suggest that things are not looking up for the BJP even in Gujarat. This however does not mean that the only significant political formation – the Congress – has much reason to celebrate. Through the 1990s, the BJP accent had been amply aided by an opposition party in disarray. Years of factionalism, destitution of the grassroots machinery, erratic ideological stances and a weak and ever-changing leadership have greatly undermined a once strong Gujarat Congress. In recent years, it has welcomed disgruntled ex-BJP members, lost chunks of its own membership to the BJP and flirted with ideas ranging from 'soft Hindutva' to secularism. Congressmen (and they overwhelmingly are men) have tried out political tactics as far apart as re-enacting Gandhi's Dandi March in 2005 to mobilize youth, to abetting the 2002 violence aimed primarily at Muslims. After all, along with BJP MLA Madhu Srivatava, one of those involved in the infamous Best Bakery case, is Congress Corporator from Baroda, Chandrakant Bhatta Srivastava.

Finally, Sud argues that the BJP has had a long innings in Gujarat. Its politics of Hindutva, however, has run out of steam. Spin too will not be able to take it far. The people of Gujarat seem to be open to political change. It is quite clear that this change will not come from the current pattern of ossified and divisive polities. If the two main parties continue along the same old rut, they will open the field for third parties. Change, other than because of new actors and or because of churning in the big two, can only be good thing for Gujarat.

We shall refer to two more reticent appraisals which seek to explain Modi's victory in Gujarat in the 2007 assembly elections.

Shrinking Liberal Space

G.P. Deshpande in his brief appraisal, brilliantly brings out the success of Moditva in Gujarat in terms of the shrinking of the liberal space in the state. In his election campaign, Narendra Modi focused on the celebration of the anti-political in the highly urbanized state of Gujarat. Eight of its 182 constituencies are urban or semi-urban. Depoliticization of this area has been a resounding success. Modi has achieved that. The Modi slogan this time was, "I am not corrupt nor is anyone else under my dispension". Thus, the slogan that an entire state was corruption-free is believed to be a measure of Modi's charisma. There is also a comfortable and anti-political belief that these politicians under Modi are kept out of the largesse. The western Indian middle class is almost pathologically against the political class of the anti-political.

The only political thing that Modi's BJP did was to offer a heady blend of the pride of being Hindu and that of being a Gujarati, that is why among other things Modi's extraordinary mastery of the Gujarati language was a major factor.

Deshpande traces the root cause for the success of Modi and BJP in recent election in collective failure or in finding a strategy for combating Hindu chauvinism as communism cannot be fought only on a regional and religious basis. He concludes his critique with the observation that Moditva prospers in liberal space shrinking in every community.[18]

Lastly, we refer to observations of Tridib Suhrad[19] who attributes Modi's victory in 2007 assembly elections to his success in convincing his electorate that he is the true bearer of Gujarati identity. But he argues that this identity does not even acknowledge the values of Mahatma Gandhi, identity for which ethics is negotiable and that revels in Modi's hyper-masculine politics.

Gandhi left Sabarmati Ashram in 1930 and never returned and Gujarat is no more the land of Gandhi anymore. Gandhi's insistence on caste-less existence perturbed the Gujarati middle class then as it does now. It is conviction that one could be a Sanatani Hindu only when one is simultaneously a good Christian, a devout Muslim and a faithful Parsi, went against our narrow, sectarian way of being religious.

Our speculative tendencies, Suhrud argues, are very profitably employed in the bullish stock market. In this scheme, the poor are forgotten and are being looked upon only as a source of cheap labour supply.

Also, Suhrud remarks that the other phenomenon is the loss of certain kind of speech. Gujarat has created unanimity of opinions around key issues that is unprecedented in any society. Be it Narmada, be it what we call development, be it over-capacity to turn against ourselves in frenzied violence with unnerving regularity, we have attained a unity in our self-perception that produced speech of another kind.

While referring to Modi's projection of the Gujarati Asmita Suhrud argues that the 'Asmita' we speak of is not rooted in either the Gujarati language or creative expression. Most Gujarati writers express dismay that we do not read serious literatures, at least not even in our own language. The Gujarati film industry has died and so has the Gujarati theatre, with the exception of some commercial theatre groups in Mumbai. Even the best apologist for Gujarat today would admit that studies/writings about Gujarat in Gujarati in the field of social science are non-existent. We speak less and less about ourselves in our tongue. In this Asmita, the west as a source of consumption and opportunity plays a role. Ahmedabad is dotted with buildings that bear the name 'New York' and believe it or not we also have a very unaesthetic and stunted 'Statue on Liberty' in the main shopping artery of Ahmedabad. And yet, we wish to create an identity that is aggressively exclusive and not inclusive. Instead of a dialogue with those who challenge us, we would prefer their annihilation.

Thus, to conclude, it becomes evident from the above appraisals that the Modi phenomenon and the BJP's successive victories in last two assembly and one Lok Sabha elections could also largely be attributed among several other factors to the absence of any effective alternative to Modi and to his party in Gujarat. Congress, neither in terms of its policies, nor even of leadership, organization or any effective strategy could provide any alternative to the BJP. One would even hesitate to use the term 'alternative' for such weak political formation. Apart from this, as we tried to bring out in the beginning of this appraisal, Gujarat is one such state which historically has not witnessed any strong, effective or even cohesive anti-caste or tribal movement that could challenge the hold of the conservative, commercial, feudal domination. The far-reaching influence of the Hindutva forces in all cultural, social, political, economic, educational and religious spheres is evident since over several decades. The Sangh Parivar has successfully extended its influence among all sections such as tribal, rural and especially urban of the state population. This is far more evident particularly among upper castes and even in the middle classes in Gujarat. Hindutva influence is strong in literary, cultural as well as academic circles. As we brought out earlier, in terms of material benefits also, higher castes such as Bania, Brahmin, Rajput and especially Patidar, have benefited in terms of expanding opportunities in industrial, commercial, agricultural and other areas by financial, technical assistance and similar other concessions. It is also equally true of the administrative, judicial, academic and cultural spheres that have been monopolized by them.

Thus, all subjective as well as objective factors have facilitated the growth and domination of the Sangh Parivar and the BJP in Gujarat.

Modi success in Gujarat has to be viewed in this context. These factors, although enable us to understand socio-political and economic scenario in Gujarat, but as several critics have argued that one has to keep in view some distinct features that have played far more crucial role in achieving the victory of Modi in the last two assembly and recent Lok Sabha elections.

The Modi phenomenon has to be viewed in the context of the acceleration and the outcome of the globalization process in the state. The actual figure of the flow of the foreign capital in Gujarat may be a disputable issue, but the state has created every possible condition in terms of its flexible labour laws, availability of cheap land, cheap labour, tax exemption, financial assistance, simpler procedures, infrastructure and such other facilities, which may not be easily available in other states. Gujarat has acquired notorious distinction for its anti-labour, anti-Dalit, anti-tribal, anti-farmer policies, along with opportunities for tax evasion of industrial, commercial, tycoons, nexus with bureaucracy, mafias and politicians that certainly work in attracting Indian as well as foreign corporate who take advantage of such golden opportunity for exploitation, oppression and extraction of maximum surplus from their ventures. These factors also largely account for the distinct image of Modi's and BJP's success in Gujarat.

NRIs in Gujarat Politics

Apart from the above, the crucial role of the NRIs in propping up Modi's image and also in promoting the Hindutva agenda cannot be overstressed. The influence of the NRIs in Gujarat politics is not a recent phenomenon. Migration of people from the upper castes, especially of the Patidars, earlier to South Africa and subsequently to the UK and in last few decades to the USA in large numbers, and their influence not only on the polity, but economic as well as in social and religious arena too, has been enormous in Gujarat. It has been otherwise also widely noted that NRIs in other countries and especially in USA and UK have been experiencing identity crisis and this phenomenon has become far more pronounced in recent past. Upper caste as well as middle caste/class migrants settled otherwise comfortably in countries like the USA and the UK. The inability to adjust with the western culture and value system based on individualistic aspirations and the kind of freedom they exhibit in selecting their career, as independence permitted not only in choice of career but choice of life partner to their lifestyle etc., and also its impact on family and social life and even status as second-class citizens, along with sharp competition and economic insecurities experienced in these countries as a result of the growing economic crisis and problems magnified by flimsy solutions offered by the monopoly finance capitalism, which ultimately lead to further gravity of the situation that could be seen in the USA in the last decade, earlier crisis in IT sector in the 90s. Subsequently, in stock market crisis in the initial phase of the present century, followed by sub-prime crisis in housing sector and now global deep economic crisis probably graver in terms of its consequences and the absence of any viable solution in the short run.

The overall outcome of this grave situation is increasing insecurity alienation, anarchy in family, marital relationship and other related problems which probably drive our NRIs to find solutions in terms of going back to their roots, falling back on their traditional institutional set-up, reverting back to their religious moorings or seeking securities in religious conglomerations, social and cultural get-togethers of the caste mates, reviving the traditional customs, rituals and ceremonies, restoring their religious, civilizational heritage and magnifying their achievement in terms of their old Vedic, cultural or religious legacies.

The state in India also has been making conscious attempt to restore and boost traditional religious festivals and glorifying our religious and cultural legacy with distinct pronounced Hindu bias at a national level. Gujarat with its dominance of the Sangh Parivar and with its extensive hold of the traditional as well as new religious sects in all aspects of life, also indulges in this revivalism and restoration of the old religious festivals, rituals and ceremonies in a very pompous way.

Religious Resurgence

In this context, it is also equally imperative to bear in mind the increasing influence of the religious cults initiated by modern gurus and God men in India as well as abroad. Some of the cults like that of Bhagvan Rajnish and Chinmayanand were quite popular in this country, but subsequently spread their influence extensively in other countries such as the USA, the UK and other western nations. Some cults such as ISKCON and Mahesh Yogi's Transcendental Meditation attracted wide publicity and much larger following abroad and then developed deeper roots in this country. But NRIs especially from Gujarat follow their traditional cults such as Swaminarayan or sects of Jainism, also Chinmayanand, particularly in the USA and the UK. Temple-building activities have acquired such wide popularity especially in the USA that scores of huge, impressive temples are found in several parts of the country and they draw large audience and the following. In Gujarat, the role of some of the new gurus such as Asaram, Morari Bapu and others in sustaining and extending the influence of the BJP and especially of Narendra Modi cannot be underestimated. It is not surprising that Asaram's ashrams with all their nefarious, illegal, perverse practices and involvement in physical assaults on their erstwhile followers, and death of two kids and extensive protest of people in Ahmedabad and filing of criminal cases against Bapu and his notorious son Narayan Swami, could get away from punishment because of their proximity with Chief Minister Modi and his bureaucracy. Asaram openly boasts about his hold over two to three crore vote bank in the country. Morari Bapu also does not hide his love and admiration for Narendra Modi and support for various activities and programme of the Sangh Parivar from these eminent gurus and God men. One finds mushroom growth of such gurus all over the state. As a matter of fact, it is impossible to keep track of them as in a single town there would be scores of such old and new gurus. If one thinks of conducting their census it would be a huge task and preparing their directory may take enormous time and resources. By and large, this is a post-independent phenomenon and their proliferation and popularity must have occurred only in around the last three decades.

Apart from the factors which help us in understanding the Sangh Parivar in winning political power in successive elections in Gujarat, one also should keep in view the BJP's influence in Gujarat and several other regions of the country, in terms of deeper roots of the Hindu nationalism in India that could be traced right with the inception of the Indian National Congress and during the course of the freedom struggle.

Even in Nehru's cabinet, the presence of Hindutva influence was very much evident. Our first President Rajendra Prasad's pro-Hindu bias and his open indulgence in religious rituals and practices hardly need much elaboration. Thus, the thrust of the Hindu or majoritarian influence in our politics and practice of the state is an old phenomenon whose root could be easily traced in social and political movement during the pre-independence period. This influence becomes more pronounced and its blatant exhibition we could probably trace to post-1980s decades. Such bias and practices of the national and provincial Congress leadership further facilitated the BJP in expanding its influence at a national level and it found the social, cultural and political situation in Gujarat far more favourable compared to other parts of the country.

However, when one keeps in mind Modi's popularity and his deviation from the Sangh Parivar practices of the subordination of the individual leader, even very powerful to the dictates of the organization, it needs little deeper in understanding of his evolution and role in Gujarat polity.

Narendra Modi, it seems to us, exhibits various contradictory elements in projection of his personality and programme and practices of the state. Since coming into power in 2005 throughout the earlier phase, he projects himself as a blatant, ruthless, advocate and a crusader for a Hindu cause who would not hesitate to take recourse to any means for suppressing and eliminating the voice and even elementary rights of the minorities, land particularly of Muslims. It is ghastly and open indulgence of the Sangh Parivar in their drive for annihilation of Muslims in the state. In 2007 election, he projects himself as a 'Vikas Purush' at the initial stage and then in response to Sonia Gandhi's critique of his role as a butcher of minorities he took again blatant anti-Muslim postures, justifying all legal and illegal acts of his government. Thus going back to his Hindutva platform and not only defense but taking pride in his and all illegal acts of his state apparatus involving encounters and other barbarian anti-Muslim crimes, enabled him to win over the other wings of the Sangh Parivar, from RSS to the Bajrang Dal, and VHP to covertly or overtly extend support in his electoral campaign. For Modi, this switch over easy as this is the basic thrust of his rule over the state. The success comes easy as the main opposition party also extends silent at times even vocal support to his anti-Muslim tirade.

But, apart from this blatant communal policy as well as strategy, Modi's success in Gujarat has to be located in other equally important factors which have provided a quite enduring support of his rule in the state.

The globalization process initiated in 1991 and further accelerated from early 90s has also facilitated Modi's dominance in Gujarat. Besides, there are also additional factors which have further strengthened and consolidated his hold over the state. NRIs' strong influence and their advocacy of this process along with the rise of the new middle-class elites who also are the main beneficiaries of this development and have developed vested interest in further acceleration of this process (which is acknowledged almost universally as an anti-poor and also inhuman) and have extended vociferous support to this model and to Modi as the main architect and ruthless executor. The most vocal support extended by the corporate world and its leading magnates Ambani brothers and Birla and even Tata is an evidence of Modi's willingness to be used as a blatant exponent of this lobby. His invitation to Tata for Nano project and the kind of favour extended to him in terms of almost free 1,100 acre of land, and almost free loan of ₹ 9,570 crores at only 0.001 interest rate, installation of free solid waste disposal plant and solid affluent treatment plant, also free power connection and daily supply of free 14,000 cubic meter water supply. Despite such enormous concessions Tata has not given any assurance for employment of local labour. Even, the land offered to Tata is a disputable property and local farmers have challenged the government ownership of land.

The most surprising and shocking part of this car project is the extensive praise and euphoria all over Gujarat, the kind of extensive publicity and support extended by media and the new elites in the state. This also is a clear indication of the tremendous manipulation of public opinion and ability of the upper classes and dominant castes to project their aspirations as needs of the entire toiling humanity of the state. Modi's role in such projection cannot be underestimated. In this sense, Gujarat is an exceptional state where such perfect manipulation could be carried on for over such a long period.

Modi's all tall proclamations of elimination of bureaucracy, bypassing of middle channels between him and the people, transparency in administration have by and large subserved the interests of the new elites, corporate world and merchant and contractor's lobby, at the cost of poor in urban and rural areas.

Modi also identifies himself with Gujarat and his claim as an architect and defender of Gujarati 'Asmita', only full-time Chief

Minister at the service of the state, and the extensive publicity he gets in electronic, print regional as well as national media enables him to consolidate his image in the state.

Development and Displacement

But, as we have brought out earlier, during Modi's rule actually Gujarat's position in terms of human development scale has gone down with reference to health and other indicators of mortality. We will also reproduce some vital statistics of the plight of Adivasis, Dalits and other poor who constitute over whelming majority of Gujarat population. These figures reveal the real plight of humanity in Gujarat and expose the exaggerated claims of Modi and his government.

1. During the last 57 years, the state has arbitrarily collected over 33 lakh hectares of land that has resulted into displacement of over 2.5 million people from their habitat in rural and tribal areas.
2. Out of the total 19,638 villages in Gujarat, over 40 per cent of villages have been more or less adversely affected by this developmental process.
3. Out of the total land acquired, 61 per cent is supposed to be for water resources and has affected over 59 per cent of the displaced people and an overwhelming majority of those affected are Adivasis.
4. Thirty-three per cent of land is acquired for transport and communication and this involves 34 per cent of displaced population.
5. Apparently only 7 per cent of land has been acquired for industrial development, but the enormous amount of water and power sources required for facilitating such projects is always overlooked. Now, under SEZs the land obtained is to the tune of 500 to 5,000 hectares of land.
6. Developmental projects are unevenly distributed, leading to further lop-sided development in the state.
7. Compensation amount given to the landowner is so moderate and that too without any provision for their rehabilitation which has made their life miserable, uprooting them from their habitat. Amount given per hectare for irrigation protect is ₹ 1,650 and for industrial development per hectare price fixed was ₹ 2,700, which is much less than the market rate of land.

Seventy per cent of the persons displaced are Adivasis and the other major section affected by these projects is of Dalits. Thus, the oppressed and exploited plotted at the lower rung of the society have paid the maximum price for this so-called development. The globalization process has accelerated this process, which otherwise also has started since the initial phase of independence.[20]

Figures of unemployed people are also equally shocking. As per the recent official estimate, the total number of unemployed in Gujarat is around 58 lakhs and this forms actually 10 per cent of Gujarat population. This figure is much higher than national average which is around 7.2 per cent of the total population. The diamond industry is a glaring example of the plight of workers in industries for Amreli district alone which is considered one of the main centres of the diamond industry in Gujarat. Out of over 1,451 units which used to employ around 60,000 workers, hardly around 200 units are functioning, affecting almost 57,000 workers in a single district. The plight of workers in Surat, Vadodara and the so-called golden strip of Gujarat is also equally pathetic. We have referred to economic depression in Gujarat elsewhere in this appraisal.[21]

As brought out by Utsa Patnaik, people living below poverty line is over 67 per cent in Gujarat, a percentage which is much higher than Bimaru state like Bihar.[22]

When Modi claims of representing five crore Gujaratis, one certainly can raise the question: if you leave out minorities from this figure, coupled with large sections of poor being displaced from their habitat as observed earlier, a small fraction of Gujarat population would only be left. Hence, by official estimates also one could establish that Modi represents only the interest of microscopic minority consisting of the elites, corporate world and traders, and builders who thrive at the cost of poor in Gujarat as elsewhere.

One could certainly also expose the tall claim of Modi of representing Gujarati Asmita. As brought out by several critics that the eminent Gujarati writers and poets, whenever they referred to Gujarati Asmita, they invariably had in mind the entire population of Gujarat, consisting of Hindus, as well as at other communities such as Parsi, Muslim and others and certainly progressive writers such as Meghani, poets such as Umashanker Joshi, Sundram, eminent literary figures such as Ramanlal Desai, Pannalal Patel and several others in their writings gave prominence to the overwhelming toiling majority of Gujarat and identified with them. In this context, it is quite surprising that Modi could get away with his bluff in Gujarat. It also reflects the sea-change experienced in the mindsets of people who claim to represent Gujarat in last few decades.

In any case, one thing is evident that Modi has not been able to get away with his gimmicks and also what is being attempted in Gujarat as the first experiment in the laboratory of Hindu Rashtra. This has been amply demonstrated by recent happenings in the country.

Last Lok Sabha and the assembly elections held in several states in last couple of years have amply demonstrated the limitations of the Gujarat experiment when attempted in other areas of the country. In last Lok Sabha election most of the states in North as well as South flatly refused Modi to enter their area for electoral campaign. He proved to be a great liability in other areas. This was also demonstrated by the fact that wherever he gained prominence in electoral campaign as in Maharashtra, Hindutva forces and particularly BJP suffered a setback. Post-Babri demolition led to isolation of the BJP at the national level and not surprisingly leaders such as Advani and Bajpai in an apologetic mould in explaining the events. Modi's image and his kind of politics have hardly any taker elsewhere. Even right-wing forces hesitate to refer to his so-called achievement in Gujarat.

The limitation of the Hindu Rashtra experiment in a way also highlights the complexity and diversity of culture and people in this country. Nation, we call India, actually consists of multi-nations, where situation in terms of cultural, political, social and economic is not only diverse but even antagonistic that the concept of nation in this context may appear orbitary. The North-East scenario is so strikingly different from other parts of the country. This is also equally true of Kashmir. Hence, one should not rush to draw any hasty inference on the basis of any pattern in one state. Probably, this sharp contrast and diversity are largely also based on uneven socio-economic development and would not permit emergence of any monolithic structure at the national level and even in Gujarat this aberration continues largely in the absence of any alternative political formation that could really challenge Modi and his party in the state.

Notes

1. Girish Patel, "Narendra Modi's One-day Cricket: What and Why," *Economic and Political Weekly*, 30 November, pp. 4827–28.
2. Ibid., p. 4824.
3. Ibid., pp. 4831–32.
4. Ghanshyam Shah, "The BJP's Riddle in Gujarat", in Thomas B. Hanson and Christophe Jaffrelot (eds.), *The BJP and the Compulsion of Politics in India* , Oxford University Press, Delhi, 1998, pp. 245–46.

5. Irfan Engineer, *Surat Riots*, Centre for Study of Society and Secularism, 1993, pp. 2-3.
6. A.R. Desai, Expanding Government's Lawlessness and Human Right of Poor in India: Legal Perspective Documentation File No. 25.
7. Tapan Basu et al., *Khaki Shorts, Saffron Flags*, Orient Longman, New Delhi, 1993, pp. 111–13.
8. Kinshuk Nag, Tinderbox - Gujarat - Economic Woes Fuel Communal Flames, *The Times of India*, April 2002.
9. Aseem Prakash, "Re-imagination of the State and Gujarat's Electoral Verdict", *Economic and Political Weekly*, 19 April 2003, p. 1604.
10. Shinoda Takashi, "Institutional Changes and Entrepreneurial Development in the SSI Sector of Gujarat", in Indira Hirway, S.P. Kashyap and Amita Shah (eds.), *Dynamics of Development in Gujarat*, CFDA, Ahmedabad, 2002, also reproduced from Pravash's article, p. 1606.
11. Ravindra M. Dholakia, "Liberalization in Gujarat : Review of Recent Experience" in Indira Hirway, S.P. Kashyap and Amita Shah (eds), *Dynamics of Development in Gujarat*, CFDA, Ahmedabad, 2002, pp. 194–223.
12. Shinoda, op.cit., p. 223.
13. Archana Ravindra and R. Dholakiya, "Non-tax Revenues and Subsidies in Gujarat: Issues and Evidences" in Indira Hirway, S.P. Kashyap and Amita Shah (eds), *Dynamics of Development in Gujarat*, CFDA, Ahmedabad, 2002, pp. 145–50.
14. Neera Chandhoke, "Civil Society in Conflict Cities", *Economic and Political Weekly*, January 5, 2008, pp. 11–12.
15. Ghanshyam Shah, "Tenth Lok Sabha Elections and the BJP's Victory in Gujarat" in Asghar Ali Engineer and Pradeep Nayak (eds.), *Islamic Perspective: A Special Issue on Communalization of Politics and 10th Lok Sabha Elections*, Ajanta Publications, New Delhi, 1998, pp. 199-203.
16. Christophe Jaffrelot, "The Meaning of Modi's Victory", *Economic and Political Weekly*, 12 April 2008, pp. 12–16.
17. Nikita Sud, "Cracks in the Façade: The Gujarat BJP and Elections 2009", *Economic and Political Weekly*, 11 July 2009, pp. 99–108.
18. G.P. Deshpande, "Moditva and the Shrinking of the Liberal Space", *Economic and Political Weekly*, 5 January 2008, p. 9.
19. Tridip Suhrud, "Modi and Gujarati 'Asmita' ", *Economic and Political Weekly*, 5 January 2008, pp. 11–12.
20. Lancy Lobo, Developmental Terrorism or Developmental Violence (unpublished paper): the percentage of the people living below poverty line as brought out by Utsa Patnaik is over 67 per cent in Gujarat, the percentage which is much higher than the BIMARU state like Bihar.
21. Digant Oza, Lapod Shunkh's Vibrant Gujarat (in Gujarati), Nisbat, Mumbai, 2009.
22. Utsa Patnaik, *Economic and Political Weekly*, 23 January 2010.

2 Hindutva and Human Rights

A Case of Gujarat

Ram Puniyani

The current national scene has been dominated by the growing assertion of politics in the name of religion, Hindutva and violence in the name of religion. Communal violence, the biggest violator of human rights, is the festering wound on the body politic of the Indian society. The nature of these riots reveals a lot about this phenomenon. First, the number of victims is more from Muslim community and partly from Christian community, second, the loss of property is also more of Muslims and third, police plays a heavily partisan role tolerating the anti-minority violence. Initially it used to be mainly the poor Muslims who were the major victims, but lately even the middle- and upper-class Muslims have also been drawn into this vortex.

The Ram Janambhoomi campaign left a big trail of blood in which more than thousand people lost their lives in 1989. The massacres of Bhagalpur, Hyderabad and Aligarh heralded the onset of bloody 80s, which has seen the peak of communal violence. The post-demolition riots gripped Mumbai, Surat, Bhopal in a major way and many other places in a significant way. With post-carnage Gujarat pogrom, the communal violence went to new lows in the violation of human rights.

Communal Politics

Communal violence is the superficially visible component of communal politics. Undoubtedly, the Muslim communal politics, which is a junior partner in the game, has provided enough ammunition to provoke the ongoing march of the chariot of Hindutva. The response of a section of Muslim community to Shah Bano judgment gave the much-needed pretext to the communalists. Also, especially since 1990s, the ghettoization and its adverse effects on Muslim community had been very serious.

The communal politics is the anti-thesis of democracy. Democracy is based on the concept of liberal space where the concept of human rights is central to the values and norms of the society and polity. In contrast, communal politics derives its legitimacy from the identity of religion and here, on the pretext of religious values the concept of rights is totally abolished and substituted by duties, duties to be performed by the weaker sections of society. This politics also assumes that people belonging to one religion have similar interests and these are opposed to the interests of the people belonging to 'other' religions.

During our freedom struggle, these trends, which wanted an Islamic state (Pakistan) or a Hindu Rashtra, had hardly any popular support. These outfits were essentially representing the interests of the Landlord-Clergy who were feeling threatened by the rising struggle for India's freedom. India's struggle for freedom was an ensemble of three basic processes. One, drive away the British colonial powers. Two, build India as a nation-state and three, to bring in democracy with caste and gender equality. This also contains the concept of human rights in its embryonic form. The spirit of freedom struggle did get enshrined in the Indian Constitution.

Roots of Communalism

During this period, the followers of religion-based politics, Muslim communal politics, Muslim League and Hindu communal politics, Hindu Mahasabha and RSS did not take part in freedom struggle as freedom struggle was for secular democratic India, while their goal was either Islam-based nation, Pakistan or Hinduism-based nation, Hindu Rashtra. After partition, most of the Muslim communal elements left for Pakistan, while mainly poor Muslims and those who chose to live in secular democratic state stayed here. The partition was on strange basis, on one hand Muslim majority area, Pakistan and on the other a secular democratic state, India. Close to half the Muslims of pre-partition India (11.4% out of 25%) remained here as Indian citizens. Immediately after independence one of the followers of Hindutva politics, Nathuram Godse murdered Mahatma Gandhi. It is interesting to note that Godse was one of the persons who had been in both RSS and Hindu Mahasabha. These organizations are not based on democracy and do not have any faith in the Indian Constitution and so do not accept the concept of equal citizenship rights for all. The concept of human rights is totally missing in these political ideologies. As per these, Indian

Constitution, which is essentially a product of India's struggle for freedom, is based on Western values so should be done away with and be replaced by one, which is based on holy Hindu books.

Hindutva: Hinduism

In due course, this politics started getting stronger. It threw up multiple formations to Hidutvize different aspects of the Indian society. Let us be very clear that Hindutva is not Hinduism. Hinduism has multiple traditions such as Brahmanism, Bhakti, Tantra, Shaiva, etc., while Hindutva is a politics of the Hindu elite based on race, language, culture, geography and Brahminical stream of Hinduism. Hinduism of Gandhi and most of Indians is tolerant and all embracing, while Hindutva is opposed to the culture of tolerance and spreads hatred against the followers of other religions. It is also opposed to the Indian Constitution, as its agenda is Hindu Rashtra, as opposed to secular democratic India, a value which is the basis of Indian constitution. The notion of Hindutva abolishes even the citizenship rights of minorities,

Golwalkar, the major ideologue of Hindutva, RSS, points out, 'From this stand point sanctioned by experience of shrewd old nations, the non-Hindu people in Hindustan must either adopt the Hindu culture and language, must learn to respect and revere Hindu religion, must entertain no idea but the glorification of Hindu nation, i.e., they must not only give up their attitude of intolerance and ingratitude towards this land and its age old traditions, but must also cultivate the positive attitude of love and devotion instead; in one word, they must cease to be foreigners or may stay in this country wholly subordinated to the Hindu nation claiming nothing, deserving no privileges far less any preferential treatment, not even citizen's rights' (Golwalkar, 1938).

RSS Combine's Intimidation

Due to communalization of social space and other socio-economic changes from 1980s, a dominant section of the society has been responding to the campaigns of Hindutva outfits, Vishwa Hindu Parishad, Bajrang Dal, Vanavasi Kalyan Ashram, BJP, etc. Though externally these organizations may show differences with each other, internally they, Sangh Parivar, is a cohesive whole as all these are controlled by trained RSS volunteers. The realization that Ram temple campaign of VHP is getting response from a section of Hindus, led the BJP to make it as a political agenda. In a country riddled with the problems of poverty, misery, disease and hunger, Lord Ram's birth-place became the central political issue due to offensive of Sangh Parivar. And, all the campaigns – Rath Yatra to Babri demolition – became bloody events. Lord Ram and then the communal violence became the vehicle on which the success of RSS's political progeny, BJP, depended. Last few years it was losing electoral appeal and now the events of Godhra-Gujarat has brought it back to the electoral reckoning. The carnage/genocide has been projected to be the Hindu pride and the process, which is anticipating to fish for votes in the rivers of blood is being planned meticulously.

The major onslaught of this politics manifested through the Babri Masjid demolition and post-demolition riots. It also brought to fore the communal party into the fold of power. Lately it was seen that the appeal of this politics was declining, as manifested in the results of elections in the northern states. And that is when Godhra came in handy. And communalists used this pretext for their nefarious designs. What took place was the process of killing and maiming, burning of people and violating the being of women. The central aim of all this is to polarize the society along the lines of religion. That is what the communalists want. Akshardham did come in as an aftermath of the massive anti-minority pogrom and it was not followed by any 'spontaneous Hindu hurt' as post-Godhra events were projected to be.

Godhra

On February 27, the S-6 coach of the Sabarmati Express got burnt, with 58 persons being killed. The true facts came out from the Bannerjee Commission report. The bogey was full of *Ram Sevaks* returning from the pilgrimage to Ayodhya where different rituals around the *Ram Shila Puja* were going on. Many news reports pointed to the provocative behaviour of Bajrang Dal volunteers travelling in the train (Jan Morcha, February 25, 2002). A Muslim tea-stall vendor was humiliated on the platform at Godhra station. One Muslim girl was being forcibly taken by the *Kar Sevaks* but was rescued. The district collector Jayanthi Ravi stated that the tragedy was unplanned. Soon, Narendra Modi, the Gujarat Chief Minister, stated that it was a pre-planned act of terrorism and linked it to global terrorism and ISI. He also called a meeting of top Gujarat officials late on February 27 and told them that revenge will be taken for Godhra and that they should not try to prevent any local retaliation (*Outlook*, August 19, 2002).

The burnt bodies of the victims were brought to Ahmedabad and the communal temperature was raised by slogan-shouting mobs. It was said that the local Ghanchi Muslims living near the station and Signal Falia had poured the inflammable material from outside and torched the bogey. Later, the Forensic Science Laboratory report came to the conclusion that the coach got burnt from inside, as the amount of inflammable liquid needed could not have been sprinkled from outside. The lower part of the compartment was intact from outside and the maximum damage due to fire took place on the floor of the coach from inside (*The Week*, July 7, 2002). Sixty-two local persons including seven boys were arrested under POTO.

Godhra: Aftermath

Two-and-a-half years after the tragic incident, Justice U.C. Bannerjee came out with the truth of Godhra. According to the report of this commission, this tragedy was a mere accident and was not a pre-planned one as claimed by Narendra Modi and the RSS combine. During the BJP-led NDA regime, the mandatory commission to inquire into this major accident was not appointed.

Immediately from next day, February 28, massive rioting – actually a planned genocide of Muslims – began in different cities of Gujarat. Ahmedabad was the major city to be affected. Out of 24 districts of Gujarat, 18 were involved in violence. Mobs, generally comprising two to three thousand people, sometimes as large as 10 thousand, were seen. They were armed with swords, *trishuls* (tridents) and agricultural implements that could kill. 'The manner of arson, hacking and killing was chillingly similar in pattern, all this suggested a well laid out plan behind the attack. It is only trained cadres who can spill out such and organized fashion' (*Communalism Combat*, March 2002, p. 18). The household and business establishments of minorities burnt during the violence were on lists that were with rioters. Even the business establishments which had Hindu-sounding names but had Muslim owners came under the attack.

The majority of business establishments owned by the Muslim community were destroyed. Homes and business establishments were burnt using gas cylinders and special powder which raises the temperature to a great extent. In the loot of business establishments, large sections of the middle classes merrily participated and the looting was coordinated on mobile phones, people came even in their Mitsubishi Lancers to do their bit in the service of the 'Hindu nation' by looting Muslim establishments. In the industrial area of Ahmedabad, 43 people including ex-MP Ahsan Jaffery were killed by a mob of over 10,000 people and the same evening a mob of over 15,000 killed 84 people in the Naroda area. The number of dead in the violence is estimated to be over two thousand. It was not just killings – those who were killed were subjected to extreme torture. Women and children were special targets.

Women were humiliated and then burnt. Also under special attack were places of religious worship, particularly *dargahs*, symbols of syncretic culture. Many holy places were destroyed and roads were built overnight on those sites. At places, Hanuman temples came up overnight where the mosques or *dargahs* were located. The *dargah* of the famous Gujarati sufi saint and poet Wali Gujarati was also not spared. The loss due to burning of business enterprises is estimated to be close to ₹ 3,800 crores. Hotels, transport businesses, industries and textile shops came under special attack.

The brutality towards children and women was sparked off by the rumour that Hindu women were molested in Godhra. The rumours were found to be totally baseless by numerous investigators. But by the time that the newspapers contradicted the news in small columns, the intended 'aim' was achieved. 'The handiwork of mobs is recorded in chilling detail in women's panel report. The women's testimony is perhaps most devastating and damning accounts of brutality in any riot in independent India. However the inaction of police and administration speaks for itself' (*The Times of India*, Editorial, April 26, 2002).

Citizens Tribunal Report

Godhra, Gujarat and Akshardham have been the major blots on our democratic ethos in post-independence India. In the din of the tragedies which gripped Gujarat for over a period of 10 months, different versions were floating around about who were guilty. The state leadership had one version, while the events themselves were either difficult to decipher or were indicating the cause of the carnage in some other direction. It is at this point that Concerned Citizens Tribunal was conceived. The most outstanding legal brains of the stature of Justices V.K. Krishna Iyer, P.B. Sawant, Hosbet Suresh and Adv. K.G. Kannabiran; eminent sociologists such as Professor Ghanshyam Shah and Professor Tanika Sarkar; and social workers such as Aruna Roy formed this tribunal.

The task was mammoth and the need for knowing the truth paramount. That is what prompted the tribunal members to examine 2,094 oral and written testimonies (both individual and collective) from the victim-survivors and human rights groups involved in relief and rehabilitation. It also examined volumes of relevant material and all this is put together in two volumes – *Crime Against Humanity* (Report of Concerned Citizens Tribunal, *Citizens for Justice and Peace*, Mumbai, 2002) which is in a way a landmark investigation in situations like these, where vested interests not only try to hide the truth but also to distort it.

The findings of the tribunal at one level are close to what many leading human rights activists and scholars suspected. The immaculate method of investigation leaves no doubt about the high merit of the report. Its findings point to the complicity of the state leadership in the whole tragedy. The tribunal in all fairness wanted to hear the version of the state government, central government and many individual ministers. Most of them did not respond, while a few of them did meet the tribunal and opened their hearts. This two-volume report gives interim findings and also recommendations about relief, rehabilitation and punishing the guilty. But the list of those named by the witnesses is so large that it is practically a 'Who's Who' of the Gujarat political and administrative machinery.

The central point of Godhra which was made the pretext for the riot comes out very clearly in the report. The tribunal concludes that the Godhra incident does not seem to be pre-planned. Neither is there any proof of a 'foreign hand', which was propagated with confidence. The tribunals' tentative conclusion that the fire was lit from inside and not outside will force us to review the whole action – reaction thesis, which was used to give legitimacy to state inaction in the face of one of the most severe riots in independent India.

Why the state political leadership was so eager to jump at make-believe conclusions, and what might have been the deeper design behind the whole carnage becomes slightly clearer after going through the twin volumes. The tribunal also makes it public that witnesses deposing before the tribunal informed it about the meeting called by the Chief Minister in which instructions were given not to take action against the 'Hindu reaction' to Godhra. This speaks volumes about the real mechanics of the whole tragedy.

During the carnage, from the beginning the complicity of the state government was obvious. The statements of Narendra Modi were the key igniting factors. His instructions to the top officials to keep aloof from the anticipated retaliation were very significant. Also, trained volunteers led the rampaging mobs and most of them knew no action would be taken against them. Since there was systematic erosion of the rule of law in maintaining state 'neutrality', the anti-minority bias had come to become part of the state policy. Since the last more than four years, in the context of uninterrupted BJP rule, the RSS had ensured that Gujarat becomes the laboratory of Hindu Rashtra. While Modi propagated the fiction that the Godhra incident was a pre-planned act by terrorists, his Home Minister Gordhan Zadaphiya saw the hand of 'enemy country' Pakistan in the whole episode. This laid the base for the attack on Muslims, as in the popular mind the link between international terrorism, Pakistan and Muslims is simple.

Truth Behind Carnage

The International Women's Tribunal summarized the situations as follows: '… the various arms of state were complicit both in the initial attacks on Muslim community as well as the later continuing violence.

The state and central Government both played a major role in Gujarat violence causing sexual violence to women, destroying property and killing members of Muslim community. The acts of continuing violence and denial of all rights to Muslim community could not have happened without the complicity of the state and its institutions. The role and functioning of Gujarat Government has directly been influenced by the penetration of Sangh Parivar. This fact underlies the conduct of the state before, during and after the peak period of the pogrom' (www.onlinevolunteers.org/gujarat/reports/iijg/2003/fullreport.pdf).

The National Human Rights Commission charged the Gujarat government with 'comprehensive failure' to control persistent violation of the rights of life, liberty, equality and dignity of the people of the state, and demanded that the violators be brought to book.

In its final report on the communal violence in the state, the Commission also expressed its displeasure over the Gujarat government's lack of response to the confidential report of the NHRC team's visit to the state despite reminders and extension of time for a detailed reply. Stressing that it was essential to heal the wounds and to look to a future of peace and harmony, the NHRC said, 'but the pursuit of these high objectives must be based on justice and the upholding of the values of the Constitution of the Republic and the laws of the land ... That is why it remains of fundamental importance that the measures that require to be taken to bring the violators of human rights to book are indeed taken', the NHRC said in its proceedings presided by its Chairman Justice J.S. Verma (http://202.54.124.133/news /2002/ may/31train1.htm).

The Godhra incident was propagated as a planned attack by terrorists. Even before people could realize what was happening, the bodies of the victims were brought to Ahmedabad with great amount of publicity. The report of the railway police debunks the theory that Godhra incident was pre-planned and executed by the hawkers and the residents near Godhra station who are mostly Ghanchi Muslims. On the contrary, the report of the Forensic Science Laboratory is clear that the bogey was burnt from the inside, leaving many a question marks about who started the fire. The government had failed to act, it deliberately did not take any precaution in the context of *Ram Sevaks* travelling by the train and raising provocative slogans. The report of Jan Morcha where the *Kar Sevaks* had done mischief at stations on the way was ignored. National Human Rights Commission observed, 'the Commission is constrained to observe that a serious failure of intelligence and action by the State Government marked the events leading to the Godhra tragedy and the subsequent deaths and destruction that occurred. On the face of it, in the light of the history of communal violence in Gujarat, recalled in the Report of the State Government itself, the question must arise whether the principle of "res ipsa loquitur" ("the affair speaking for itself") should not apply in this case in assessing the degree of State responsibility in the failure to protect the life, liberty, equality and dignity of the people of Gujarat'.

The VHP-called bandh was fully backed by the BJP and the state. Modi, in tune with his history as a RSS *pracharak*, was keen to see the consolidation of Hindus behind Sangh Parivar. In response to the rising anti-Muslim pogrom, he said that there is a reaction to every action and this statement of his encouraged the rampaging mobs. In addition, despite evidence to the contrary, he kept on repeating that the situation is under control. In the initial period, he even went on to claim that the violence had been brought under control within 72 hours. Nobody bought this claim, but his fellow *swayamsevaks* sitting in the Home Ministry in Delhi patted him on his back for his 'efficient' work. All the criticism of his policies was deflected by him by asserting that people are defaming the five crore people of Gujarat.

Many ministers of the Gujarat government personally went to the police control room to ensure that the rioting mob was left free to do what it was doing, to ensure that the mob was not controlled in any way. Many of them led the mobs: 'Gujarat ministers Nitin Patel and Narav Laloo Patel allegedly led violence against women in Kadih and Unja in Mehasana respectively (*Communalism Combat*, March 2002, p. 109). The government's callous attitude towards this is also manifest from the fact that Modi visited the biggest camp, Shah Alam, only when Vajpayee (the then Prime Minister) paid a visit to Gujarat, a good two months after the whole tragedy began. Close to a lakh persons living in the camps braved it out without basic minimum necessities. The examination centres of majority community students were shifted away from the minority-dominated areas while such 'care' could not be taken for the students of the minority community who had to appear in the examination in such a traumatized state of mind. The distinction of communities was not spared even in death. The victims of Godhra were to be paid a compensation of ₹ 2 lakhs, while the victims of the 'retaliatory violence' were to be paid ₹ 1 lakh. After popular protests and media criticism, a uniform amount of ₹ 1 lakh was fixed. To get the compensation there was so much running about. The appointment of Justice Shah to investigate the episode also revealed the intentions of the government. Justice Shah has the 'reputation' of delivering an anti-Minority judgement in TADA, Dabgarwad-Laliwala, case, which was later reversed by Supreme court. The apex court questioned the very reasoning of the TADA court in convicting the accused.

The attitude of the government filtered down to the civil service. A former Cabinet Secretary T.S.R. Subramanyam (*Indian Express*, April 10, 2002) went on to say, 'There is no civil service left in Gujarat ... Over the years civil service has changed from steel frame to non-existent'. This was equally evident in the partisan attitude of police, which not only assisted those conducting the pogroms but also refused to register the FIRs. Harsh Mander, a civil servant on deputation to Action Aid, was so disgusted after seeing the role of his professional colleagues that he decided to quit the civil service. Also to quit the disgraced service were 20 Muslim officers of ONGC who could tolerate it no longer. P.C. Pandey summarized the attitude of the civil service very well, 'These people also, they somehow get carried away by the overall general sentiment. That's the whole trouble. The police are equally influenced by the overall general sentiments' (*Communalism Combat*, March 2002, p. 115). That the carnage, which has been termed an upsurge of Hindus by the VHP and other RSS affiliates, was not spontaneous is also proved by the fact that cranes, trucks and shovels were used extensively for the whole operation. Also, the extensive use of gas cylinders, the lists of Muslim households and business enterprises and the import of trucks of swords and dangerous chemicals also point to the fact of extensive planning which went into preparation of this pogrom.

A section of the media – *Sandesh*, *Gujarat Samachar* and other publications – added fuel to the fire by spreading rumours and by carrying these tragedies as sensational headlines. This supplemented many poisonous leaflets distributed by different wings of Sangh Parivar. The most notorious of this was the one distributed by the VHP calling for a boycott of Muslim business establishments and of the Muslim community as a whole. Many of these called for attacking the Muslims in the name of self-defence ('Reply Bricks with stones', *Communalism Combat*, March 2002, p. 136). The training in firearms, distribution of *trishuls* (tridents), which were basically disguised knives, went on unabated before and during the pogrom.

'Deliverance of Justice' in Hindu Rashtra Laboratory

Post-riot Gujarat again showed the high-handedness of its administration. Justice Nanavati was appointed to probe the whole episode. Initially, Justice Nanavati stated that there was no serious lapse in controlling the communal clashes. He went on to state that there is no evidence against the Bajrang Dal and VHP workers in participating and instigating riots. The Best Bakery core witnesses turned hostile under pressure from the local BJP-VHP workers. Some poor Muslims were made to depose in camera and also in the heavy presence of police officials, forcing them to praise the role of the police in protecting them. The People's Union for Civil Liberty – Vadodara Shanti Abhiyan – boycotted the commission and a delegation led by senior Gujarat journalist and human rights activist Digant Oza submitted a memorandum drawing the attention of National Human Rights Commission to the gross violation of human rights of minorities in Gujarat and of the need to restrain the Gujarat government in its acts of commission and omission in the violation of basic democratic rights of minority communities.

After the riots, the local people put a condition to the Muslims that they would be allowed to return to their homes if they withdrew the First Information Reports (FIRs) in case they have been filed, or if they gave an undertaking not to file FIRs if they had not yet been filed. The civic groups and Citizen's Tribunal showed without any doubt the role of the state machinery and police in aiding and abetting the riots. It was a state-sponsored riot. As the state is totally in the grip of the RSS Combine, the wall of hatred is sealing the borders between the two communities and the boycott of Muslims in employment and trade is close to total. It is in this situation that police finds it easy to tutor the witnesses. The Best Bakery witnesses turning hostile was a result of all these factors. To begin with, there was a simple realization that in such a ghettoized atmosphere it may not be possible to survive while bearing witness against the authorities and the political elements. Besides, more direct threats from different sources are regularly forcing the victims to keep quiet. The Vadodara episode where police has taken the witnesses to depose is the best example of travesty of justice.

The collapse of justice delivery system by now is more than obvious. Of the over 4,000 cases filed in 2002, hardly 10 have reached judgment state. Most have not even entered trial stage. 'In spite of so much interest taken by Supreme Court there is, to be honest, a complete breakdown of in the justice delivery system in Gujarat. The picture looks very bleak ... The FIRs filed were so badly tempered that main accused were not even mentioned ... in Ahmedabad, of approximate 1580 people detained in 2002 cases about 1550 were tribal, Dalits and backward class. Upper caste names simply disappeared. To play it safe, saffron forces saw to it that the prosecutors were from VHP'. (J.S. Bandookwala, *DNA*, January 5, 2008)

The Supreme Court saved democracy in this adverse scenario. Its observation that Gujarat government has not done its duty in prosecuting the guilty of the riots came as a big slap to Modi, who all through behaved like a rampaging bull. Its judgment to get the cases of Zahira Shiekh heard again with due protection is a landmark. Zahira Sheikh was lured by money and kept changing her statements at the drop of the hat, leading the Supreme Court to sentence her for a jail term.

While the Nanavati-Shah commission appointed by the Government is still on the job, the investigative sting conducted by *Tehelka* magazine brought out the truth for all of us to see for ourselves. The following summary of its investigation gives the totality of the picture.

Tehelka Expose, November 2007

(from the special issue November 3, 2007)

The sting investigation conducted by *Tehelka* magazine showed the guilty of the riots boasting of their crimes on the camera.

- Modi visited Godhra on 27th and his outburst provided the first sign to Sangh workers that the time to corner Muslims has come.
- That very night BJP and Sangh workers met at Ahmedabad, Vadodara and Godhra, and gave the green signal for an all out assault on Muslims across the state.
- A strategy was decided on how to shield the attackers from the law after the riots. Prominent lawyers were briefed and senior police officers taken into confidence. Workers were told that Modi was squarely behind them.
- The mobilization of under castes, something the Sangh has been engaged in for years, dovetailed into the deep penetration of Hindutva already had among the upper castes of Gujarat. Godhra provided the perfect spark to fuse them together.
- From the very beginning, the police played a very partisan role, often joining the mobs. Officers who tried to do their duty found their hands tied. The complicity was led by the then Ahmedabad Commissioner, P.C. Pandey who ensured compliance by a swathe of junior officers.
- Weapons from bombs to *trishuls,* were manufactured and distributed by workers of RSS combine. They were also smuggled by them from all over the country.

- BJP and Sangh leaders led the bloodthirsty mobs through Ahmedabad's by lanes, Sabarkantha's villages, Vadodara's localities. The police stood guard to the mayhem.
- BJP MLA Mayaben Kodnani drove around Ahmedabad's Naroda locality all day directing the mobs. VHP leaders Atul Vaid and Bharat Teli did the same at Gulbarga Housing society. None of them ever went to jail.
- Fire was the most favoured weapon in rioters hands. That cremation is considered an Islamic fuelled their frenzy to burn. Petrol and kerosene were lavishly used, as were victims own gas cylinders.
- Babu Bajrangi reveals that he collected 23 revolvers from Hindus in Naroda Patiya. He called Jaideep Patel 11 times and informed Gordhan Zadaphia the then minister of state for home about the death toll.
- Government counsel before Nanavati-Shah Commission, Arvind Pandya, himself worships Modi and describes Justice Shah as 'our man'.

Genocide

The violence in Gujarat showed the extent to which the communal politics can go. Hindutva, the Indian version of Fascism, has been built up around the similar lines. It is a movement which sustained itself through molecular permeation over a period of time and now is dominating the political scene. The ideological constructs against the minorities have laid the ground on which the popular consent and support for anti-minority pogrom can be easily whipped up. The violence this time, in Gujarat as in the earlier anti-Sikh violence, 1984, did fit into the definition of Genocide as laid down by UN. The cleverest part of this pogrom against minorities was that Adivasis and Dalits were manipulated to play the foot soldiers of the violence unleashed by Hindutva forces. The second point is that RSS combine was already gearing up for a massive violence against minorities as discernible through the preparations, which were already afoot and the systematic work, to kill the minorities, as seen during the carnage. In Gujarat it has become a sort of war against the minorities, 'in the undeclared was being waged by the state against minorities, the Government has deployed a wide arsenal of weapons. Amongst these are genocide, sustained demonization by innuendo and falsehood, ghettoization, and economic boycott ... it has succeeded in enduring mass psychology of terror among them most of all by instrument of POTA' (Mander, 2005).

The team of lawyers was already on hand to defend the culprits. And this time around all the state functionaries, from low to the high were the trained RSS swayamsevaks (volunteers of high rank). Gujarat government's home minister, Gujarat chief minister, the central home minister and the prime minister all came from the same Hate University, the RSS *shakha*. The popular sentiments were whipped up against a small minority which was known to be more peaceful than in other states.

Violence Against Women

The communal ideology is founded on the patriarchal notions. Atrocities on women of 'other community' are regarded as punishment against 'the other' community. The communal violence while very traumatizing for the men from minority community has manifold worse impact on the lives of women. During the violence, they are subjected to rape and other sexual assaults with impunity. After Gujarat episode, different women rights groups came together as International Initiative for Justice in Gujarat and after thorough investigation came out with a report, *Threatened Existence – A Feminist Analysis of the Genocide in Gujarat*' (Forum Against Oppression of Women, Mumbai, 2003). The report points out that the deliberate shaming, especially of girls and women, by raping them publicly or in front of other family members, including children speaks of intentional attempt to subjugate a community by attacking female body. In Chapter II, it makes a chilling observation, which was seen in its rudiments in case of Mumbai violence also, 'In Gujarat as in Bosnia or Rwanda earlier, the widespread and furious attacks against women of minority community were regarded as legitimate not only by male attackers but also by women of majority community. We heard from testimonies that in some places the rapists were actively supported and even instigated by women of majority community'.

Forms of violence against the women also were reflective of the social common sense which by now has become the base of its operative methods. VHP leaflets, openly circulating in Gujarat, signed by the state general secretary, Chinubhai Patel, promise: 'We will cut them and their blood will flow like rivers. We will kill Muslims the way we destroyed Babri mosque'. This is followed by a poem

'The volcano which was inactive ... has erupted
It has burnt the arse of miyas and made them dance nude
We have untied the penises that were tied till now
We have widened the tight vaginas of the bibis ...'

One of the most spectacular forms of sadism in the recent events had been the way Muslim female and infantile bodies were made to function in the drama of Hindutva terror. There had been earlier anticipations of that. The investigations made by the All India Democratic Women's Association in 1992–93, especially in Surat and Bhopal, had pointed out several similar features. Women were 'tortured, molested, raped, and then burnt to death'. Sometimes, their children were killed before their eyes. At the same time, more often than not, such atrocities were whispered about and not always confirmed openly. This time, rape victims as well as their male relatives have no inhibition about reporting rape and sexual torture (Sarkar, 2002).

It is propagated that Muslim women have more children, are more fertile, causing the increase in population which is a threat to Hindus. In the violence what was seen was that women's private parts were mutilated, weapons introduced into them and the abdomen of woman was cut to throw the baby in the fire, as a symbol of attack on minority women's fertility.

'Gujarat violence once again proved a bit more sternly that while minority men feel humiliated and defeated the minority women, abruptly understood their vulnerability not just in the face of outsider but within their own worlds of familiarity and intimacy' (Robinson, 2005).

Post-Violence Gujarat

The BJP Government of Gujarat did not care at all about the norms of rehabilitation. The efforts were put together by the Muslim trusts who tried to put together the facilities and provisions with great difficulty, against the odds posed by the hostile state. The compensation given to riot victims was meagre and deliberate harassment was meted out to the victims. The disbursement was of the small amounts.

The few state-run refugee camps were closed down soon enough. The pretext given was that state does not want to run the child production factories, the humiliating insinuation being punched was that Muslim produce more children and are a demographic threat to the Hindu nation. The violence resulted in great intimidation of the

Minority community. The fear of minority was systematically cultivated in the psyche of majority community. Today, the cleavage between communities along religious lines seems to be complete. Muslims have been pushed to the ghettoes which are poor in hygiene and distant from the civic amenities. Many a social facilities such as banking, schools, mobile-phone services are denied to them and the large chunk of society is living in fear.

Even before the violence, Gujarat was being groomed in to the laboratory of Hindu Rashtra, different towns and villages of Gujarat state started putting the boards at various places 'welcome to so and so village of Hindu Rashtra' now this has gone up in number tremendously.

The state of justice was well-reflected in the Zahira Sheikh case. The witnesses were harassed and forced to turn hostile and change their statements. There are many cases, which are neither investigated properly nor are being pursued. The justice system also shows lots of holes in the pattern of justice delivery. The FIRs were not registered, cases were not pursued properly, and the judgments if at all were not upright.

With the victory of Modi (2007), Gujarat has more or less become Hindu Rashtra factory.

Gujarat: Hindu Rashtra

The status of minorities is the index of state of democracy in a particular nation. Today in Gujarat, minorities have been relegated to the status of second-class citizens. As a matter of fact, Gujarat is the 'model' base of RSS combine. It is not for nothing that it was chosen as the laboratory of Hindu Rashtra. The regrouping of social layers in Gujarat has been taking place since last three decades in an intense fashion. Along with urbanization, there has been a parallel process in which the rich peasants of Gujarat have achieved an enhanced social status. These Patidar's caste (cash-crop farmers) has been upgraded by a process of religious maneuvring. The polarization of middle class (Brahmin, Bania) and Patidar occurred around 1980, around the issue of reservations for the lower castes. In 1980, Gujarat witnessed an extreme form of caste violence directed against the lower castes. This was the major move of Hindutva base which was opposed to the affirmative action for the Dalits. It was argued that due to these 'son-in-laws' of the government. who are good for nothing, the children with real merit are suffering in jobs and in admissions in professional colleges. These anti-Dalit riots were the alarm bell of the times to come.

These anti-reservation agitations played a key role in consolidating the base of upper castes and upwardly mobile middle classes. RSS Combine supported these upper caste onslaughts. By using clever strategies, the RSS Combine was able to give an upwardly mobile channel to a section of Dalits, who were aspiring for a better place within the Hindu society. In Gujarat, one can clearly see the social functionality of creating the 'other' (Muslim). Here earlier, the ultimate object of hate was the Dalit, by a clever maneuver, the Muslim was substituted for that, the Dalit has been unleashed upon the 'other', an atmosphere of terror was created, which helped to maintain a 'status quo' of social hierarchy. Various Yatras and campaigns of VHP gave cohesion to this social base. Sangh Parivars ideological manipulation of the situation played a major role. It operated on two levels. At ideological level it regarded all those who are not Muslims and Christians as Hindus. This negative definition was given further twist by asserting that Hindus worship Cow, Ram, Vedas, Gita and Acharyas. So in turn, all Adivasis and Dalits have to adopt these symbols and ideologies. This was able to give a new identity to a large section of subalterns. The large proliferation of different Vanvasi Kalyan Ashrams, Shishu Mandirs and other institutions occupied the cultural space lying vacant due to absence of major reform movements. The major challenge, as Shah (*EPW*, 2002) rightly points out for the proponents of Hindutva is to build unity among all Hindus without disturbing dominance of the upper castes and class. Hindu Mahasabha had launched the Bharat Hindu Milan Mandir in 1920s and they have been more active in Gujarat since 1970s. Besides undertaking activities to unite various sects and organizing religious festivals, they take up welfare and relief measures for the poor. The main thrust of these organizations is to build unity and harmony among the upper and lower castes.

Similarly, the RSS has also floated the organization called Samajik Samrasata Manch (SSM) Social Assimilation Platform to attract Dalits for the purpose of developing Hindu unity. Here we observe two separate strategies, one for Dalits and the other for Adivasis. In both, the common factor is that their material problems are not addressed and an assertive cultural identity is brought to the fore. Among Dalits the new middle class aspired for higher status within the Hindu social fold. Sanskritization process made them ape for imitating the upper caste, to ignore and forget the material plight of their deprived brethren. While the deprived one's among them got swept in the cultural whirlpool of Swadhyay, Asaram Bapus, Swaminarayan type sects and Pandurang Shashtris who proliferated in Gujarat duly supported by the affluent middle class. They did bring the traditional Brahminical values in modern garb, laced in sugary syrup. These outfits have spread the idea of Hindutva and the pride in being Hindu based on Hindutva cutting across different communities. Mcwan (2002) points out that 'enamored by their wealth and power the Ambedkerite Dalits turned towards BJP. Those who aligned themselves with RSS also managed to acquire power'. The core of RSS project through all these mechanisms have been to turn all the castes against Muslims and Christians. Dagger in the velvet cloak was pierced through the material aspirations of Dalits, the ideology of status quo; Hindutva was shoved in a most respectable form.

The politics of the type of Hindutva harps on the insecurity of middle classes. This is utmost clear in the social scene of Gujarat. The repeated victory of Narendra Modi in Gujarat, despite the *Tehelka* sting, despite knowing his major role in the anti-Muslim pogrom is reflective of the political needs of the middle class. The Modi/RSS combine/Hindutva politics has succeeded in instilling the fear of a minority in the minds of majority community, more so the middle classes. They have accepted the propaganda that it is only because of the 'brave' Modi that they are safe, also that it is the mass murderer Modi who alone can show these anti-national Muslims and Christians their place in the society that of a second-class citizen. Gujarat is also a future trajectory of India if things do not change for better. The adverse impacts of globalization are creating an insecure affluent middle class, very conservative, very much opposed to social change and hostile to the interests of struggling and deprived classes. In a way, the Indian Constitution is no more applicable in Gujarat.

A section of Gujarat Muslims are reconciling to their second-class citizen status, their deprivations as citizens, the absence of social welfare for them and other elementary civic facilities which go with a democratic set up. In these situations, the age old conservative religious associations provide the succor and solace to survive in the heartless world. The culture, the mixed heritage, has been uprooted and elite modernized Brahminical culture rules the roots. The urban middle class or middle class with urban aspirations, is the real beneficiary of this division in the society, this partition which has taken place in Gujarat, after the cycle of communal strife leading to the massive pogrom in 2002. 'The clashes found in militant religious nationalism a new self respect and a new virtual identity as a martial community ... In Gujarat, this class has smelt blood, for it does not have do the killings but can plan, finance and coordinate them with impunity ... The middle class controls the media and education, which have become the hate factories of recent times. And they receive support from most non-resident Indians who, at safe distance from India, can afford to be more nationalist, bloodthirsty, and irresponsible' (Ashis Nandy, *The Times of India*, January 8, 2008).

Gujarat Today: India Tomorrow?

The Gujarat carnage and the consequent victory of the party which led the pogrom, is a signal for the deeper societal processes, which are operating at subterranean level. While RSS began in 1925, it kept working for the concept of Hindu nation all through. Its basic agenda of opposition to the process of transformation of caste and gender relations has been cloaked in very sophisticated language of Hindutva, and Hate other has given it the sharp edge in unleashing sections of deprived against another section of deprived. With the ascendance of identity politics World over from the decade of 1980, the legitimacy of this type of politics has gone up and middle classes are the biggest beneficiary of this. RSS has laid the mines in the form of divisive ideology all over the country. That it can succeed has been demonstrated in Gujarat, and that it can spread to other parts of the country is visible with the increasing clout of BJP at political level and sustained work of RSS in spreading its branches all over from last many decades.

This politics not only abolishes democracy it has no concept of human rights, and tramples on the human rights of weaker sections of the society with impunity, and labels the whole exercise as a nationalist one. This is more than a wake up call for those upholding democratic and secular values, time that they marshal all their intellectual and political resources to defend democracy and pick up the courage to defend the human rights of workers, women, Dalits, Adivasis and minorities.

References

Bandookwala, J.S., *DNA*, Mumbai, January 5, 2008.

Golwalkar, M.S., *We or Our Nationhood Defined*, Bharat Prakashan, Nagpur 1938, p. 27.

International Initiative for Justice in Gujarat, "Threatened Existence: A Feminist Analysis of the Genocide in Gujarat", Forum Against Oppression of Women, Mumbai, 2003.

Magazine, *Communalism Combat,* Genocide, March–April 2002, April–May 2006, June–July 2007.

Mander, Harsh, The Knockings of Hate Gujarat, Anhad, Delhi 2005.

Mcwan, Joseph, Society Under Siege, *Seminar,* May 2002.

Nandy, Ashis, *The Times of India,* January 8, 2008.

Puniyani, Ram, *Communalism: Illustrated Primer*, Bombay Sarvodaya Friendship Center, Mumbai 2007, p. 19–26.

Puniyani, Ram, *Fascism of Sangh Parivar,* Media House, Delhi, 2004, pp. 72–74.

Robinson, Rowena, *Tremors of Violence*, Sage, 2005, p. 124.

Sarkar, Tanika, "Semiotics of Terror", *EPW*, July 13, 2002.

Shah, Ghanshyam, "Caste, Hindutva and Hideousness", *Economic and Political Weekly*, 15 April 2002, p. 1391.

Tehelka, November 2007.

Web Sites

http://cac.ektaonline.org/resources/reports/nhrc.htm

(www.onlinevolunteers.org/gujarat/reports/iijg/2003/fullreport. pdf.)

National Human Rights Commission

(http://202.54.124.133/news/2002/may/31train1.htm)

Section II
Development Model

3 Gujarat

Screaming Fiction and Mute Facts

Anand Mazgaonkar

Welcome to *numero uno* Gujarat, the most industrialized state in the country, largest producer of drugs, chemicals, petrochemicals, biggest polishing centre of diamonds, largest manufacturer of soda ash, salt, the first state to enter into a carbon trading agreement with the World Bank, the only state to have an integrated state-wide gas grid,[1] the veritable growth engine of the country. In the past we had deities installed in temples and shrines. We now have them (actually only one, the self-proclaimed deity to five crore Gujaratis) smiling grandly from billboards broadcasting those claims. It would seem from those advertisements and claims that there was no life on earth before him. The 'State CEO' could perhaps sign an agreement with World Bank or some other state trading its skewed gender ratio, high hunger and malnutrition rates, its 'worse-than-sub-Saharan' HDI just as they do carbon emissions.

Slick slogans, grandiose launching of programmes, pledging of thousands of crores for never-to-be-heard-again schemes, a 'sammelan' at the drop of a hat, in 'our deity's' mind compensate for a disappearing Public Distribution System, crippling public health services, dwindling educational allocation and collapsing public transport. We have been there before as far as sloganeering, suppressing inconvenient facts and public relations offensives are concerned. It is a direct pick from Mrs Indira Gandhi's mid-70s Emergency manual. However, much one may delude oneself of one's invincibility, facts and reality do catch up with the bluff and bluster. It did with Mrs Indira Gandhi. It has done with all showmen and dictators.

It has been said that part of the people can be fooled all the time, all the people can be fooled part of the time, but one cannot fool all the people all the time. The reality is that some people cannot be fooled any of the time. An alternative report card of the reality on the ground is therefore entirely in order.

Industrialization

Gujarat boasts of 202 industrial estates, 83 product clusters, 60 Special Economic Zones (SEZs), 42 ports, the toxic 'Golden Corridor', and 'Silver Corridor', upcoming Japanese and Korean townships at different places along the coast, apart from the upcoming Special Investment Region (SIR), Dedicated Freight Corridor, Delhi–Mumbai Industrial Corridor (DMIC), and Petroleum, Chemicals, Petrochemicals Investment Region (PCPIR). All this is made to sound like giant strides in a development journey that leaves behind the 'Asian Tigers' and competes with the one and only China. One would be at pains to detect any major difference between the respective Gujarat Industrial Policy documents of the year 2000, 2003 or 2009 except that it bends over backwards evermore than earlier, throws in more jargon such as PCPIR, DMIC, SIR, etc. and aggravates process of dispossession via existing laws such as the Land Acquisition Act or by the more nefarious SEZ Act and all that goes along with it. The humungous environmental and human costs, the disastrous effect it has on water-scarced Gujarat, the salinity ingress it causes and the demand it has on power supply simply find no mention.

Advertised as 'a leading investment destination', the gross value of Industrial Entrepreneurs Memoranda filed between 1991 and 2008 was $ 125.3 billion[2] (₹ 563,850 crore). According to government claims, 50 per cent of those would be actually implemented. The Vibrant Gujarat (Table 1) jamborees to showcase Gujarat as an ideal investment destination were launched with great fanfare in 2003 (Table 1).

Table 1

Vibrant Gujarat[3]

	MOUs	*Investment $ Billion*	*Investment in Crore ₹*	*Employment Potential*
2003	76	14	63,000	–
2005	226	20	90,000	–
2007	675	152	6,84,000	13,26,387
2009	8663	243	10,93,500	26,29,672

How much of this promised investment actually materializes is questioned occasionally and forgotten until the next inflated balloon of investment figures is released in the sky. The reality is that no more than 21 per cent of the tom-tommed numbers see the light of day.[4]

Figure 1
Industrial Estates in Gujarat[5]

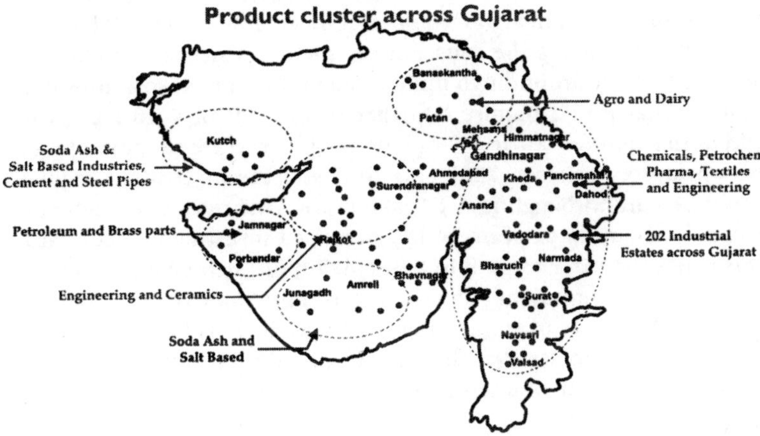

800 large industries and over 3,20,000 micro, small and medium industries

Enticements for the Hard Sell

Single window clearance, reliable power supply, privatization of ports, power, rail and road infrastructure, creation of Special Government Institutions Act, amendment in Industrial Disputes Act, 1947 for flexible labour employment in SEZs and Gujarat Infrastructure Development Act, 1999 to encourage private sector participation are some of the explicit allurements which the corporates are promised. In fact, each state advertises such a package to pretend that it is the only one that has thought of it.

If the 'Golden Corridor' – from Vapi in the south to Patan in the north of Gujarat, roughly 500 km – and the 'Silver corridor' along the Saurashtra coast – from Dholera (north of Bhavnagar) to Jamnagar (roughly 500+ km) are the Government's description of the success of its pattern of industrialization, it seriously begs the question whether normal human life and the environment on the one hand and development through the current mode of industrialization on the other have to be at such odds with each other.

Employment

Given the craze for 'everything mega', the state focuses on bending over backwards for the big and powerful names. Hence, we mainly have capital-intensive, highly polluting industries which for the most part only provide casual, non-permanent employment. There is therefore a very large informal or unorganized sector with its attendant vulnerabilities. And all kinds of claims are made regarding the employment potential of SEZs, SIR, PCPIR, DMIC, etc., but it is safe to assume that the creation of each new job would require at least ₹ 40 to 50 lakh (₹ 4 to 5 million)[6]. Taking the conservative unemployment rate to be eight per cent we have around two million unemployed in a workforce of 25 million. That would require a further investment of ₹ 10 lakh crore. Add to that another 2.7 to 2.9 million people who are supposed to join the workforce[7] between 2007 and 2012 and the investment required would be a mind-boggling ₹ 54 lakh crore. One must also remember that only about 25 per cent of the promised investments materialize. This is not the place to go into a discussion on such vital issues as the veracity of government figures regarding employment potential, quality and security of employment, whether there is full employment, etc., so suffice it to say that this pattern of industrialization is unlikely to solve the problem of unemployment in Gujarat.

Water

If there is one problem everyone of whichever political persuasion and geographical location would agree on it is the water crisis. People have been fed the myth that the Narmada waters will be the panacea to all their woes. But scarcity is not the only problem. There are decreasing rainfall, depleting groundwater due to overdrawn to feed unsustainable agricultural practices, salinity ingress, contaminated groundwater, polluted rivers and criminal waste by promoting water parks and such activities in places where better widom should prevail. Rivers that are supposed to have nurtured cultures have only two functions today: have a dam upstream and a gutter to carry effluent from cities and industries downstream. This is especially true of all rivers (Kolak, Daman Ganga, Par, Tapi, Narmada, Mahi, Sabarmati) between Vapi and Ahmedabad.

The international organization Green Peace carried out various tests of the effluent discharged into rivers by industrial estates in Vapi, Ankleshwar and Baroda in the late 1990s and found '"treated" and untreated industrial wastewater from rivers and Common Effluent Treatment Plants (CETPs) – promoted as a magic solution to combat pollution. The areas were contaminated with highly toxic poisons, including persistent and life-threatening pollutants – polychlorinated biphenyls, hexachlorobenzene and toxic heavy metals such as lead, cadmium, chromium, copper and mercury.[8]

The efficacy of Common Effluent Treatment Plants has often been tom-tommed since then, but recent findings tell a story that is no different. The Central Pollution Control Board data in response to Right to

Information applications by a Paryavaran Suraksha Samiti representative shows that the Effluent Treatment Plants in Vapi, Ankleshwar, Baroda and Ahmedabad have not met the State Pollution Control Board's norms between 2006 and 2009, even on the most basic parameters. It would be voluminous to include all the data here, therefore one need only look at the latest information at the time of this writing (Table 2).

Table 2
Status of Effluent Disposal Infrastructure at Various Industrial Estates[9]

Industrial Estate	*Date*	*Details of violation of norms*	*Remarks*
Sarigam	4 Dec 09	Consent granted by GPCB lapsed in 2004 SS, BOD, COD, Chloride, Ammonical Nitrogen, Phenolic Compound, Zinc, & Sulphides, are most of the time higher than the permissible limits specified by GPCB	GPCB notice to Sarigam Waste & Effluent Management Co. Ltd.
Vapi	29 Mar 10	Effluent discharged into Damanganga river shows COD: 869, i.e., 347.60 per cent more (GPCB norms 250 mg/l), TDS: 9088, i.e., 432.76 per cent more (GPCB norms 2100 mg/l), and NH3-N: 98, i.e., 196 per cent more (GPCB norms 50 mg/l)	CPCB Report
Ankleshwar	10 Mar 10	Effluent discharged into the Gulf of Cambay shows COD: 1241, i.e., 248.20 per cent more (GPCB norms 500 mg/l), and NH3-N: 664, i.e., 1328 per cent more (GPCB norms 50 mg/l)	CPCB Report
Baroda Effluent Channel Project	Mar 10	Effluent discharged into estuary of Mahisagar river shows pH: 4.6 (GPCB norms 6.5–8.5), TSS: 361 (GPCB norms 100 mg/l), TDS: 14,458 (GPCB norms 5000 mg/l), COD: 1826 (GPCB norms 250 mg/l), BOD: 334 (GPCB norms 100 mg/l), NH3-N: 387 (GPCB norms 50 mg/l), Cyanide: 2.857 (GPCB norms 0.2 mg/l), and Phenols: 15.37 (GPCB norms 1.0 mg/l)	CPCB Report
CETP, Vatva, Ahmedabad	27 Jan 10	Effluent discharged into Sabarmati river shows COD: 2189, i.e., 879.20 per cent more (GPCB norms 250 mg/l), TDS: 16,141, i.e., 768.60 per cent more (GPCB norms 2100 mg/l), and NH3-N: 190, i.e., 380 per cent more (GPCB norms 50 mg/l)	CPCB Report

Cont'd...

...Cont'd

GECSL, Vatva, Ahmedabad	27 Mar 10	Effluent discharged into Sabarmati river shows COD: 1100, i.e., 440 per cent more (GPCB norms 250 mg/l), and TDS: 2506, i.e., 119.33 per cent more (GPCB norms 2100 mg/l)	CPCB Report
GVMSAVL, Odhav, Ahmedabad	28 Mar 10	Effluent discharged into Sabarmati river shows COD: 7315, i.e., 292.6 per cent more (GPCB norms 250 mg/l), TDS: 6928, i.e., 329.90 per cent more (GPCB norms 2100 mg/l), and NH3-N: 1260, i.e., 2520 per cent more (GPCB norms 50 mg/l)	CPCB Report
NEPL, Naroda, Ahmedabad	28 Mar 10	Effluent discharged into Sabarmati river shows COD: 2471, i.e., 988.40 per cent more (GPCB norms 250 mg/l), TDS: 11,971, i.e., 570.00 per cent more (GPCB norms 2100 mg/l), and NH3-N: 190, i.e., 380 per cent more (GPCB norms 50 mg/l)	CPCB Report

GPCB : Gujarat Pollution Control Board
TDS : Total Dissolved Salts
COD : Chemical Oxygen Demand
CETP : Common Effluent Treatment Plant
CPCB : Central Pollution Control Board
BOD : Biochemical Oxygen Demand
NH_3N : Ammonium Nitrate
SS : Suspended Solids

It has to be borne in mind that even this rudimentary pollution control infrastructure was put in place because of the rising public pressure and a lot of it was subsidized by public funds, e.g., Ankleshwar CETP was subsidized up to 50 per cent by the state and central governments. An excellent profit-privatization and cost-externalization model! On being asked by Paryavaran Suraksha Samiti as to why the Chief Minister Narendra Modi himself inaugurated the Ankleshwar Final Effluent Treatment Plant in January 2007, though it had not been meeting the pollution control norms, his office stated that records had been destroyed as there were new elections in December 2007!

Farmers living along the effluent channels and fisher people are the worst affected. The fishing industry in Daman and Diu has seen a drop of 64.3 per cent in the last decade, says the superintendent of fisheries for Daman and Diu Abhilasha Agarwal and she blames the polluted effluents from the Vapi industrial estate for this huge loss. Agrees Arvind Tandel of the Matsaya Udyog Society (MUS) at Daman, 'just till a decade ago, there were 600 boats that went into the sea.

Today, there are only 226 boats that are registered. Only 29 boats of the 226 venture into the sea. Besides, the number of the fishing labourers were 18,000 till a decade ago'.[10]

Table 3

Fish Catch at Daman Coast[11]

Year	*Catch in tonnes*
2000–01	2,526
2001–02	1,557
2002–03	1,404
2003–04	1,115
2004–05	1,090
2005–06	1,241
2006–07	1,217
2007–08	1,347
2008–09	1,031
2009–10	910.3

Various tests of groundwater in Vapi, Ankleshwar and Baroda carried out by Centre of Science for Environment and Paryavaran Suraksha Samiti showed the presence of heavy metals.

Table 4

Groundwater Tests Done by Down to Earth in 1999[12]

Village	*Mercury Level*	*Chemical Oxygen Demand*
Permissible limit	0.001	250
Machua village (Vatva, Ahmedabad)	0.115	47
Lali village (Vatva, Ahmedabad)	0.211	25
Chiri village (Vapi)	0.096	263
Sarangpur village (Ankleshwar)	0.118	164
Bapunagar (Ankleshwar)	0.176	47.000

Note: All units in milligrams per litre. The permissible limit for mercury is for drinking water and the limit for COD is for industrial effluent, not drinking water.

Source: Padma Vankar et al., 1999, Faculty for Ecological and Analytical Testing, Indian Institute for Technology, Kanpur, June 21, mimeo.

The Supreme Court Monitoring Committee on Hazardous Wastes visited Gujarat in April 2004 and stated, 'in the case of Vapi, Ankleshwar, Nandesari (Vadodara) and villages around the Effluent Channel Project (ECP) (District: Vadodara and Bharuch) the

Committee itself has physically verified that the groundwater in all these areas is unfit for drinking, displays colours of bright red, orange and chocolate, and cannot be used for drinking water purposes or even for washing clothes as they get stained. Villagers are forced to use the coloured water for agricultural (purposes) and this has led to the contamination of agricultural products'.[13] Taking into account the gravity of the situation, the Supreme Court was constrained to order the Government of Gujarat to provide drinking water to 26 villages around Vapi, Ankleshwar and Nandesari industrial estates.[14]

A detailed study carried out by the Central Pollution Control Board (November 2003) on the 'groundwater collected quality around common effluent treatment plants and common secured landfill sites in Gujarat' states that the groundwater collected not only in these three areas but also at Vatwa and Odhav (Ahmedabad) Industrial estates is not fit for drinking or even for irrigation because it is coloured and contaminated.[15]

Hazardous Wastes

Gujarat produces about 6,60,000 tonnes (1.2 million tonnes according to Chairman, CPCB, New Delhi) of hazardous solid waste which is 15 per cent of the country's waste.[16] When the indiscriminate dumping of such wastes on open public and private lands in the vicinity of industrial estates across the state was highlighted, the industry – government – expert nexus marketed the idea of landfills (TSDF: Treatment, Storage & Disposal Facility) and incinerators. It is an accepted fact that effluent treatment plants, landfills and incinerators are end of the pipe solutions that do not deal with the problem, do not destroy the toxics, they only transfer it from one form and place to another. Yet, the powers that pretend as if they have cracked the problem. Experience has shown that it is not only the small-scale industries that violate environmental law, but big ones do it with enviable impunity. A cursory visit to any of the big industrial estates in the 'golden corridor' bears testimony to our collective criminality as far as the environment is concerned.

Water samples in the vicinity of the landfill sites show that 'safe disposal' is indeed a myth and pollutants from it are leaching into the groundwater in the surrounding areas. Reports obtained from Central Pollution Control Board for samples from leachate wells at landfill sites for periods pertaining to years 2009 and 2010 suggest that Sachin (Surat), Ankleshwar, Nandesari and Ahmedabad do not conform to norms.

As if Gujarat did not have enough of a problem of hazardous waste lying around everywhere, there was more problem afoot to transport

Union Carbide waste – 67 MT initially, then jacked up to 350 MT – from Bhopal to Ankleshwar for incineration. Documents available under the Right to Information show that the Union Government, the State Government, the Gujarat Pollution Control Board, the Government of Madhya Pradesh and Mr Ratan Tata were all complicit in transferring the problem from Bhopal to Gujarat and exonerating Dow Chemicals from its responsibility of cleaning up the Union Carbide mess. Ratan Tata went so far as to offer setting up of industry-led remediation fund to 'clean up' the Union Carbide site – all to please Dow Chemicals. That is how public policy is formulated and it does not matter which party is in power. Paryavaran Suraksha Samiti activists who opposed the transport of Union Carbide waste to Ankleshwar were threatened with defamation for opposing.

Air

Industrial estates such as Vapi, Ankleshwar, Nandesari (Baroda) seem like the stench capitals of the state. The state boasting of being the most developed industrial state in the country monitors only Sulphur Dioxide, Oxides of Nitrogen, Suspended Particulate Matter, Carbon Monoxide and at most a couple of other parameters, whereas every individual chemical manufacturing unit would be emitting myriad complex compounds. There is neither the infrastructure nor there will be to deal with what is being released into the atmosphere. Ignorance is indeed bliss, for the moment at least, and for some!

Paryavaran Suraksha Samiti in collaboration with the International Bucket Brigade took three air samples in Ankleshwar and Baroda industrial estates in the year 2005 and had them analysed at the Columbia Analytical Services, Inc., US. The list of chemicals found among the three samples[17] was Carbon Disulphide; Acetonitrile; Isopropyl Alcohol; Acrylonitrile; Methyl Ethyl Ketone (2-Butanone); 1,2 Dichloroethane; Toluene; Acetone; Chloroform; Methylene Chloride; Benzene; Ethanol; Hydrogen Sulphide; Methyl Mercaptan; Dimethyl Disulphide; n-Hexane; Carbon Tetrachloride; Trichloroethene; Toluene; Ethyl Benzene; m, p-Xylenes. From a lay person's point of view it can only be pointed out that at least four of the chemicals found in the Ankleshwar sample, and two chemicals in one and three chemicals in the other Baroda samples are known carcinogens. Repeated requests to the regulatory agencies to clean up their act have fallen on deaf ears.

Gujarat's Coasts

The whole 'silver corridor' along the Saurashtra coastline, and Kutch have been marketed as the theatre of Vibrant Gujarat-action and may well put the environmental disaster-in-making in the golden corridor to shame. Vibrant Gujarat and its MOUs can brook no interference from such wisdom as sensitivity to coastal ecology, marine diversity, the role of mangroves in acting as barrier to cyclones and storms and breeding ground for fish, coral reefs or sea weeds. Large-scale limestone mining along coast for cement factories was known to exacerbate salinity ingress. Cement plants, other industries and ports are sought to be established with a redoubled vigour trampling up people's resistance to save their lives and livelihoods. A look at the government's upcoming plans is a veritable bull-in-a-china-shop story.

Mithi Virdi, about 40 kms from Bhavnagar city, is slated to have a 6–8000 MW nuclear power plant. Existing nuclear power plants in the country typically are of 500 MW size. The sheer size is mind-boggling. People of at least five villages have been resisting Government moves to acquire around 1,200[18] acres for the last two years. The area has prosperous agriculture with three crops a year and is known for an excellent fruit-growing area famous for its mangoes. The government tries to characterize the area as wasteland.

Vadodara Zala village in Junagadh district has been resisting the proposed hand over of the village's remaining grazing land to a large corporation. It first lost 38 acres to a cement company, the remaining 650+ acres is sought to be turned over to a huge industrial group for a port. About 6000 people of the village have nonviolently prevented government officials from undertaking surveys in the area to protect the grazing lands for their 5000 cattle heads. The government policy used to be demarcating at least 40 acres of land for every 100 cattle heads.

People of Mocha in Porbandar district have valiantly fought illegal limestone mining for the last few years.

Over the last two years, at least 15 villages near Mahuva in Bhavnagar district have fought Nirma company's planned 1.91 million tonne cement plant at a site where public funds where expended to construct water conservation structures. It is also an area with prospering three-crops-per-year agriculture such as Mithi Virdi and is again sought to be characterized by government as wasteland. While Nirma Cements will employ only 418 people, the 51 existing onion dehydrating plants employ around 10,000 people and 18 cotton ginning units employ 3,000 people. The combined turnover of these units is estimated to be around ₹ 3,800 crore.[19]

Kutch

The Gulf of Kutch which abounds in marine wealth is considered one of the biologically richest marine habitats. It had the best mangrove cover after the Sunderbans. A Gujarat Forest Department report by H.S. Singh,

Chief Conservator of Forest, in early 2007 claims that 340 square km (34,000 hectares) of mangroves along the state coastline have either disappeared completely or are on the verge of disappearing. These drastic losses of mangrove forest stem mainly from industrial activities, specifically in the Gulf of Kutch. Mundra SEZ had 3,000 hectares of mangroves out of a total of 13,000 hectares and much of these had already been cleared.[20] It is now the target of corporates' attention especially after the earthquake in 2001 and all kinds of incentives and special packages.

The coastline is home to 3,500 fishing families, mainly from the Muslim wagher community, who spend eight-nine months in the extreme weather conditions by the coast, away from their villages. They have done so for at least last 200 years. And at current prices, their fish catch of 12,000 MT was valued at over ₹ 60 crore.[21] Their lives and livelihoods are now seriously threatened by Adani's Mundra Port SEZ, 3,300 MW power plant and the 300 MW OPG power plant. The poor fisher people have waged a long struggle to protect their right to life and livelihood. It is not only the fisher people who are dispossessed. A total of 14 villages have lost more than 1,400 acres of grazing land (under panchayats) to the SEZ. Tunda, Vandh and Siracha villages dominated by Rabaris (a traditional cattle/buffalo-rearing community relying entirely on animal husbandry) have lost 1,800 acres of revenue wasteland and 311 acres of grazing land to the Adani Power SEZ and are now living in perpetual fear of losing the rest of the gauchhar to Tata company's proposed 4,000 mw ultra mega power plant coming up on the other side of the village on approximately 1,250 hectares of land, two kilometres from the main Mundra SEZ.[22]

Kutch was also at the wrong end of the stick as a result of the government policy of turning over village 'wastelands' to corporations for farming on 20-year leases for a measly ₹ 40/acre/year.[23] While the policy applied to all of Gujarat, Kutch was likely to be the worst affected as it had the highest amount of 'wasteland'. Estimates suggest that at least 4.5 million hectares of land was targeted. At least 1.8 million hectares of that was cultivable land being tilled by Dalits and small and marginal farmers.[24] The plan was likely to impact hundreds of thousands of landless people, charcoal makers, animal herders and others. Stiff resistance was put up against the decision and there is apparently a go-slow at the government level.

Delhi–Mumbai Industrial Corridor, SEZs, Land Acquisition and Scams

The Delhi–Mumbai Industrial Corridor is a $ 90 billion infrastructure project in collaboration with the Japanese Ministry of Economy, Trade

Figure 2

Fish Catch Details[25]

Location of different Marine Fishing Villages *(Bandars)* in Mundra Coast superimpose on the map of the proposed MPSEZL (WFDP)

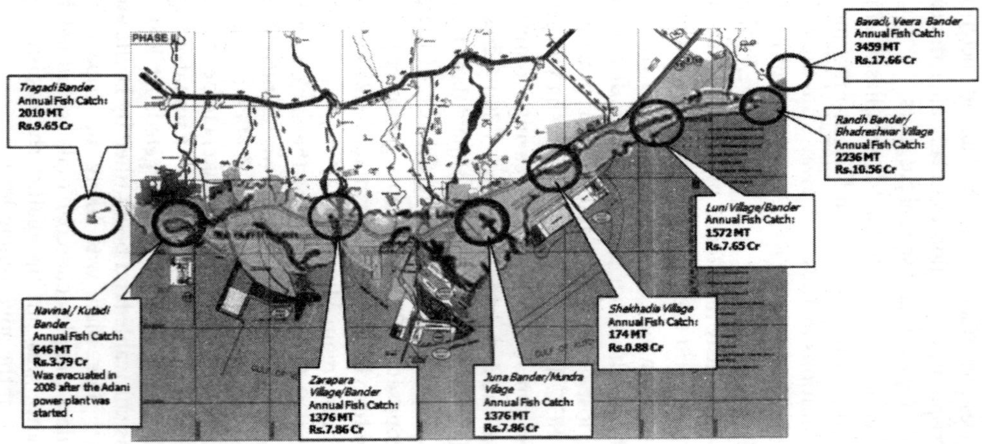

Annual Fish Production in the area affected by the MPSEZL/WEDP

12027 MT. Rs. 60.8 Cr

Note: 1. Average annual fish catch for the period 2000–2005 has been mentioned.
2. Total Fish catch includes Fish catch by mechanized boat and Pagadia fishing.
3. Value of fish catch has been calculated on basis of current market prices.

Source: (Annual Fish Catch in MT): Fisheries Department Bhuj.

and Industry. It is supposed to be a 1,483 km long, and 150 km wide belt on either side of the Dedicated Freight Corridor from Mumbai to Delhi as shown in Figure 3.

Figure 3
Delhi-Mumbai Industrial Corridor (DMIC)[26]

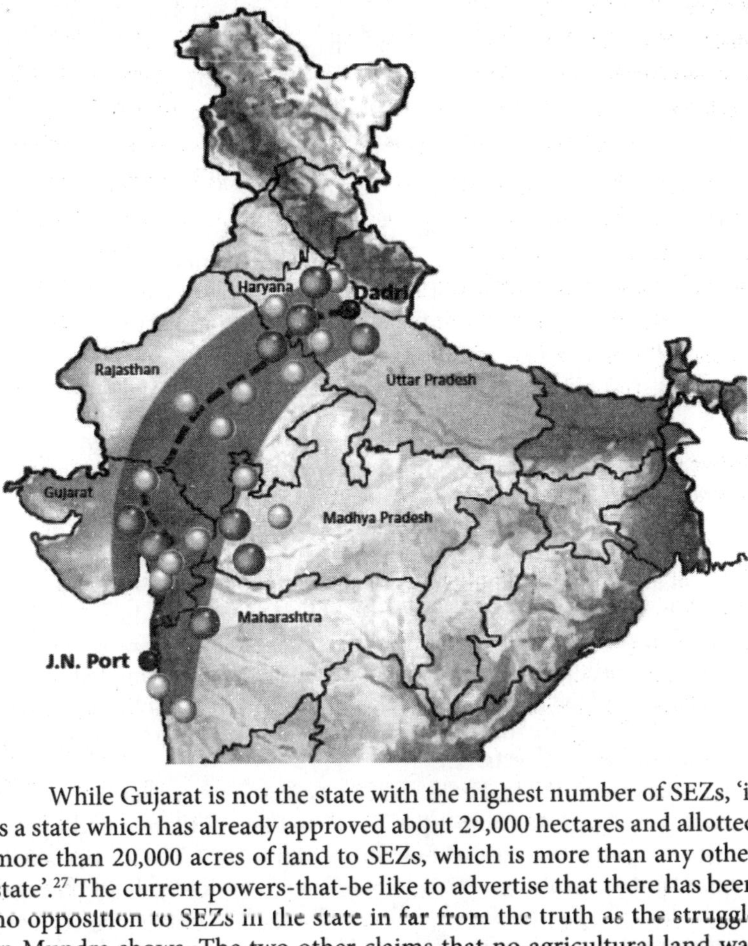

While Gujarat is not the state with the highest number of SEZs, 'it is a state which has already approved about 29,000 hectares and allotted more than 20,000 acres of land to SEZs, which is more than any other state'.[27] The current powers-that-be like to advertise that there has been no opposition to SEZs in the state in far from the truth as the struggle in Mundra shows. The two other claims that no agricultural land was given for SEZs and that private developers themselves dealt with the farmers to their satisfaction is patently false too. Of the 20,000 hectares allotted to SEZs at least 17,300 hectares were handed over by the government, only 3,500 hectares were privately acquired by private promoters of SEZs.[28]

Land deals seem to be a win-win situation if you are either a businessman, a government official in the right place at the right time, local agent facilitating land takeover to the detriment of the local community. And you are doomed if you are a farmer, fisher person, pastoralist or anyone who has to toil for a living and that would be 99 per cent of the people. Here is a prospectus if you do belong to the small section of scamsters. Adanis were given some land at ₹ 1 per square metre. If you are Adanis in Dhrub village you get land at between ₹ 12.5 and ₹ 25 per square metre and at ₹ 25 in Mundra, while other companies were charged ₹ 60 to 70 per square metre. After levelling, zoning, etc. Adanis sold the same at ₹ 800 to 2,000 per square metre. The PSUs such as IOC and HPCL too had to buy it at ₹ 1,200 per square metre.[29]

Similarly, Tata Motors got 1,100 acres for its Nano car project for a pittance. The largesse they got from the Government of Gujarat as allurement to come to Gujarat is enviable: a 20-year loan of ₹ 9,570 cr at an interest of 0.01 per cent for a ₹ 2,900 crore project (i.e., 330 per cent of what they are investing), exactly one-hundredth of one per cent! The conditions they imposed on the government read like an MOU was being signed with the East India Company: 14,000,000 litres of water per day (Narmada water?), 200 KVA power supply through double circuit feeder lines, exemption from stamp duty, registration charges, transfer fees, two/four lane road connectivity with project site, appointment of consultant to study logistics requirements of the project, acquisition of land for rail connectivity to the DMIC, additional land for ancillary industries, 100 acres of land for its township near Ahmedabad, exemption from electricity duty, facilities for disposal of hazardous waste, facilities for establishment of a transportation terminal and so on.[30] Each ₹ 1,00,000 car is estimated to cost the exchequer ₹ 60,000.[31] The terms could serve as a model agreement to any business house that does not already know how to harness public funds for private interests.

What took the cake as far as scams are concerned is the Kolkata-based private company called Visa Power Ltd. that had signed an MoU with the Government of Gujarat for a 1000 MW power plant, issuing land acquisition notices to 800 farmers in Kadiyali, Bherai and Bhachadar villages near Rajula (Amreli district).[32] Despite all the liberalization and privatization, land acquisition under the 1894 law has as yet not been privatized! As if this is not all a 50,000 hectare land bank is being created for industrial houses.[33]

A study by Lancy Lobo on the scale and extent of displacement caused by various 'development' projects in Gujarat between 1947 and 2004 reveals that at least 3.3 million hectares of land has been acquired and four million people have been displaced in the name of progress and development, and over 55 per cent of them are Adivasis and Dalits.[34] One simply cannot imagine the scale of displacement and dispossession that will be caused by a project such as the Delhi–Mumbai Industrial Corridor (DMIC) or Delhi–Mumbai Freight corridor. The DMIC will take in its sweep a belt of 300 km, including the eastern Adivasi belt of Gujarat. Even if there is environmental and social impact assessment, it will only be individual project-based, nothing that will quite fathom the combined or cumulative impact of something so humungous.

Mutual Back-Scratching Arrangement

The policy of showering largesse on large corporate houses seems to have been mastered to perfection by the CEO of Gujarat. They get land and other financial and non-financial benefits in the name of development and get to accompany him on foreign junkets. It is no wonder that the Government of Gujarat does not respond to the opposition charge that nine industries were given sales tax concessions to the tune of ₹ 12,273.73 crore.[35] This has apparently enabled him to live in style as he seems to prefer private chartered aircraft more than the government aircraft. In the first seven months of 2007, he used a government aircraft for only eight of his 34 visits and used a government plane for only four of his 18 visits in the first 130 days of 2008, using chartered aircraft for the rest of his visits. Private chartered aircraft were used on nine of his 12 foreign visits along with a host of corporate captains.[36]

Another case in point – even if puzzling – is who paid for the 27 or so 'women's empowerment' public meetings that were held in various districts of the state. Neither the Women & Child Development Department, nor the General Administration Department seem to have paid for it.[37] Who paid for helicopter rides to each of these jamborees?

A Report Card Minus Bluff and Hype

1. The best that policy-makers can think of (other than public relations offensives) for the slow-motion-Bhopal that the golden and silver corridors have become or are turning into technical fixes, end-of-the-pipe solutions such as effluent treatment plants, landfills, incinerators which either worsen the problem or only transfer it out of sight.
2. The 'state-of-the-art' technologies that policy-makers and regulatory agencies advertise are only rudimentary infrastructure referred to in Point 1 above, whereas dealing with manufacture,

transport and storage of hazardous chemicals calls for level of awareness and understanding that appears simply incomprehensible for our 'worthy' decision-makers. Scientific studies have shown that man-made chemical contaminants pose extremely serious threats at even very low levels of exposure, they interfere with the body's own hormones and might cuter through various unknown pathways and build up over time. They are especially dangerous in the earliest phases of life. Moreover, they might bioaccumulate and move up the food chain.[38]

3. Regulatory bodies such as Gujarat Pollution Control Board depend too much on public apathy and absence of awareness to hide their complicity in the abysmal state of environment, using trickery to pretend that everything is alright, e.g., the river sample findings they publish in their reports pertain to sampling points that are upstream of effluent outfalls, so they simply do not take samples of polluted waters.[39]
4. All industries associations have lobbied hard for the government to foot the waste disposal costs. Private profits and costs laid at the door of the public exchequer.
5. Industry groups or their fronts try to scare away serious criticism by threatening critics with defamation, etc. They have done that with Paryavaran Suraksha Samiti activists as well as with others. Blacksmith Institute has been publishing '10 Worst Polluted Places' Reports for some time. It included Vapi in its 2007 report. Apparently, Vapi Industries Association sued them for ₹ 40 crore and they removed Vapi from that list.[40]
6. You see the spectacle of a private corporation serving land acquisition notices (as Visa Power did) or pressuring the government to change its prohibition policy (as MNCs are reported to do), of Tatas and Adanis being given massive subsidies for their Nano plant and Mundra SEZ, respectively.
7. Public health facilities and government hospitals are in shambles on the one hand, and medical tourism for rich visitors is promoted.
8. Gujarat's public debt which was ₹ 45,301 crore in 2001–02 grew to ₹ 94,000 crore[41] in 2005–06, and is reported to be around ₹ 1,05,000 crore in 2009.
9. A sampling of Gujarat's social indicators punctures the hyperbole about being No. 1:
   Water: 74 out of 184 tehsils (sub-districts) do not have safe drinking water[42]
   Malnutrition: 42.4 per cent children
   Anaemia: more than 50 per cent of the population

Sex ratio: 883 females to every 1000 male children
Public transport: Services operated per day fell from over 20,000 in 2001 to 6,700 in 2008 (65 per cent drop)
Sarva Shiksha Abhiyan expenditure fell from ₹ 12,020.2 crore in 2007–08 to ₹ 11,940 crore in 2008–09 and to ₹ 11,933 crore in 2009–10.[43]

10. Environmental and occupational health issues find absolutely no place in the policy discourse of the rulers. The plight of communities such as in Kolak village (Valsad district) suspected to report disproportionally high incidence of cancer, or at least 29 gemstone workers dying of silicosis in Khambhat area, or the respiratory and skin diseases people near Ankleshwar and Vapi suffer from.
11. The pattern of industrial development followed causes many social imbalances such as skewed gender ratio.

Table 5

Gender Ratio in the Villages in the Vicinity of Industrial Estates[44]

Village	*Industrial Estate in Vicinity*	*Males*	*Females*	*Number of Females to Every 1,000 Males*
Salvav	Vapi	2,743	2,251	820
Balitha	Vapi	4,301	2,918	678
Chharwada	Vapi	2,341	1,650	704
Rata	Vapi	1,268	1,042	821
Chhiri	Vapi	6,949	3,541	510
Sarangpur	Ankleshwar	7,727	4,804	622
Bhadkodra	Ankleshwar	5,050	3,570	707
Jitali	Ankleshwar	2,037	1,827	896
Bakrol	Ankleshwar	842	662	786
Sanjali	Panoli	3,327	1,512	454
Dashrath	Baroda	5,640	4,990	885
Koyli	Baroda	4,988	4,592	921
Sherkhi	Baroda	4,425	4,000	904

Experts, policy-makers, scholars may need statistics as arguments but the primary producers, the toiling people – the farmers, farm workers, Adivasis, fisher people, factory workers – experience reality 3-D. And the 21st century reality for the overwhelming majority is:

- pay and use: only those with the means have the right and access to services;
- we are content to be a satellite economy, content to serve and be dependent on others;

- universalization of middle-class norms, lifestyle, aspirations and selling of dreams that most people will never fulfil;
- politically correct and catchy language, mouthing of platitudes such as 'sustainable development', 'participation', 'social justice', 'rights-based approach' and so on, without the ground reality changing;
- a clinical insensitivity to the violence and iniquity around;
- the self-defence/violence of the victim is magnified, whereas the violence of the system is justified;
- 'corporate social responsibility' is only a technique to whitewash corporate crime and buy over opposition, that is the flavour of the times;
- absence of space – one can have symbolic protests as at Jantar Mantar in Delhi, but if the opposition to the State – corporate – media nexus becomes any more effective one is likely to be reviled as anti-development, anti-national, militant, Naxalite, etc. (remember the 'foreign hand' in Mrs Indira Gandhi's times?);
- an overwhelming majority of the people are condemned to doing the same monotonous, non-stimulating work all their working lives that can neither do justice to human creativity nor is good for physical and mental health; and
- an atmosphere where the efficacy of non-violence is in serious doubt.

Notes

1. Vibrant Gujarat 2011 brochure by iNDEXTb accessed at www.vibrant gujarat.com on March 19, 2010.
2. Secretariat of Industrial Assistance Statistics, July 2008, Department of Industrial Policy & Promotion, Government of India, quoted in 'Gujarat: The Growth Engine, published by iNDEXTb for Vibrant Gujarat'.
3. Gujarat: The Growth Engine, published by iNDEXTb for Vibrant Gujarat and Vibrant Gujarat 2011 brochure by iNDEXTb accessed at www.vibrant gujarat.com.
4. http://www.indianexpress.com/news/report-by-own-govt-punctures-modis-gujarat/413765/, accessed on 17, June 2010 .
5. Gujarat: The Growth Engine, published by iNDEXTb for Vibrant Gujarat and Vibrant Gujarat 2011 brochure by iNDEXTb accessed at www.vibrant gujarat.com.
6. Calculated from the Vibrant Gujarat Investment & Potential Employment Generation Claims in Gujarat: The Growth Engine, published by iNDEXTb for Vibrant Gujarat and Vibrant Gujarat 2011 brochure by iNDEXTb accessed at www.vibrantgujarat.com. Currency conversion: US $1= ₹ 45.

7. NCEUS working draft 'The Challenge of Employment in Development in India: An Informal Economy Perspective', Table 5.15, p. 121.
8. http://www.greenpeace.org/india/press/releases/waste, accessed on June 1, 2010.
9. Based on information received by PSS under RTI Act.
10. *The Times of India,* Ahmedabad, June 5, 2010; Section: Gujarat; 10.
11. Ibid.
12. *Down to Earth*, August 31, 1999.
13. 'Bahut Ho Gaya – Take Action Now', Greenpeaceindia.org, accessed on June 1, 2010.
14. See Supreme Court order, dated May 7, 2004 on Writ Petition 657 of 1995.
15. 'Bahut Ho Gaya – Take Action Now', Greenpeaceindia.org, accessed on June 1, 2010.
16. MoEF's State of Environment Report-2009, p. 52.
17. Paryavaran Suraksha Samiti Press Release, August, 2005.
18. http://imowatch.blogspot.com/2010/04/alang-faces-choice-between-devil-deep.html, accessed on June 3, 2010.
19. See http://searchlight-is-on.blogspot.com/2010/02/mahua-weeps-nirma-smiles-in-narendra.html, accessed on 3 June '10.
20. http://www.india-seminar.com/2008/582/582_manshi_ patrik.htm.
21. http://masskutch.blogspot.com/2009/05/fishing-in-kutch-coast.html, accessed on June 4, 2010.
22. http://www.india-seminar.com/2008/582/582_manshi_ patrik.htm.
23. Government of Gujarat, Revenue Department Resolution, JMN/3903/453/A (Part I), dtd. May 17, 2005.
24. http://janpathnetwork.org/land_right.htm, accessed on June 4, 2010.
25. http://2.bp.blogspot.com/_4ZunwuGITKU/SfwU7ojxCMI/AAAAAAAAAAU/6BoXG8rf0es/s1600-h/Impact+on+Fishing.jpg, accessed on June 4, 2010.
26. DMIC Concept Paper. Department of Industrial Policy & Promotion, Ministry of Commerce, Government of India.
27. Manshi Asher in "Unravelling the Gujarat Special Economic Zone (SEZ) Model", http://www.indiasezpolitics.org/article.php?id=41, accessed on June 4, 2010.
28. Ibid.
29. http://www.environmentportal.in/node/247960, accessed on June 4, 2010.
30. http://shaktisinhgohil.com/press-release/attachments-for-press-note-date-02062010, accessed on June 14, 2010.
31. http://www.indianexpress.com/news/each-nano-will-cost-rs-60-000-to-gujarat-exchequer-gohil/411297/0, accessed on June 14, 2010.
32. http://www.indiaenvironmentportal.org.in/node/6493, accessed on June 16, 2010.
33. https://www.namoleague.com/Gujarat-Development-Business-Details?page=18, accessed on June 5, 2010.

34. Lancy Lobo quoted in Walter Fernandes' paper, can be accessed at http://onlineministries.creighton.edu/CollaborativeMinistry/NESRC/Walter/BANGALORE.doc.
35. http://gujaratcongress.org/distinfo_files/Chargesheet.pdf, accessed on June 17, 2010.
36. Press note dated March 12, 2010, issued by Mr Arjun Modhvadia's office on his speech in Gujarat Assembly.
37. Information obtained by Dr Trupti Shah through RTI applications.
38. See 'Our Stolen Future' by Theo Colborrn, Dianne Dumanoski & John, Peterson Myers.
39. See any GPCB Report over the years.
40. http://en.wikipedia.org/wiki/Vapi, accessed on June 22, 2010 and http://www.blacksmithinstitute.org/projects/display/61.
41. http://www.sacw.net/article836.html, accessed on June 5, 2010.
42. Gujarat Ecology Commission Report: State Environmental Action Plan, Chapter 3, p. 75.
43. http://www.sacw.net/article836.html, accessed on June 5, 2010.
44. Census of India, 2001.

4 Land Acquisition and Displacement in Gujarat, 1947–2004

Lancy Lobo

Insatiable Demand for Land and Displacement

Planned development in post-independent India, especially the growth of the core sector, including power, mining, heavy industry, irrigation and related infrastructural developments, came about at an enormous cost, borne by millions of persons who were displaced involuntarily or otherwise deprived of their livelihood. Even conservative guesses of the numbers of such people vary between 30 million and 50 million. Nearly 40 to 50 per cent of them are tribals. According to estimates, not more than 25 per cent of the displaced since the First Five-Year Plan have been resettled. Indeed, the experience of the first four decades after independence shows that development projects benefit primarily a few at the cost of many. The projects, instead of promoting even and holistic development of the society widen the gap between the haves and the have-nots, between regions, communities and sections of society, contributing to widespread unrest, conflict as well as extensive socio-environmental crises.

All this has happened in the name of larger or national interest. Millions are forcibly uprooted from their homes, habitats, communities and not even resettled, leave alone rehabilitated. Sometimes, even bare minimum compensation is denied to these people, bringing into question the validity and sanctity of the so-called national interests. The fact that they are denied fundamental rights guaranteed by the Constitution and several international covenants, and the growth of people's movements against such practices, brings into focus the unjust nature of the principles of eminent domain that get predominance in what is considered protection of national interests.

The Land Acquisition Act of 1894 (LAA 1894) introduced the concept of the 'public purpose'. The government could acquire land from private owners for public purposes or for a company. The agency vested with the power to make the acquisition was the District Collector. He was charged with surveying the land required, establishing the nature of the individual claims on it, settling any disputes among the existing right-holders, and any that may arise between the owners and the body acquiring the land, and awarding compensation. The landowners and right-holders of the land to be acquired were to be compensated in cash.

Land Acquisition and Displacement in Gujarat Over Time and Space

Since independence the state of Gujarat has been undertaking developmental projects such as water resources (large, medium and small dams), transport and communications, industries, mines, non-hydel, defence and security, environment protection, human resources, farms and fisheries, urban development, refugee resettlement, social welfare, tourism, government offices and so on. Land was acquired for these projects by the state during 57 years have been of three types: revenue (private), forest and government (common property resources). Data for this chapter are largely drawn from an earlier study (Lobo and Kumar, 2009), titled, Land Acquisition, Displacement and Resettlement in Gujarat: 1947–2004. While revenue land is acquired by the state with some compensation, the forest and government lands are transferred to the projects. Therefore, people dependent on forests and government land are likely to suffer the most.

The study by Lobo and Kumar (ibid.) provides hard authentic data on number of families displaced and deprived by various so-called development projects. It is also an attempt to study the impact of displacement and deprivation on various strata of the society. The data cover a span of nearly 60 years from 1947 to 2004. Since no secondary data were available from any one department of the Government of Gujarat, the scholars had to scan nearly 80,000 gazette notifications and then to code and re-code the information for maintaining uniformity in measurements of land. They also examined land acquisition documents, and visited project offices in the different parts of the state to get information about monetary compensation under various projects. Moreover, the study has carried out a sample survey of the households affected by different categories of projects, to understand the conditions of the displaced people in the new locations. Hence, this study is not merely a compilation of primary and secondary data, but it also provides analysis of different aspects of the problem at various levels.

This study shows that nearly 2.5 million households, one-fifth of the population, have lost their land and/or habitat, and fall in the category of displaced in the post-independent Gujarat (Table 2). Eighty per cent of the displaced are powerless and belong to the lower strata of society. Irrigation and industries are the main development projects, which caused a large number of displacements. The authors rightly demonstrate, with enough empirical evidence that 'Gujarat's model of development is a shadow of the model prevalent in India and in the world at large. This is a model that relies heavily on the use of non-renewable energies, increases urbanization at the cost of rural life, and causes environmental damage and destruction. This model helps a few to gain at the cost of the pain and misery of many. A large number of people face the risk of losing their knowledge just as they lost their lands, resources, languages and lives'. Sixty-one per cent of the land acquired in for water resources which are mostly in tribal areas in the eastern forest regions of Gujarat. Subsequently, 59 per cent of the total families displaced or affected are tribals. Table 1 shows the distribution of phase-wise revenue land acquired for different categories of projects and the families displaced and affected.

Spatial/Regional Analysis

Gujarat can be divided into two: mainland Gujarat, and Saurashtra and Kutch. Mainland Gujarat can be further divided into north, central and south Gujarat. One can see the differential character of development in these regions.

North Gujarat

North Gujarat provides connectivity to northern India, especially with the recent strengthening of the national and state highways. The region has three major dams: Dantiwada, Meshwa and Dharoi, which generate electricity, as well as water for irrigation. This has benefited the State, which would not otherwise have been able to cope with the drought faced by the north Gujarat region during 1964–74, when more than 70 per cent of the villages suffered human and material losses.

Water resource projects in the region have taken 60 per cent (4.2 lakh hectares) of the total land acquired, affecting 48 per cent of the families. Transportation projects, such as the national and state highways in the region, have affected an estimated 40,000 families or 2.2 lakh persons. The region has the lowest land acquisition for industries, urban development and water resource projects in the state.

Table 1

Phase-wise Distribution of Land Acquisition and Families Affected by Categories of Projects

Categories	*1947–60*		*1961–80*		*1981–90*		*1991–2004*		*Unknown*		*Grand Total*	
	LAQ[1]	*FAM*[2]	*LAQ*	*FAM*	*LAQ*	*FAM*	*LAQ*	*FAM*	*LAQ*	*FAM*	*LAQ*	*FAM*
Water Resources	32,261 (13.89)	30,306 (40.48)	674,051 (56.55)	76,119 (52.61)	689,958 (66.93)	78,700 (64.43)	522,12 (78.22)	68,919 (76.09)	2,794 (71.33)	75 (21.25)	1,921,188 (61.45)	254,119 (58.74)
Industries	2,891 (1.24)	369 (0.49)	40,741 (3.42)	4,844 (3.35)	87,181 (8.46)	6,291 (5.15)	49,415 (7.40)	3,541 (3.91)	68 (1.74)	11 (3.12)	180,296 (5.77)	15,056 (3.48)
Mines	24 (0.01)	85 (0.11)	30(0.00)	1 (0.00)	2,090 (0.20)	98 (0.08)	4,918 (0.74)	257 (0.28)	0 (0.00)	0 (0.00)	7,062 (0.23)	441 (0.10)
Non Hydel	179 (0.08)	332 (0.44)	5,727 (0.48)	317 (0.22)	8,507 (0.83)	394 (0.32)	1,874 (0.28)	118 (0.13)	639 (16.31)	51 (14.45)	16,926 (0.54)	1,212 (0.28)
Defence & Security	60 (0.03)	42 (0.06)	861 (0.07)	64 (0.04)	4,981 (0.48)	109 (0.09)	890 (0.13)	46 (0.05)	81 (2.07)	3 (0.85)	6,873 (0.22)	264 (0.06)
Environment Protection	17 (0.01)	23 (0.03)	1,543 (0.13)	240 (0.17)	289 (0.03)	17 (0.01)	0 (0.00)	0 (0.00)	0 (0.00)	0 (0.00)	1,849 (0.06)	280 (0.06)
Transport and Communication	168,625 (72.58)	40,753 (54.43)	309,046 (25.93)	56,201 (38.85)	175,049 (16.98)	34,236 (28.03)	67,081 (10.05)	13,574 (14.99)	216 (5.51)	116 (32.86)	720,017 (23.03)	144,880 (33.49)
Human Resources	9,634 (4.15)	495 (0.66)	51,045 (4.28)	954 (0.66)	9,372 (0.91)	271 (0.22)	374 (0.06)	26 (0.03)	0 (0.00)	0 (0.00)	70,425 (2.25)	1,746 (0.40)
Farms & Fisheries	1,080 (0.46)	362 (0.48)	1,837 (0.15)	355 (0.25)	826 (0.08)	45 (0.04)	3 (0.00)	1 (0.00)	0 (0.00)	0 (0.00)	3,746 (0.12)	763 (0.18)

Cont'd ...

... Cont'd

Urban Development	13,605 (5.86)	693 (0.93)	75,258 (6.31)	3,244 (2.24)	32,137 (3.12)	1,306 (1.07)	15,918 (2.38)	3,861 (4.26)	0 (0.00)	0 (0.00)	136,918 (4.38)	9,104 (2.10)
Refugee Resettlement	8 (0.00)	4 (0.01)	67 (0.01)	22 (0.02)	0 (0.00)	0 (0.00)	794 (0.12)	43 (0.05)	0 (0.00)	0 (0.00)	869 (0.03)	69 (0.02)
Social Welfare	1,023 (0.44)	330 (0.44)	23,602 (1.98)	1,392 (0.96)	5,444 (0.53)	443 (0.36)	317 (0.05)	22 (0.02)	0 (0.00)	0 (0.00)	30,386 (0.97)	2,187 (0.51)
Tourism	131 (0.06)	27 (0.04)	284 (0.02)	26 (0.02)	99 (0.01)	7 (0.01)	112 (0.02)	9 (0.01)	0 (0.00)	0 (0.00)	626 (0.02)	69 (0.02)
Government Offices	772 (0.33)	305 (0.41)	2,953 (0.25)	226 (0.16)	14,626 (1.42)	139 (0.11)	3,361 (0.50)	125 (0.14)	0 (0.00)	0 (0.00)	21,712 (0.69)	795 (0.18)
Unknown	2,020 (0.87)	749 (1.00)	4,860 (0.41)	670 (0.46)	286 (0.03)	96 (0.08)	351 (0.05)	39 (0.04)	119 (3.04)	97 (27.48)	7,636 (0.24)	1,651 (0.38)
Total	232,330	74,875	1,191,905	144,675	1,030,845	122,152	667,532	90,581	3,917	353	3,126,529	432,636

1. Land acquisition in hectares
2. Estimated families affected (figures in bracket = %)

Note: Families affected is based on the assumption that one plot acquired is equal to one family dependent on it.

Table 2
Category-wise Regional Distribution of Land Acquisition and Affected Families in Gujarat, 1947–2004

		Regions										
Project Category		*North Gujarat*	*Per cent*	*Central Gujarat*	*Per cent*	*South Gujarat*	*Per cent*	*Saurashtra & Kutch*	*Per cent*	*Unknown*	*Per cent*	*Gujarat*
Water Resource	LAQ	4,35,226	22.65	7,56,454	39.37	5,28,135	27.49	2,01,005	10.46	368	0.02	19,21,188
	FAM	49,252	19.38	1,02,075	40.17	89,021	35.03	13,696	5.39	75	0.03	2,54,119
Industry	LAQ	14,192	7.87	50,311	27.90	91,685	50.85	24,040	13.33	68	0.04	1,80,296
	FAM	1215	8.07	5613	37.28	6879	45.69	1338	8.89	11	0.07	15,056
Mines	LAQ	29	0.41	100	1.42	2268	32.12	4664	66.05	0	0.00	7061
	FAM	8	1.81	88	19.95	116	26.30	229	51.93	0	0.00	441
Non-Hydel	LAQ	73	0.43	2939	17.36	12,443	73.51	833	4.92	638	3.77	16,926
	FAM	2	0.17	498	41.09	617	50.91	44	3.63	51	4.21	1212
Defense & Security	LAQ	510	7.42	1059	15.41	199	2.90	5105	74.28	0	0.00	6873
	FAM	92	34.85	77	29.17	32	12.12	63	23.86	0	0.00	264
Environment Protection	LAQ	51	2.76	1359	73.50	439	23.74	0	0.00	0	0.00	1849
	FAM	13	4.64	179	63.93	88	31.43	0	0.00	0	0.00	280
Transport & Communication	LAQ	1,66,005	23.06	2,75,332	38.24	2,18,078	30.29	60,387	8.39	215	0.03	7,20,017
	FAM	40,353	27.85	65,156	44.97	30,389	20.98	8866	6.12	116	0.08	1,44,880
Human Resources	LAQ	14,838	21.07	18,751	26.63	36,664	52.06	172	0.24	0	0.00	70,425
	FAM	576	32.99	881	50.46	277	15.86	12	0.69	0	0.00	1746

Cont'd ...

... Cont'd

Farm & Fisheries	LAQ	188	5.02	1139	30.41	2049	54.70	370	9.88	0	0.00	3746
	FAM	29	3.80	416	54.52	302	39.58	16	2.10	0	0.00	763
Urban Development	LAQ	5213	3.81	55,328	40.41	66,643	48.67	9735	7.11	0	0.00	1,36,918
	FAM	390	4.28	3680	40.42	1577	17.32	3457	37.97	0	0.00	9104
Refugee	LAQ	65	7.48	748	86.08	56	6.44	0	0.00	0	0.00	869
	FAM	19	27.54	40	57.97	10	14.49	0	0.00	0	0.00	69
Social Welfare	LAQ	2150	7.08	7182	23.64	20,159	66.34	895	2.95	0	0.00	30,386
	FAM	16	0.73	743	33.97	1309	59.85	119	5.44	0	0.00	2187
Tourism	LAQ	117	18.69	384	61.34	72	11.50	53	8.47	0	0.00	626
	FAM	11	15.94	44	63.77	10	14.49	4	5.80	0	0.00	69
Government Office	LAQ	1561	7.19	10,606	48.85	8682	39.99	864	3.98	0	0.00	21,712
	FAM	106	13.33	236	29.69	414	52.08	39	4.91	0	0.00	795
Not Known	LAQ	1659	21.73	3323	43.52	1481	19.39	1054	13.80	119	1.56	7636
	FAM	359	21.74	713	43.19	390	23.62	92	5.57	97	5.88	1651
Total	LAQ	6,41,876	20.53	11,85,015	37.90	9,89,052	31.63	3,09,177	9.89	1408	0.05	31,26,529
	FAM	92,441	21.37	1,80,459	41.71	1,31,431	30.38	27,975	6.47	350	0.08	4,32,636

Note: LAQ = Land acquired (in hectares) and FAM = Families affected (numbers).

Central Gujarat

Central Gujarat, also known as the 'food bowl' of the state, was in need of irrigation alternatives, and land was acquired mostly for the canals located upstream of major rivers such as the Sabarmati, Watrak and Mahi. Though the canal network was constructed by land acquisition, the canals themselves proved to be beneficial to the farmers. Large areas of land also had to be given up for the Wanakbori thermal power project.

Central Gujarat also has the highest amount of land acquired for roads, with the purpose of connecting the villages to boost the cooperative movements and participate in 'Operation Flood'. Later, the massive acquisition for the National Expressway after 1985 resulted in the loss of 10,000 hectares or more of prime agricultural land. The green revolution in Gujarat began through agricultural initiatives in the Anand and Kheda districts, and ushered a high productivity phase in Vadodara, Surat, the south of Ahmedabad, Mehsana, the north of Rajkot, Jamnagar, Junagadh and Amreli in Saurashtra. The Charotar belt did not complain about the land acquired for canals and roads. The utilization of government and *gauchar* (grazing lands) land, on which the Dalits and OBCs depended, had an adverse effect on these people.

Apart from agricultural production in Central Gujarat, the eastern hilly districts of Panchmahal and Dahod have numerous mineral resources. The main minerals extracted are limestone, marble, stone, sand, bauxite, manganese, etc. Located in the tribal-dominated forest tracts, these areas were leased for mining till recently, when the courts restricted mining in forest tracts.

The massive canal network of the major irrigation projects was a Godsend for Central Gujarat. Even though there were numerous check dams, bore wells and *khet talavdi*s (lakes); the state had created irrigation problems in the region. Industries around the Vadodara sub-region acquired nearly 2,500 hectares of land for various industrial uses, the most prominent being the petrochemical complexes. The region accounts for 37 per cent (11.85 lakh hectares) of the total land acquired in the state; of these, 64 per cent (7.5 lakh hectares) were for water resources, 22 per cent (2.75 lakh hectares) for transportation, nearly five per cent for industries, and the remaining for other uses. An estimated 1.8 lakh families or one million persons were affected by these development projects: nearly 51 per cent by the water resources projects and 36 per cent by the transportation ones. Industries/projects have deprived 5,000 families or 27,000 persons in the region of their cultivable land.

South Gujarat

South Gujarat seems to have borne the brunt of the development demands of the state. Being one of the rich forest and mineral reserves of the state, the region was exploited to provide the much-needed water for irrigation. Presently identified as a chemical zone, South Gujarat is also known for the cultivation of sugarcane for Gujarat's sugar factories. The canal network in the region was mainly developed to facilitate sugarcane farming and horticulture. Developed after the 1980s, this region is home to the chemical and hazardous industrial estates of Gujarat. The golden corridors of the region, from Bharuch to Vapi, have been experiencing rapid industrial development. The region has the largest chemical estates in Ankleshwar, Vapi and Surat, in addition to the traditional diamond and textile industries in Surat. The textile trade in the region has received a serious setback, with states such as Tamil Nadu and Maharashtra contributing a larger share to India's textile trade post in the 1990s. The development of the industries in South Gujarat is certainly not based on the region's skills and human resource availability, but largely due to the state's incentives to industries, cheap labour and lax environmental policies.

The transfer of forestlands to development projects, including mining and the timber trade, has also seriously affected South Gujarat. A major cause of displacement of the tribals is the activities of the Forest Department; people are treated as 'encroachers' in their own land and their presence within the forest is challenged. Of the 35,000 hectares of forestland transferred to the State, nearly 14,000 hectares have been transferred from the Surat, Bharuch and Valsad districts.

The 9.2 lakh hectares of land acquired for the water resources and industrial development projects in the region have affected an estimated 1.31 lakh families, 7.2 lakh persons. Of the thin stretch of cultivable land available in the region, one lakh hectares were acquired for industries, accounting for 50 per cent of the total land acquired for industries in the state. An estimated 5.2 lakh hectares of land have been acquired for water resource projects, mainly for the dam and canal networks of three multipurpose and a dozen medium dams.

Saurashtra and Kutch

Till 1965, the region had developed a small and medium irrigation scheme which resulted in its becoming a major contributor to the food-oil seed production in the State and in the country. The development of the road network resulted in the penetration of the industries into the region. The Kutch district had developed a hub for the Export Processing Zone (EPZ) in Kandla Port since the 1970s.

Industrial development in the district is mainly related to the services required at Kandla Port Trust, under the Free Trade Zone, which has been converted to a Special Economic Zone (SEZ) to extend the benefits provided to the industries. Traditionally, during British India, Saurashtra – especially Jamnagar, Junagadh and Rajkot – was also a developed region for manufacturing diesel engines, brass parts, clocks and tiles. The development of cement and lignite industries provided the development potential for other ancillary industries in the region. After the 2001 earthquake, the government invited industries to Kutch by easing the region's already lenient tax regime. Salt and chemical industries were widely developed in the Great and Little Rann of Kutch. The fragile ecosystem was disturbed and damaged by leasing more than 1,000 hectares of land to large corporates, for salt pans, mining/farming.

The Jamnagar Petrochemical Complex is one of the largest concentrations of private and public petrochemical industries in the country. The people in the region were evicted to accommodate the oil and gas terminal imported by the industries. After the earthquake, the government facilitated industrial development near the Marine National Park and the coastal zones of Saurashtra and Kutch. The State Government transferred nearly 10,000 hectares of the Marine National Park to the industries for salt pans.

The region had figured low on the development priority till 1980, and so had received little attention from policy-planners. Since the 1990s, the industrialization policies boosted investment along the Silver Corridors (Ahmedabad–Jamnagar and Rajkot–Bhavnagar). Of the total 3.2 lakh hectares of land acquired for development projects, nearly 66.6 per cent, i.e., 2.3 lakh hectares were used for water resource projects. The industries in the region have acquired 24,000 hectares of land, mainly for the petrochemical industries around Jamnagar and for the medium industries around Rajkot, Jamnagar, Bhuj, Mundra and Kandla.

The Gujarat state with a population of 50 million (year 2001) has a geographical area of 1,96,000 sq km (19.6 million ha) and the cultivable area of 12.36 million ha. Of these, nearly 28 per cent (3.5 million hectares) of the cultivable land was acquired for various development projects in the State directly affecting 2.5 million persons (5% of the total population of the state). Since late 1990s, 2002 general election and 'Vision 2020' campaign, and a significant section of the middle class and media have become terribly impatient 'to make India a developed country' and in pursuit of this goal they are willing to take blatantly anti-poor stance. This is evident from the recent demolition of the slums in Mumbai, Delhi (for commonwealth games), Ahmedabad (for Sabarmati River Front Development), etc. Twenty years ago, big industries were wary for asking government apart from the designated required land for setting industries, now they do not hesitate in asking for 60,000 hectares of land for setting up Special Economic Zone (SEZ). The state being a party to not only anti-people adventures in being a facilitator for the large-scale industries, but also falling into the trap laid by the multinational corporations and industries. The recent red carpet welcome received by the industries in the Vibrant Gujarat 2007 summit attracting 4.1 lakh crores worth investment makes one of the preferred investment destination in the country. The dual need of the multipurpose project such SSP has created a body of water, which enables to fulfil not only the agricultural requirement but also water consumption in industrial and urban areas. The state planners for the new development projects now capture the areas, which were earlier considered to be natural barriers for development.

Impact of Land Acquisition and Displacement

Displacement and poverty have been linked together by social scientists such as Michael Cernea, a sociologist who has researched development-induced displacement and resettlement for the World Bank. He points out that being forcibly ousted from one's land and habitat carries with it the risk of becoming poorer than before displacement, since a significant portion of the people displaced do not receive compensation for their lost assets and the assistance required to re-establish themselves productively. Cernea (1999) has identified eight interlinked potential risks intrinsic to displacement. Others have suggested the addition of other risks such as the loss of access to public services, schooling for children, and civil rights or the abuse of human rights such as loss of property without fair compensation, or violence from security forces or risks of communal violence in resettlement areas to Cernea's list.

Eight interlinked potential risks intrinsic to displacement are:

1. *Landlessness:* Expropriation of land removes the main foundation upon which people's productive systems, commercial activities, and livelihoods are constructed.
2. *Joblessness:* The risk of losing wage employment is very high both in urban and rural displacements for those employed in enterprises, services or agriculture. Yet, creating new jobs is difficult and requires substantial investment.

3. *Homelessness:* Loss of shelter tends to be only temporary for many people being resettled; but, for some, homelessness or a worsening in their housing standards remains a lingering condition. In a broader cultural sense, loss of a family's individual home and the loss of a group's cultural space tend to result in alienation and status deprivation.
4. *Marginalization:* Marginalization occurs when families lose economic power and spiral on a 'downward mobility' path. Many individuals cannot use their earlier-acquired skills at the new location; human capital is lost or rendered inactive or obsolete. Economic marginalization is often accompanied by social and psychological marginalization.
5. *Food insecurity:* Forced uprooting increases the risk that people will fall into temporary or chronic undernourishment, defined as calorie-protein intake levels below the minimum necessary for normal growth and work.
6. *Increased morbidity and mortality:* Displacement-induced social stress and psychological trauma, the use of unsafe water supply and improvised sewage systems, increase vulnerability to epidemics and chronic diarrhoea, dysentery or particularly parasitic and vector-borne diseases such as malaria and schistosomiasis.
7. *Loss of access to common property:* For poor people, loss of access to the common property assets that belonged to relocated communities (pastures, forest lands, water bodies, burial grounds, quarries and so on) result in significant deterioration in income and livelihood levels.
8. *Social disintegration:* Displacement causes a profound unraveling of existing patterns of social organization. This unraveling occurs at many levels. When people are forcibly moved, production systems, life-sustaining informal networks, trade linkages, etc. are dismantled.

The study on Gujarat (Lobo and Kumar, 2009) corroborates the risks identified above that are intrinsic to the character of development pursued in the State.

Policy Issues in Gujarat

Our study on development-induced displacement in Gujarat during the period 1947 to 2004 has uncovered a mottled picture in the state, which may be looked into while formulating the R&R policy of the state. The Gujarat Ecology Commission reports readied in 1995 on the status of air, water and land are yet to be released by the government as they are damning to its growth-centric development. It is said that

Gujarat's GDP is 14 per cent, and that of the rest of the country is 10 per cent. Few however, speak about the rapid rate of the depletion of Gujarat's resources. A policy should look into the sustainable development policies having minimum negative implications on the land and human resources.

1. *People displaced and deprived by development projects:* In Gujarat, four lakh households (2.5 million persons; 5 per cent of the state's total population) have been displaced or affected by developmental projects such as water resources, transport and communications, industries, mines, defence, sanctuaries, human resources, government offices, tourism, etc., during 57 years. On the recent land earmarked for by the special economic zones, the Chief Minister has repeatedly stated that barren, waste and saline lands will be used. But it is believed that the 60 SEZs and the proposed Special Investment Regions will take away quite a bit of the agricultural land. The state should balance the land utilization for agricultural as well as industrial uses based on the regional social, resources and economic evaluation of the state.
2. There has been a gradual shift in the pattern of land utilization in Gujarat, moving from the primarily agricultural to the non-agricultural. The consequence of the present pattern of development is the continuing powerlessness of the weaker sections of society: they are often displaced without getting any benefits from the projects. Since independence, development projects of the five-year plans have displaced about five lakh persons each year in India, primarily as a consequence of land acquisition. This figure does not include displacement by non-plan projects. In addition, changes in land use, acquisition for urban growth and loss of livelihood have also caused environmental degradation and pollution. Hydro-electrical and irrigation projects have been the largest cause of displacement and the destruction of habitat. Policy on the R&R should look into the long term negative fallout of such development approach and appropriate initiatives to mitigate them.
3. *Decadal change:* As mentioned earlier, after the formation of Gujarat, the state's focus shifted from transportation projects to water resources projects. The highest land acquisition in the state was during 1981–90 for both water resources as well as industrial projects; it amounted to 10.3 lakh hectares, and directly affected 1.22 lakh families. Between 1971 and 1980, the state had acquired 70 per cent of the total land acquired till 2004. The quantity of the land acquired should be minimized for the industrial projects

especially for the special economic zones. Policy should look for restrictive areas subject to Social and Environmental clearance from the concerned departments.

4. *Sub-regions affected:* The regional spread of development projects reflects the land acquisition trends in the state. For instance, though water resources projects have more land acquisition in South Gujarat (dams) as compared to Central Gujarat (canal network), the latter region has benefited from the canals more. The policy should make effort to minimize the sub-regional imbalances.
5. *Social groups affected:* From the sample data of the study, it may been seen that the victims of the development projects have been, for the most part, the tribal communities, especially in the water resources, mining and forestry projects. The Dalits and the backward communities in Central and South Gujarat have often had to part with their small landholdings for canal networks and industrial complexes. The industrial regions of Saurashtra and Kutch have seen the larger, agriculture-dependent communities (who worked as agricultural labourers) especially in Jamnagar, Rajkot, Bhavnagar and Kutch districts, suffer due to land acquisition. Our survey across the state reveals that the communities already economically and socially neglected by the state could not regain their livelihood, and lost both their lands and their pride. The policy should consider the R&R specific to the different social groups affected.
6. *Gender:* It is women who suffer the most from the process of displacement. A great number of women who were mostly dependent on agricultural land, forests and water bodies for their livelihood have been forced to work against their wishes. The female workforce from tribal communities was forced to work in the sugarcane fields in South Gujarat; women from Central and North Gujarat were uprooted from their own fields and had to work as labourers in factories; some are even pushed into becoming a part of the urban mainstream and work in cities as domestics. Women have thus been made to feel insecure and have been subject to violent atrocities not only at home but also outside. The policy on R&R should be able to address the problems of women and children.
7. *Linear/site-specific projects in situ:* The character of the project has also contributed to the nature of displacement and deprivation. Site-specific projects requiring large areas of land (dams, industrial complexes, urban centres and other social

infrastructure) have a greater potential for displacing people. Projects such as industrial complexes, power plants and townships may benefit the displaced both in the short and long term. The mining projects have varied impacts depending on the nature of the mining taking place. In such cases, land is permanently lost to the project; the landowners' only economic gain is the compensation received. Land loss may be less for linear projects such as roads, canals or pipelines: such projects rarely displace people. However, the better compensation policy of the SSNL and the Highway Authorities has helped land losers to get good value for their land. The impact of linear projects may be high only when land loss is caused by multiple projects. Such cases have occurred in Central and North Gujarat where the loss of the village land is so high that it has deprived people of all cultivable land. The policy should be specific to the nature of the project. Project-specific strategies need to be formulated for the R&R in the state.

8. *The inadequacy of compensation:* Those displaced or affected by development projects seldom receive a satisfactory return on the land acquired. The Land Acquisition Act does not recognize the 'displaced', or recommend resettlement and rehabilitation packages for the project-affected except in terms of monetary compensation which can never be commensurate with the value of the land. Till the early 1980s, the general trend of compensation in the state was low as compared to the current rates where people's awareness and government policy have played a significant role in raising the compensation amount. This amount was smaller in tribal regions due to two factors: (a) the non-transferable character of tribal lands lowered the value of land (as compared to marketable lands); (b) the low price of land was also due its location and lack of productivity. Since valuation is largely dependent on sale instances of the land under question, the valuation of certain lands may be lower than others at the same site. As mentioned earlier, compensation also depends on the type of agency and the nature of the project: industrial projects for instance, have higher rates of compensation than others. It is necessary to observe if compensation is based on the current value of land (as seen from the revenue perspective) or on its earning potential over the next 10–15 years. Is the compensation paid to farmers comparable with the Voluntary Retirement Scheme offered to various public sector undertakings which compensates employees not only for the loss of income but also

for the income they might have earned until their retirement? Similarly, if land acquisition makes farmers retire from their occupation, how is the payment of the current market price of their land as compensation justified what could be the price of land after 10 years? Thus, either the state needs to reconsider its compensation policy or formulate a rehabilitation plan for landholders who have been deprived by development projects. Most projects might not be capable or willing to rehabilitate project-affected persons. In such cases, mandatory compensation and rehabilitation by allowing projects to pay costs to the state or local bodies for the development of the affected is highly recommended.

9. The Central Government plans to amend the Land Acquisition Act of 1894 and remove the section inserted in 1984 during Indira Gandhi's regime that empowered the government's acquisition of land for private parties for the purpose of industrial development in backward regions. The Amendment also redefines the public purpose for which the government is allowed to acquire private land. It is thought that this will terminate the government's right to acquire land for promoting industrial estates and SEZs. The government will, however, retain powers to intervene if vested-interest elements adopt malafide means to prevent the establishment of the SEZ or that of any other project. While one of the key amendments will require private parties and developers to buy land from the owners through negotiations without any government help, the government will step in if 90 per cent or more land has been acquired, but there is resistance against the purchase of the remaining 10 per cent. Under the proposed amendment, the government can notify resisting landowners to compulsorily sell their land. In such a case, the owners would be entitled to the highest price that the project promoters had paid for any part of the land acquired for the project.

10. The *public purpose* in the United States is known as the *eminent domain*. Eminent domain is generally defined as the power of the nation or sovereign state to take, or to authorize the taking of, private property for public use without the owner's consent, conditioned upon the payment of just compensation. The exercise of the power of eminent domain is subject to all the prohibitions found in the Constitution of the United States and of the several states. The provisions by which the power is chiefly limited are: (a) that property shall not be taken for public use without just compensation, and (b) that no person shall be deprived of his life,

liberty or property without due process of law (for elaborate discussion see Dias, 2006: 61 ff).

11. *The concept of 'public purpose'*: The Land Acquisition Act does not define the term 'public purpose' – this is left to the discretion of the 'concerned authority'. The government often misuses this term. The original owner of land is, of course, entitled to compensation for the loss of property. Compensation is calculated as per the market value of land at the time of the notification. It is the concerned authority that conducts the valuation, not an independent agency. For the effective utilization of the term 'public purpose', the Supreme Court has been helping the government by making a controversial judgment wherein it states, 'by contributing a trifling sum, the character and pattern of acquisition could be changed by the government. In the ultimate analysis, what is considered to be an acquisition for facilitating the setting up of an industry in the private sector could get imbued with the character of public purpose acquisition, if only the government comes forward to sanction the payment of a nominal sum towards compensation' (*Business Standard*, March 21, 2007).
12. The expropriation of tribal land in Gujarat smacks of the *terra nullius* (literally 'no one's land or unoccupied land'). Saurashtra had *zamindari,* mainland Gujarat (especially British districts) had ryatwari, while eastern Gujarat had a kind of community ownership of land. They had customary laws and the civil law came much later. British had expropriated much of this tribal land and after independence too only the state could allow the tribal to sell land through the permission of the Collector. Thus, the tribals were doubly vulnerable with reference to their land ownership and transfer. The poor implementation of PESA in scheduled tribal areas added to the tribal misery.

References

Antony, M.J., "Sore Points in Land Acquisition," *Business Standard*, March 21, 2007.

Cernea. M., "Why Economic Analysis Is Essential to Resettlement: A Sociologist's View". In Michael M. Cernea, ed. *The Economics of Involuntary Resettlement: Questions and Challenges,* The World Bank, Washington, D.C., 1999.

Dias, Anthony, "Development-induced Displacement and its Impact". In Tharakan Siby, ed., *The Nowhere People: Responses to Internally Displaced Persons*, Books for Change, Bangalore, 2006.

Fernandes, Walter and Niraj Naik, *Development-induced Displacement in Goa 1965 to 1995: A Study on its Extent and Nature,* Indian Social Institute, New Delhi and Panjim: INSAF (mimeo), 2001.

Iyer, Ramaswamy, "Towards a Just Displacement and Rehabilitation Policy", *Economic and Political Weekly,* 28 July 2007, pp. 3103–07.

Lobo, Lancy and Shashikant Kumar, *Land Acquisition, Displacement and Resettlement in Gujarat: 1947–2004,* Sage Publications, New Delhi, 2009.

Prabhu, Pradip, "Land Alienation, Land Reforms and Tribals in Maharashtra". In Ghanshyam Shah and D.C. Shah, eds. *Land Reforms in India: Performance and Challenges in Gujarat and Maharashtra,* Sage Publications, New Delhi, 2002.

Ramanathan, Usha, "Public Purpose: Points for Discussion". In Walter Fernandes, ed. *The Land Acquisition (Amendment) Bill 1998: For Liberalisation or for the Poor?,* Indian Social Institute, New Delhi, 1999, pp. 19–24.

5 A Kaleidoscopic Panorama of Agrarian Struggles in Gujarat

Kiran Desai

Prologue: Pre-Independence and Post-Independence Scenario of Agrarian Resistance in India

This paper makes an effort to delineate various forms of agrarian struggles that have taken place in Gujarat. As it is not possible to cover each and every spurt of action that took shape around agrarian issues, a few major struggles would be highlighted along with specific implications, each of them indicates in terms of its character and effects with reference to micro as well as larger context. In order to get comparative scenario pertaining to agrarian unrest, a brief sketch in relation to India as a whole is relevant here.

For the generalization purpose, it can be deduced that issues related with land alienation as well as policy measures pertaining to land reforms have been the major causes and factors that have sparked agrarian unrest not only in Gujarat, but in various parts of the country. With reference to pre-independent India, renowned historian David Hardiman has mentioned that according to Eric Stokes there were two major kinds of agrarian protest: '(1) by rich peasants in areas of "high farming" who were seeking to extend their power, and (2) by pauperised peasants who had suffered badly as a result of colonial rule' (Stokes, 1976, cited in Hardiman, 1992). In the same volume, Hardiman himself has identified five areas of agrarian resistance for the same period with reference to India as a whole as well as antagonistic interest groups, namely, '... (1) peasants against European planters; (2) peasants against indigenous landlords; (3) peasants against professional money-landers (sahukars); (4) peasants against the land-tax bureaucracy; and (5) peasants against forest officials" (Hardiman, 1992: 11). Covering both pre- and post-independence periods in general, A.R. Desai in his seminal work has distinguished two kinds of agrarian struggles: one, launch by proprietary class, mainly consisting of big and middle-level landholders and the second, struggles of those who are at the lower levels of rural agrarian hierarchy. The former is to gain more concessions, support and facilities from government in order to buttress the income and profit of this, by and large, prosperous group, whereas the latter category of struggles is mainly launched by agrarian poor and toiling groups (Desai, 1986). This chapter will mainly cover this latter kind of agrarian unrest, though the former would be featured as and where it is required. In other words, the depiction pertaining to agrarian movements involving mainly lower echelons of rural population and that too of recent time in Gujarat, especially post-independence era, would be featured in this chapter. In order to get comprehensive and holistic picture, it is imperative to have a glimpse of peasant struggles in India from historical perspective.

Agrarian struggles have a long history in India. They date back to as long as 16th century. In most cases of these revolts land revenue, tenants' rights and their exploitation had remained the main issues for discontent. As typified by Hardiman, mainly the peasants had to wage battle against big landowners, *sahukars* and/or the various agencies of the State. Often, all the agrarian strata jointly launched struggles against the authority, either local or foreign (Dhanagare, Guha and Hardiman have depicted, compiled and analysed them in their work, see Dhanagare, 1983; Guha, 1983; Hardiman, 1992). Hardiman (1992), in his edited volume, has included which he considered as the major eight struggles that took place in pre-independent India covering the period of second half of the 19th century to earlier part of the 20th century. In his introduction of the volume, he has delved on and brought out complexities pertaining to socio-economic characteristics and specificities of these unrests keeping in focus the five categories he has carved out (as mentioned above) for analytical purpose. In his long essay (Hardiman, 1992: 1–59), the author at one point has cited Partha Chatterjee's observation wherein the latter has suggested that Indian peasants had behaved and perceived themselves as a community not necessarily in a sense of a class. Taking this reflection further by deciphering the 'community' as a complex category, Hardiman argues that, '... the boundaries of the perceived community were never closed: peasants could at one moment be inspired by their religion as well as fight for the peasant community as a whole against those seen as their exploiters in a way that cut across religious boundaries' (Hardiman, 1992: 22). He explained his remarks by citing a few illustrations. For instance, in the case of Mappilas of Malabar religious factor did play a crucial role when mainly Muslim tenants resisted against Hindu landlords. Similarly, in Deccan revolt of last quarter of 19th century in which peasants fought against money-lenders, social background of the latter did influence the nature of wrath of peasants. Hardiman has argued that colonial regime had facilitated stronger position of *sahukars* vis-à-vis peasants and that had evoked peasants resistance in this case. Deccan revolt has been considered as one of the major struggle of pre-independence colonial period. He has also covered in his edited work (Hardiman, 1992), a struggle between peasants and planters on the issue of Indigo plantation in Bengal, mainly its eastern part during the period 1859–1862. The planters were mainly British, whereas most of the peasants were of a Muslim sect. The struggle ended with an increase in the rates for plantation work. In this introductory essay, Hardiman has mentioned various agitations by the peasants of different parts of Bombay presidency and noticed that these protests are not properly studied by the scholars (Hardiman, 1992: 44). His volume, on the other hand, has included an essay on the agitation launched by the peasants of Punjab against the water tax and which resulted into government of India intervening and getting their demands accepted by Punjab government (Barrier, in Hardiman, 1992). These two movements got strong backing from urban-based nationalists. Indian National Congress, except few individuals, never took up peasants cause. Hume, Tilak and Lala Lajpatrai were some of the prominent leaders who had given due importance to agrarian issues. The struggles of varied kinds that had taken place in the 19th century and early 20th century (before Gandhi took over leadership) had taken shape along different forms in terms of formation of peasants as an organized group. As Hardiman has put it,

> ... solidarity in these struggles was achieved not by appealing to sectional interests, but by infusing a spirit of community solidarity against outside oppression. All sorts of bonds of clan, caste, tribe, kinship, religion and locality were invoked in building such solidarities.
>
> (Hardiman, 1992: 57)

In the final analysis, all the struggles mentioned above could not achieve their intended objectives and desired results. The Bengal resistance (1859–62), though had compelled the British indigo-planters to leave eastern India as Dhanagare has pointed out new groups of exploiters in the form of money-lenders and tenant land-owners replaced them (Dhanagare, 1983). The Deccan riots (as the movement was termed then) were resulted into the Deccan Agriculturists Relief Act of 1879 to curb the exploitative methods of money-lenders. But this legislation failed to protect poor Kunbi peasants as the *sahukars* continued to have a hold on the local credit system as well as transpose. As seen above only the outcome of agitation by peasants of Punjab in 1907 was favourable for peasants. Similarly, resistance by forest dwellers got them some minor concessions only.

Dhanagare's seminal work covers agrarian struggles for the period 1920–1950 (Dhanagare, 1983). As he has put it, the Moplah revolt in Malabar region was '... in essence an expression of long-standing agrarian discontent, which was only intensified by the religious and ethnic identity of the Moplahs and by their political alienation ...' (Dhanagare, 1983: 82). The Oudh region of then United Province (now Uttar Pradesh – UP) had witnessed two agrarian agitations – one in the period of 1920–22 and the other during 1930–32. In the first one, the poor peasants and landless resorted to violent resistance against rise in prices and land rent as well as for land occupancy rights in spite of presence of Congress leadership who endorsed non-violent methods and means, whereas the 1930–32 agitation was led by the Congress to espouse the cause of rich and middle peasants as these two groups were facing agrarian crisis due to economic depression of that period. Indian National Congress since its inception in 1885 had not been taking militant and combative stance on agrarian issues and its approach was to gain concessions for peasants through moderate means of representation. As Hardiman has put it citing the observation of John Mclane, 'No attempts were made to discuss radical solutions to rural problems, such as land redistribution, a ceiling on holdings or land to the tillers' (Hardiman, 1992: 54). Only few nationalists such as B.G. Tilak and Lala Lajpat Rai took up the agrarian issues in Maharashtra and Punjab, respectively, on their own. It was Gandhi who changed the course by taking up grievances of peasants first, in Champaran in 1917 and Kheda in 1918. On the other hand, communists took up the agrarian issues by founding All India Kisan Sabha and led two known peasant movements on the eve of independence, i.e., Tebhaga movement in Bengal during 1946–47 and peasant insurrection of Telangana in the period 1946–51. The contribution of Sahjanand Swami, a Gandhian turned communist was quite extraordinary in activities of Kisan Sabha. The Tebhaga movement was launched by sharecroppers to retain two-thirds share of the produce and thereby to reduce the rent they paid to the class of rich farmers. Dhanagare considers it as '... the first consciously attempted revolt by a politicised peasantry in Indian history' (Dhanagare, 1983: 155). The Tebhaga struggle though had a potential to erupt in to a massive revolt, it did not happen due to social and communal forces and internal differences in Kisan Sabha and share-cropping continued even after the movement. The Telangana revolt which was launched and led by the Communist Party of India, began in 1946 and was withdrawn in 1951. The class alliance of rich and middle peasantry with poor took part in this insurrection under the communist leadership. The post-Second World War political developments as well as economic crisis gave impetus to this struggle. The vast number of peasants, mainly from middle-and poor-level peasants fought against Nizam government, big landlords and their agents. As Dhanagare has mentioned:

> If seizure of power for a considerable period of time is taken as the touchstone of the success then, perhaps, no other peasant revolt or movement in India was more successful than the one in Telangana. If, however, a lasting dent in the agrarian structure and change in the principal participants are viewed as the criterion, then the Telangana insurrection was no more successful then other peasant resistance movements in India.
>
> (Dhanagare, 1983: 207)

An edited volume (1986) by renowned sociologist A.R. Desai covers agrarian struggles of different hues in post-independent India. It is not probable to include them all in this chapter. But some major developments on the front of agrarian sector should be mentioned. In terms of movement, there were many notice-worthy struggles such as Girijan movement in Srikakulam, Andhra Pradesh (1967–70), peasant unrest in Bhojpur-Bihar of 70s, Bataidari movement of Bihar also of 70s, the famous Naxalbari movement of late 60s in West Bengal, all these movements led by various hues of Communist ideology; agitations in various states lead by Samyukta Socialist party and Praja Samajwadi party; struggles steered by Kisan Sabha and Bhartiya Khet mazdoor union as well as land related tribal movements especially in north-east region. The issues around which these struggles had taken place are varied and complex. Similarly, the nature and form of agitation on each instance were dependent on specificities related with region, political and ideological affiliation of the leadership and people, State's response and attitude, class differentiation and relations with reference to agrarian scenario and other factors. Many states have opted for land reforms in post-independence era and that had resulted into varied nature of upheavals and reactions. Issues emerging out of tenancy rights had also created situation of strife and tension. Wages of agriculture labourers, rights of cultivation and forest produce of tribals and other forest-dwellers are other issues that culminated into struggles of the deprived groups. On the other hand, issues such as irrigation facility, prices and marketing of crops especially commercial crops, land tax, water cess, extension of electrification and subsidy in its rates, demand for subsidies and better prices as well as demand for credit facilities are some of the main issues around which peasants of varied strata have been raising their voice in the forms of representation, meeting, seminar, rally, satyagraha as well as prolong agitation. Various organizations have been active for the cause of peasants. All India Kisan Sabha, Bhartiya Khet Mazdoor Union and peasant organizations associated with different political parties and ideologies have been vouching for the cause of various agrarian groups at all India level. At the same time, regional level organizations have also been effectively making their presence felt. For instance, Kashtakari Sanghatna in Thane district of Maharashtra has been organizing Varli tribe for their problems pertaining to rights over land and forest. Similarly, spontaneous local level mass agitations were reported from each and every part of the country.

Agrarian Unrest in Gujarat

In Gujarat, the agrarian struggles launched by and for the deprived groups reflect and represent rights and issues pertaining to land with reference to various tribal groups in most cases. Though the essay chiefly portrays post-independence scenario, two major peasant struggles of pre-independence period which were very much associated with freedom movement under the leadership of Gandhi would also be mentioned to get a comparative picture in terms of a set of characteristics especially the nature of class affiliation. These two agitations were known as 'Kheda Satyagraha' and 'Bardoli Satyagraha' denoting the places where the Satyagraha movement took place. Along with these two agitations, it is pertinent to take into account a series of protests that took place in various parts of Gujarat (then part of Bombay province) at the end of the 19th century. During the period of 1899–1900, Gujarat was under a spell of severe famine and peasants expected a relief in land tax. But the British government refused to give any relief in land tax and throughout the region peasants had to resort to protest by way of refusing to pay the land tax. Kheda, Surat, Broach (Bharuch) everywhere peasants declined to pay tax and in most of the cases leadership was provided by local people, mainly from peasants themselves. The resistance though was soon collapsed, due to intimidating tactics and stern response of the British regime.

Kheda district was located in Central Gujarat. In the latter part of the year 1917, the district received torrential rain and the peasants, cutting across various, strata, suffered heavy losses as their harvested kharif crops got wet and rotted. Two local level activists, Mohanlal Pandya and Shankarlal Parikh, who were inspired by Gandhi after attending Gujarat Political conference held at Godhara decided to take up the demand of the peasants for suspension of land revenue for the year by preparing a petition in which 22,000 peasants signed. Later on, Gujarat Sabha under the leadership of Gandhi decided to take up the issue after Gandhi and Vallabhbhai Patel toured the villages of the district to assess the situation and when they found that the demand of the peasants was just, the Satyagraha was launched. Patidars as a caste was a dominating force among peasants of various strata. Gandhi asked the peasants to sign a sacred vow pledging to undergo all the sufferings by not paying land revenue for the year, even allowing the government to confiscate their land. If the rulers would gracefully postpone the collection of revenue, those peasants who can afford would be prepared to pay up revenue. But, the government did not heed to the request and Satyagraha was on. Hardiman considered Kheda Satyagraha less organized in terms of leadership and strategy (Hardiman, 1981), and with regard to participation of peasants cutting across various caste, class and village configuration too the movement had a patchy record. Though it should be mentioned that in some parts of the district, Patidars of different strata as well as backward social group such as Baraiyas had joined hands in pledging and fulfilling the vow. Gandhi had among his followers figures and individuals of varied kinds such as Vallabhbhai Patel who represented land-owning Patidars and also mass-leader such as Indulal Yagnik who had a strong influence among the unprivileged groups such as Baraiyas, and due to that various segments of the social order in the district could come together. The government did not want to displease Gandhi during that period as he was helping the British in the recruitment drive for war and hence, district authorities were instructed not to take harsh actions against Satyagrahis. However, in stead of seizing land of satyagrahi defaulters at many places, the authorities confiscated moveable properties such as vessels, ornaments, furniture, etc. The agitation ended in June 1918 when an order was issued that impoverished that peasants should be acquitted from paying their revenue. Hardiman has observed and argued that '... the real victory (with regard to the final outcome of the movement) lay with Gandhi who had built for himself a powerful political base in the villages of the district (for his larger cause of independence struggle against the British)' (Hardiman, 1981: 108).

The second Satyagraha took place in the Bardoli taluka of Surat district in the late 20s. As is the case now, at that time too Bardoli was known for its agricultural prosperity. In January 1928, the British government raised the land tax by another 30 per cent. The land-owners, mainly of Patidar caste, first, resolved to hold back payment of only the enhanced rates and expressed willingness to pay tax at old rates. However, later after seeking counsel from Gandhi and Vallabhbhai Patel, they decided to withhold revenue dues completely until the increase ordered was suspended, or the government made fresh inquiry and thereafter revision. Petitions and representations were made but the government did not succumb and the Satyagraha was launched under the leadership of Vallabhbhai Patel. The local leaders such as Kunvarji Mehta and others made great efforts to associate poor peasantry including agricultural labourers and share-croppers mainly consisting of tribals in the movement. The constructive activities that already had been going on gandhian line proved extremely helpful in this initiative. Compare to Kheda satyagraha, the Bardoli Satyagraha was carried out in highly organized way. As mentioned above, the leaders took immense care to forge an alliance of all the communities cutting across social and economic categories in the struggle so that no group felt alienated. Even though the Patidars and Anavils were the main land-owning social groups who were affected by the revenue hike, as mentioned above not only Adivasis were mobilized to join the movement, but external leadership of communities such as Muslims, Parsis was invited to mobilize these communities to join hands and those efforts yielded desired results. People were effectively mobilized through the means of regular meetings, distribution of pamphlets and cultural programmes in which artists and groups from various parts of the country took part to inspire and mobilize the local people. As Dhanagare has noted (Dhanagare, 1983) all the three tiers of leadership; national in the form of Gandhi, regional in the form of Patel, and Kunvarji Mehta and others at local level, operated cohesively to steer the movement in the right direction and as planned. Though they were waging a battle for a local issue pertaining to main economic and livelihood activity of the rural population, they too had larger political objective of mobilizing and associating various peasant groups to the national independence movement against the British Empire. But, as Dhanagare (1983) has pointed out, the government could not fathom the political dimension of Bardoli Satyagraha and acted strongly with repressive methods. The defaulters were served notice and then their land and crops were seized and moveable properties were confiscated. The government officials and purchasers of auctioned property were boycotted by Satyagrahis, some of the *talatis* and *mukhis* who were incharge of collecting revenue quit the job and on top of that the Gujarat members of the Bombay Legislative Council resigned together, and all these had put the British government under enormous pressure. The Viceroy, due to larger concern, also coerced the Bombay Government to go for settlement. On the other hand, Vallabhbhai too understood and gauged the situation, and he too was keen to reach at some compromise. So in August 1928, the Satyagraha was called off and revenue increase was reduced to 6.25 per cent from 22 per cent. Similarly, the auctioned properties were returned to the original owners. Dhanagare has analysed the Bardoli Satyagraha with reference to its social character thus:

> The Bardoli Satyagraha thus symbolised agrarian class alliance against the government, but the cooperative endeavour was encouraged only insofar as it did not give rise to consciousness along class lines, and only to the extent that it did not disturb the traditional social structure.
>
> (Dhanagare, 1983: 107)

Assessing the above two agrarian movements which were inspired by Gandhian method and even led by Gandhi and his close associates such as Vallabhbhai and Indulal, is a complex subject even from the academic point of view. A scholar with Marxian perspective such as Dhanagare has critical view on them as is evident from the above observation. He was of the view that in both the instances Gandhi took up minor local issues to garner support of various peasant groups and that he knowingly or unknowingly promoted the cause of the specific social segment, mainly dominant and groups placed at upper level of social and economic echelons were those who supported Gandhi. He was also critical of Gandhi's strategy to terminate agitation prematurely, even when it had gained momentum and without achieving much in terms of the objectives that it had launched with. These critical points certainly are quite valid. But at the same time, Gandhi's own world-view and perspective should also be taken into account while assessing these movements. It is true that for Gandhi, these two agitations were not separate local issue-based struggles, but they were parts of larger scheme of national independence movement. However, he was never oblivious of local social oppressive setting. Similarly, for him, non-violence and truth were of prime importance and he was very upset with Patidars of Kheda district for indulging into violence and vengeance, and that was the reason he was not very positive and enthusiastic while giving nod for launching the Bardoli Satyagraha (Dhanagare, Ch. IV, 1983). Perhaps he also had realization from Kheda experience that rich and elite group of peasants had manipulated the movement for their narrow cause. And hence, in Bardoli Satyagraha, extra and conscious efforts were made not only to forge alliance of the weaker sections of agrarian relational structure with other groups, but welfare or 'constructive' activities to ameliorate their conditions were given due emphasis. Dhanagare has argued that 'constructive activities' for deprived groups worked as a device and construct that thwart any revolutionary or radical mobilization against oppressive agrarian relations (Dhanagare, Ch. IV, 1983). Gandhi had never espoused or endorsed existing exploitative agrarian relations and had advocated change. But one, during that period his main priority was India's independence, though at the same time not overlooking or ignoring inherent social problems and contradictions of Indian social order and hence, advocacy and sincere implementation of 'constructive activities' which were based on his ideas and vision of desired social order that he has succinctly and sharply put in 'Hind Swaraj' (Gandhi, 1995) not as a device or a strategy to pacify revolutionary outburst by the deprived groups. And that relates to second and very crucial point. Gandhi believed in innate nobility and goodness of human beings and accordingly professed and put into action his ideas and programmes for social change; 'constructive activities' was a very significant component of that entire scheme. Another significant organized attempt from Adivasis of Vyara Taluka region of then the Surat district, the area was then under Gaekwadi princely state, needs brief mention here. In earlier part of the 1930s, the Adivasis under the leadership of one Kotla Mehta who was not much influenced by Gandhian thoughts and methods, and was rather radical in terms of his ideas, took out a long march from Vyara to Vadodara, the capital of Gaekwadi state, to present memorandum pertaining to problems of Adivasis tenants. Kotla Mehta had prepared a draft of proposed tenancy act and the representatives who took part in the long march had submitted that draft to the Gaekwadi state and which was accepted and an enactment was formulated based on that (Chaudhari, 2006). We would stop here and move to extremely significant policy measure in post-independence Gujarat which had a far-reaching effect in terms of social implications.

Gujarat state was born in the 1960s, created from then Bombay state, which was bifurcated into Maharashtra and Gujarat. Gujarat can be divided on the basis of geographical peculiarities as well as historical-socio-cultural background into two sub-regions; Mainland Gujarat and Peninsular Gujarat – the latter is also known as Saurashtra and kachha region. Mainland Gujarat was a part of the Bombay state during colonial rule and even after independence till its birth in 1960. Saurashtra–Kutch, prior to independence was consisting of nearly 500 kingdoms of different size and all of them were merged into a separate state of Saurashtra in an independent Indian union. It too became a part of the Bombay state in 1956. During colonial rule, various *rajwadas* of Saurashtra had three types of land tenure system: occupancy, *girasdari* and *barkhali*. Only in the first system, the cultivator directly held the land from the state, whereas in other two there were intermediaries between cultivators and states such as *girasdars, talukdars, bhayats, bhagdars, mulgirasias* and *barkhalidars* (Shah, 2002). These intermediaries, a majority of them were of Rajput caste, had been enjoying property rights and land, and were collecting their agricultural shares without tilling the land. One of the first policy measure which the Saurashtra government in the independent era took to give occupancy rights to the cultivators abolishing intermediary system. Of course, the Rajput landlords tried their best to subvert the legal enactments by removing the tenants by hook or crook. The situation became socially tense as most of the tenants were Patidars. After many deliberations between the contestant groups and even intervention from the union government, the dispute could be resolved. According to Shah, land reform measures in Saurashtra had resulted into evenly distribution of land ownership from earlier highly skewed one and the patidar tenants had benefited mainly as they got support from the state which was keen to get rid of the *zamindari* system and feudal social order with an intention of smooth transition to capitalist mode of agricultural production. The rajputs though did not become landless, were compelled to till their land. But mainly they lost power and their sumptuous lifestyle. But as Shah has pointed out that the kolis and other deprived groups who were also land tenants did not get much benefits (Shah, 2002). However in overall terms, the process of land reforms, especially pertaining to tenancy rights to the actual cultivators had created enormous social upheavals and tension in the Saurashtra region. The girasdar rajputs had resorted to almost revolt and some of them became dacoits, resulting into situation of robbery, murders and frightening and tense social milieu. A sizeable number of patidars left the region and a significant portion of them joined the diamond industry of Surat. They have prospered substantially through diamond industry and not only have enhanced their social status, but have become an extremely potent powerful and influential force, both politically and economically through it (see Engelshoven, 1999 and Desai and Nikhil Raj, 2001).

So far as mainland Gujarat is concerned, the Congress government had enacted Bombay Tenancy Act 1939 which was amended by introducing new provisions in order to overcome some difficulties in its effective implementation. The act was called the Bombay Tenancy and Agricultural Lands Act 1948, but it too failed to have any impact and ejection of tenants by landlords on excuse of intention of self-cultivation could not be curbed. The tenants on their part too did not show interest and enthusiasm to purchase the land even at a reasonable price due to certain reasons, main being lack of resources. Later on, concession in price was offered but that too did not produce much effect. The Act was further amended in 1972 in order to block loopholes. However, as Ghanshyam Shah has noted:

> ... One, nearly half of the tenants belonged to lower castes including scheduled castes and scheduled tribes. Since they were poor and less exposed to the outside world, they found it difficult to understand the intricacies of law ... they were subdued and found it difficult to raise their voice against the landowners of the dominant castes. In the absence of an organised movement, ... they succumbed to the pressure of the dominant upper caste to surrender their tenancy to the landlords. They either did not declare themselves as tenants or did not present themselves before the tribunal to prove their claim. Many of them did not have the confidence that they would be able to pay instalments to the landowners.
>
> (Shah, 2002: 137)

Shah is of the view that one of the reason for weak implementation of the tenancy act in the mainland Gujarat after Gujarat is formed, was that the act was having unfavourable effect on land-owners of dominant castes who were controlling both the government as well as the Congress party. After the formation of Gujarat state, Land ceiling Act came into effect in September 1961 which stated the fixation of a ceiling on land-holding. The act was amended in 1974 lowering the ceiling further. The Act was even more poorly implemented as the big landholders, mainly belonging to dominant castes, divided their land-holdings artificially among relatives. Thus, in all the apparently progressive measures of land reforms could not provide much relief and benefits to the weaker sections of the agrarian social order.

The first major agrarian struggle of post-independent period in Gujarat region commenced in the year 1952, i.e., eight years before formation of the Gujarat state and it ended in 1967, after six years of formation of Gujarat state.[1] The movement is known as 'Ghasia Satyagraha' or 'Annakheda Satyagraha'. The location of the struggle was Pardi Taluka of Valsad district in South Gujarat region. It was predominantly a tribal area with around 60 per cent of Adivasis population. The area was primarily a plane area and the Adivasis were the original owners of most of the land. However, they became debtors once Parsis and higher caste Hindus who entered the area for selling liquor and money-lending. Godavari Parulekar (1976) in her autobiography has vividly narrated how the outsiders exploited the local Adivasis and took away their land with reference to the neighbouring Talukas of Pardi of Thane district. In 1952, almost three-fourths of the total cultivable land of Pardi taluka was owned by around 100 landlords who were mainly Parsis, Banias and Anavils. These non-cultivating landlords were not interested in agriculture and hence, the vast cultivable land was not utilized to grow crops. Their primary interest was commercial and though a small portion of the land had been tilled by Adivasis tenants, '... a large amount of the land had been left as waste so that grass could be harvested annually for the profitable Bombay fodder trade' (Hardiman, 1996: 307). Thus, the original inhabitants, Adivasis, were reduced to landless labourers and worst of it, they could not get employment as wage labourers for a major part of the year as most the land was used for growing grass. The Adivasis almost starved for eight to 10 months in a year. Though Kisan Sabha under the leadership of Indulal Yagnik took up the cause of Adivasis of Pardi in the late 1930s and initiated a series of protest actions which were participated by the Adivasis in huge number, by early 40s the movement got submerged and fizzled out due to 'Quit India' movement of 1942. It was the Praja Samajwadi Party (PSP) under the leadership of Ishwarlal Desai who later on took up the issue of grassland of Pardi and prolonged satyagraha of 15 years took place. As the term 'Satyagraha' indicates the 'Ghasia movement' was planned and accordingly series of actions and protests were organized within the Gandhian framework, of which non-violence and peaceful resistance were the basic tenets. Given the particular socio-economic and political context, the movement was confined to two demands: bringing the grasslands under crop production and implementing the tenancy act. The series of actions were immaculately planned by the leadership. Minute detail was taken care of; which includes date, time and place of the Satyagraha, the leader of that particular event, the names and number of the participants as well as the observer who most often was the renowned figure and who would subsequent to the particular Satyagraha put forward her/his report on whether the tenets of Gandhian method were strictly adhered to or not and how far the objectives of the Satyagraha were served. The Satyagrahis would enter the land of a big landlord and till the land in each event of Satyagraha. Later on as the movement progressed, call of boycott of grass-cutting operation was also included. The Bombay provincial government was run by the Congress and the party leaders sided with the landlords and tried their best to crush the Satyagraha. This was obvious as on one hand, the landlords had remained the party's strong allies and on the other hand, in terms of electoral politics the Congress was annoyed that PSP had been mobilizing its major support-base at the grass-root level and in turn affecting the party's major vote-bank in the Pardi region. The Congress leadership was also embarrassed and irritated as the PSP leaders were invoking and utilizing Gandhian tenets and methods in the movement of which the Congress considered itself as only and sole heirs.

Ishwar Desai and the PSP had established great rapport with the Adivasis. The government tried to win over the tribals by announcing various development programmes. But the Adivasis remained firm and the PSP leadership too did not deter in their commitment. The movement had to revitalize after the formation of Gujarat State. The movement ended in July 1967 with its objectives of bringing land under crop cultivation and redistribution among the Adivasis were largely achieved. However, not much could be attained with regard to restoration of the tenancy rights of those tenants who had been driven away by landowners using unscrupulous means.

The Pardi 'Annakhed' or 'Ghasia' Satyagraha was criticized on two to three counts. Firstly, though led by socialist leadership, the movement never raised voice against the very socio-economic structure that had shaped agrarian practice of the nature of grassland. The leadership, instead, sought to introduce varied reforms within the then existing structure. It is true that the issue of grassland was not taken up as a part of long-drawn battle of social transformation. The leadership could understand and assess the social and political context of that period. At the same time, Ishwar Desai and others were not ultra left or radical in their ideological make-up and had more faith and trust in Gandhian ideas and methods. They could see condition of extreme poverty of Adivasis and collusion of landlords, and Congress leadership that perpetuated this adversity. And hence they took up this issue. The leadership was also criticized with regard to the real motives for launching movement. Ishwarbhai and PSP leadership plunged into the satyagraha in order to create vote-bank of Adivasis in that area, it was argued mainly by the then Congress leaders. This was a typical cynical view with a tone of reductionism that rule out any value-based and ideologically driven political move. The commitment of the leadership for the cause of poor Adivasis could be easily discerned from the way the entire movement had been planned and organized as well as carried on untiringly for 15 long years. The 'Annakheda Satyagraha' or 'Ghasia Satyagraha' was initiated and led by non-tribal leaders, but conscious efforts were being made to include and involve the Adivasis not only by way of participation in the events, but they were given leadership of specific event and they were part of planning process also. All in all, 'the Pardi Annakhed Satyagraha' can be considered a significant agrarian struggle of post-independent India. Though it has not achieved much in terms of land distribution and land ownership, it certainly has brought phenomenal change in land-use practice that has helped the poor Adivasis to overcome the perennial problem concerning their survival and has also strengthened their political status. In another way, the 'Pardi Satyagraha' proved that the Gandhian method of protest can be effectively used in post-independent India too for just cause and even against Gandhi's own so-called heirs.

As elsewhere in Gujarat too, the agrarian struggles by deprived groups concerns tribal assertions for rights related to land in most cases. Stany Pinto has explained elaborately how land is conceived and perceived by tribals in his Ph.D thesis (Pinto, 1999). He quoted Pathy in this regard thus,

> (For the tribals) ... Land is a comprehensive generic term which includes not only the soil and territory but a living entity with environment, spirit, cosmos and all else in reciprocal relationship, linking the present with both the past and future generations of humans, animals and plants.
>
> (Pinto, 1999: 13)

He has also delineated various forms of tribal assertion against the encroachment of outsiders in Gujarat during pre-independence period. The form of struggle might not be addressing vital issue of land alienation directly and instead expressed itself in social or religious idioms, he observed. For instance, 'Devi Movement' of South Gujarat region apparently urged Adivasis to live pious and simple life by abstaining from consuming liquor, following a goddess's sermons, etc., but as David Hardiman has argued, it was an expression of resistance against British imposition of heavy tax on liquor, a part of regular diet of

Adivasis, due to which they were exploited by Parsi liquor-shop owners, many losing land to them (see Hardiman, 1987 and Lobo-Mecwan, 2003). Stany Pinto has chronicled a prolonged series of protest and resistance of Adivasis of Bharuch district against Rajpipla princely state and the British regime for dispossession of land, the first of that was reported way back in 1885 (Pinto, 1999). The protest and response to it by the British rulers turned violent, a British official was killed and in a retaliatory and brutal state action, five tribals were killed, several injured and the leaders were hanged to death. But the unrest did not fizzle away and the Adivasis continued their struggle over losing their land to non-tribal landlords, mainly from Rajput, Muslim, Patel and Vania social groups. In order to pacify and woo them, they were offered land far away from their villages and often in the unreachable forest of interior Valia and Dediapada talukas (Pinto, 1999), which was responded by the Adivasis in a mixed way. Some of them had preferred to till their fore-fathers, land on tenancy basis, another group accepted the option of shifting to remote area, whereas a section of the Adivasis got involved in robbery and looting. Valia and Jhagadia were the main Talukas from where various forms of resistance were expressed. The British tried to quell the situation both by pacifying as well as intimidating measures. As Stany Pinto has mentioned, the assertion in various forms were continued even after independence and as a matter of fact Valia Taluka was called and mentioned as 'Chambal of Gujarat', 'Telangana of Gujarat' and 'Chicago of Gujarat' by state apparatuses and landlord class. Kisan Sabha also got active in Bharuch region to create awareness among tribals about their rights as tenants and as owners of the land after 'Land to the Tiller Act'. Landless labourers or *Chakars* were sensitized about minimum wages act. The situation took dramatic turn in the 70s and 80s with impact and influence of Kisan Sabha receded and the leadership of the on-going movement went into the hands of tribal leaders who changed the tracks of the struggle from mainly agrarian and land-alienation-related issues to issues pertaining to tribal identity with regard to their deprivation in various spheres of social sector and their location in politics. Interestingly, again efforts were made to weave a set of religious idioms and symbols around a crucial issue of tribal identity. It was the movement called 'Sati Pati' which was started with a purpose to reform tribal life through religious tenets. But later on a leader with a name Kesrisingh brought in radical issues such as spurning relationship with non-tribals, proscribing non-tribal institutions such as school, election, government agencies, etc., and egged on his Adivasi supporters to grab land of non-tribals under the land tenancy act and advocated not to pay land revenue. In

Bharuch district, assertive articulation of these agrarian-land-related and political components of the movement had given rise to very assertive, strong and highly inspiring leadership such as Narsing Vasava, Manga Supad, Chhotu Vasava, Daoud Bhura, Amarsinh Vasava and others Adivasi figures given rise to situation of tension and conflict between tribals, on one hand, and non-tribal landlords and state machinery, on the other hand, culminating into harassment of the former by the latter, and killing and murdering many of the above leaders and brutal attacks on villages, though it were the tribals who were branded as 'dacoits'. It, thus, can be summed up that the Bharuch movement have gone through many phases and turmoil. The issues related to land alienation and land rights of tribals have remained central throughout the struggle though many more issues have been incorporated in between. Similarly, the symbols and idioms used have undergone changes during a prolonged struggle; from issue related to land to religious preaching and then to politics of tribal identity in recent time. Thus, in all, the movement has taken a chequered path. With reference to Gujarat, the Bharuch agrarian struggle has remained the most significant movement where the deprived groups, the Adivasis have waged fierce battle for their rights and justice against the state and dominant groups suffering enormous casualties and pain. It is difficult to analyse the movement in terms of effect and impact. Nevertheless, it could be said that the state oppression and the domination of socially above placed groups as well as propertied and landed class who have been allies of the state, have been seriously challenged through rare assertiveness and courage. Of late, however, the tribal leadership that has been steering the struggle is trying through manipulative means to gain appropriate political advantages of the struggle for their personal political benefits with reference to mainstream politics of parliamentary democracy.

The Dangs district is located in the southern most part of the Gujarat state. It is a predominantly tribal district with almost 90 per cent of its population as Adivasis, mainly consisting of tribes of Bhil, Kunkna, Varli, Kotwalia and few others. Geographically, it has a hilly terrain and almost 98 per cent of the district is forest. In pre-British period, the Dangs was ruled by Bhil chieftains. British invaded the region in the first quarter of the 19th century and got lease of forest from Bhil chieftains and deviously as well as forcibly not only increased their power over forest but simultaneously curbed the rights of Adivasis of concerning shifting cultivation, grazing their cattle and collection of forest produce for domestic purpose over forest. The British wanted to exploit forest for their narrow interest of revenue and commercial purpose. Ironically, as Irfan Engineer has candidly brought out the government of independent India's policy is not much different, and often appears even worse from colonial regime as more and more forest areas have been brought under reserve forest category and thereby restricting availability of land for Adivasis for their shifting cultivation and other purpose as well as even curbing their free movement in the forest (Engineer, 2002). Engineer juxtaposes this policy measures against census data which indicate that almost nine out of every 10 Dangis depend on agriculture for livelihood. The government not only has encroached the cultivable land through legal means, but even used extra-legal method. Engineer has succinctly put the adversity of the Adivasis of the Dangs thus;

> The net result of encroachment of the law as well as forest department on the livelihood of the Adivasis and on their land is that they are left with small uneconomic landholdings, which are not sufficient for subsistence of majority of them, who are then forced to migrate out as migrant labourers in semi-bonded conditions as cane harvesters and informal labourers in other rural and urban sectors.
>
> (Engineer, 2002: 317)

Dangi Adivasis have been protesting first against British and then successive state governments and their forest departments, though earlier the resistance was more sporadic and spontaneous, and not carried out in an organized manner. In the 80s 'Bhoomihin Kisan Hakka Sanrakshan Samiti' was formed and a series of protest were organized under it. The Adivasis entered the forest land and started tilling the land. The state government suppressed the resistance using brutal force. The activists and leaders were not only jailed and tortured but were branded as 'naxalites'. Even though the Dangs struggle on rights of Dangi Adivasis on forest land was led and steered by non-Dangi activists, local Adivasis whole-heartedly supported the movement and many Adivasis were part of core group of the movement. The movement though had fizzled out mainly due to repressive and brutal measures of state government; a committee was formed by the government in 1992 to look into the problems of Dangi Adivasis. The committee's main recommendation was to bestow upon ownership of that strip or plot of forest land to each Adivasi tiller cultivating the particular plot on or before 1980. But though agreed upon principally, this recommendation was never implemented. As we would see in the coming text, after a prolonged struggle by organizations advocating for rights of Adivasis on forest land and forest produces, an act has been passed by the parliament in the very recent past. We will come to that after delineating organized struggles for the cause in Gujarat. But prior to that the struggle pertaining to land issues with reference to another deprived section, i.e., Dalits should also require mention.

Most of the Dalits in rural Gujarat have been either cultivators with small land-holdings or eke out their livelihood through toiling as agriculture labourers. Behavioural Science Centre, Ahmedabad, especially Father Heredero and others initiated awareness programme among Dalits of central Gujarat, especially of Bhal region with the purpose that they could use their land in a better way to increase agricultural production. Addressing social evil of untouchability was also on their agenda. Training was imparted to them on how to utilize various government's schemes and programmes for agriculture development. They were also encouraged and supported to form agricultural cooperatives. Dalits were able to acquire waste land from government under its poverty alleviation programme. This land and whatever land an individual Dalit cultivator owned were part of the agriculture cooperative societies. These societies were not only able to increase agricultural production by employing modern technology and inputs, but the Dalit agricultural labourers could also get better wages through them. As Ghanshyam Shah has noted, this sort of accomplishment had raised confidence of the Dalits that they could improve their condition without depending on the higher caste landlords (Shah, an unpublished report). This sort of economic independence of suppressed group and especially consequent social change had infuriated the dominant social groups such as Darbar and Patel. Mainly Darbars started harassing the Dalits. The ghastly event of Golana village that shook the Gujarat society needs mention here. Dalits had formed an agricultural cooperative society there too in 1978 and it yielded desired results by earning surplus through rise in agricultural production. In the first half of the 80s, the Dalits received 33 acres of land from the government which was a surplus land under land ceiling act and was earlier owned by the Darbars. Despite threat and fury of Darbars, the Dalits summoned courage and started tilling the land. Add into that the Dalits were allotted more than 300 house plots under the Gujarat Government's 20-point programme and that land was earlier used by the Darbars. The ensuing tension created division among Dalits with the Darbars supported and inciting one section of the Dalits. On January 28, 1986, the Vankars among Dalits were brutally attacked by the Darbars, killing four Dalits, seriously injuring another 18 and also burning houses as well as destroying domestic belongings. This bloody event created a social and political uproar in the state and in a long drawn legal battle the accused got conviction. The issue here is that in highly socially polarized and unequal rural social order the Dalits have to face stiff opposition and wage struggle on continuous basis, sometimes openly and sometimes latently, to get their fair share in agrarian agricultural economy.

Organizational Effort for Rights over Forest Land

In this latter part of the chapter, the major organizational efforts and struggles which resulted into a very significant gain for Adivasis would be delineated in brief. Gujarat's leading human rights activist-thinker Shri Indukumar Jani has graphically described how 'Disha', an organization that has been formed in 1986 by then a committed social activist and now a prominent political figure Shri Madhusudan Mistry, has organized Adivasis and others who have been eking out their livelihood either by cultivating forest land or through labouring in forest-related works, and waged a series of protests and struggles against all odds (Jani, 2009). The organization began by forming a union for forest-workers or *van-majoor* and putting a series of demands for their rights such as; not to pay them less wages by taking their signatures on blank vouchers, paying wages by complying with minimum wages act, to make them permanent after stipulated period of working and others. 'Disha' started its activities from Sabarkantha and Panchmahal districts by mainly concentrating on problems of *van-majoors* but then gradually other issues pertaining to rights of forest-dwellers especially related to forest-land utilization had also been addressed. The atrocities committed by forest department officials on forest-dwellers were vehemently fought against. Gradually, the entire tribal forest belt of the eastern region of Gujarat has been covered. Mistrybhai, as Madhusudan Mistry is popularly known as and 'Disha' assessed and studied the problems and issues pertaining to forest land very minutely, clinically and with academic rigour and then put up demands and fought for that. Apart from rights of *van-majoors,* the organization's major agenda has been to get ownership right of forest-land for forest-dwellers. The government mainly in the form of forest department officials tried very hard to crush the organization and the movement it led. Even Madhusudan Mistry was physically assaulted. As Jani has noted, the approach and method of 'Disha' is not just confining to organizing protest march or *dharna* for just demands, but also to mobilize influential political actors in power corridors of Gandhinagar and even Delhi. One of the main problems 'Disha' has to encounter is ever-changing political formation at the level of state government. Meanwhile, issues pertaining to forest land kept on piling up. In 1990–91, forest areas of Danta-Palanpur in North Gujarat region was declared as sanctuary and thereby curtailing issue of licence to collect forest products. A massive rally and dharna was organized in 1992 in Ahmedabad in front of the office of ruling party in which

Adivasis from all over Gujarat participated. The Chimanbhai Patel government acceded to most of the demands, major one being ownership right of forest land for Adivasis cultivators tilling the piece of land on or before October 25, 1980. But it required a long formal process of verification of ownership of land as well as getting sanction from the central government. Government formed a committee with renowned socialist leader Sanat Mehta as the chairperson. The major problem with regard to verification of land was concerning substantial proof that the poor and illiterate Adivasis could not have. The cunning forest department officials showed less area of land in the receipts. Moreover, those Adivasis who produced receipts were forced to grow trees in 50 per cent of the land by the forest department. For two years, not much progress was made in allocation of land and so another demonstration was planned in February 1994. But, the government of Gujarat called the leaders for discussion beforehand and after a long deliberation between 'Eklavya' (an umbrella organization formed for all the groups waging struggle for land rights) representatives and a group of ministers, it was declared that the state government was recommending regularization of some 39,750 hectares of land for 50,860 forest-dwellers and the verification process would be continued. But again, the movement got severe jolt just after the agreement, the Chief Minister shri Chimanbhai expired, the political situation again got fluid and the government machinery come at a standstill with regard to implementation of land rights of forest-dwellers. The new ministry was formed under the chief-ministership of Shri Chabildas Mehta and the leadership of the movement realized that fresh efforts had to be made to stir Gandhinagar power-corridor. Another march was planned on August 14, 1994 on the route – Ahmedabad to Gandhinagar. Around 10,000 adivasis from each nook and corner of the Gujarat, from Danta to Dharampur took part in the march along with leading intellectuals, prominent Gujaratis and also construction workers as well as agricultural labourers. Apart from 'Disha' and 'Eklavya', other organizations such as 'Navsarjan', 'Janpath', 'Vikas', 'Adhikaar', 'Gujarat Khet Vikas Parishad' and others too joined. The government of Chhabildas Mehta responded positively and the Chief Minister even addressed the rally. Mistry was made member of the committee which was to implement regularization of land to the Adivasis. On the day of November 19, 1994, the Chief Minister awarded *sanad* of land right to Adivasis symbolically at a function held at Chhotaudepur, Vadodara. It was declared that 68,000 families of Adivasis and other backward communities would get land rights over total of about one lakh hectors of forest land. But that was not the end of the torturous path of their movement. Within few days after that momentous declaration a state assembly election of Gujarat was held and Bhartiya Janata party government was formed under the leadership of Shri Keshubhai Patel. The Patel ministry of BJP too took up land issue immediately after installation but of altogether different and diametrically opposite nature. The government removed the precondition of having residence within 8 km for procuring cultivable land. Thus, a person, for instance, belonging to Ahmedabad can purchase an agricultural land even in as far a place as Surat district. The issue of forest-land right of forest-dwellers and the implementation of it as declared in Chhotaudepur was totally ignored. 'Eklavya' again had started making presentation to the proper authority. The leaders were aghast when the forest minister Mr Fakir Vaghela told them that the papers given at *sanad* were technically not the same. The government also raised some objections pertaining to cut-off date for land rights. But again, the fluidity in Gandhinagar politics changed the scenario. Shankarsingh Vaghela toppled Keshubhai's BJP government and formed a government with the support of Congress. In 1997 at a large meeting at Limkheda, he restarted the distribution of *sanad* to the Adivasis and declared that 39,750 hectors of forest land would be distributed among 54,784 land-tillers. The long drawn battle for land rights waged for Adivasis and other forest-dwellers had taught some important lessons to movement leadership, especially to Madhusudanbhai. As we have taken note of earlier also, along with non-violent means of protests, demonstrations, rallies and fasts as a strategy, the movement leaders also had been establishing contacts within power-circles of Gandhinagar and even Delhi and that had proved quite effective and meaningful. But over a period of time, Madhusudan Mistry had realized that in order to get justice and rights for deprived groups, joining mainstream politics is essential and driven with that thinking he finally entered mainstream political arena and became Member of Parliament for two successive terms. 'Eklavya' has continued its struggle on various issues pertaining to forest-dwellers. For instance, it raised demand for providing irrigation facility to forest-cultivators. Above all, the organization has to monitor procedure of allotment of *sanad* on continuous basis. Mistry has been a very active and articulate Member of Parliament. Due to his involvement in the movement and active participation in the *sansad,* he was made a member of the Joint Parliamentary Committee (JPC) which formulated 'The Scheduled Tribes and Other Traditional Forest Dwellers (Recognition of Forest Rights) Act, 2006', which came into force on December 29, 2006. The act has extended the cut-off date for land occupation for forest-dwellers up to December 13, 2005. Apart from individual right of land, it has also bestowed certain community rights for forest-dwellers with regard to utilization of forest land. Though this enactment can be considered as achieving what the 'Eklavya' movement has been aiming for, the struggle in real terms is far from over. It is the state government which has to implement the act and it seems that the present government of Gujarat is creating many hurdles in this regard and 'Eklavya' is planning a big rally on March 6, 2010 in Ahmedabad.

The Adivasis had lost land also due to large-scale irrigation projects in Southern Gujarat region, first due to Ukai dam on river Tapti and then Sardar Sarovar project on river Narmada. Ukai dam was built in 1960. Adivasis of 344 villages of Songadh, Uchchhal, Nizar and Sagbara talukas of then Surat and Bharuch districts were affected, out of that 27 villages were submerged fully under water (see Lobo-Mecwan, 2003). Adivasis had to leave their motherland and had to go to far off places. As per government figures, in all a population of 1,50,000 was affected and 40,000 acres of fertile land was lost. We would not go into details of Sardar Sarovar project as much has been written about it in the academic and quasi-academic write-ups. Nevertheless, comparison between these two large development projects in terms of protest and struggle for and by the people suggests that while in the case of latter pro-Adivasis and pro-project affected people organizations such as ARCH and Narmada Bachao Andolan (NBA) vehemently fought for the rights of the people and due to that the state was compelled to formulate and implement a 'progressive' rehabilitation policy in which all the project-affected households are entitled to have minimum five acres of land with irrigation facility as well as other infrastructural facilities and inputs at new sites, no such movement or organization had come to the rescue and support for the rights of Ukai dam oustees and most of them were forced to leave their villages and live as paupers and wretched somewhere else. Of late, a movement under the leadership of Pratibha Shinde has taken up the problems and sufferings of PAPs of Ukai dam.

Here, it is also pertinent to mention plights and hardships of a group among Adivasis whose problems have remained unaddressed due to lack of organization as well as not having outside support of committed activists as the case of 'Disha' and 'Eklavya' has shown. This community is known as Halpatis and they are based at South Gujarat districts of Surat and Valsad (now also Navsari). They have been mainly eking out their livelihood by working as agricultural labourers in the farms of higher caste landlords, mainly belonging to Anavil and Patidar castes, in prosperous plain areas. Earlier, Halpati labourers were almost in a state of bondage under *hali* system. Renowned Dutch social scientist Jan Breman has described '... this pattern of relationship ... in terms of bondage and Patronage' (Breman, 1986: 363). Living mostly with caste-Hindus and that too in plain areas, the Halpatis, on one hand, are not considered Adivasis, and on the other, nor are they included in the Hindu-fold wholeheartedly. H*ali* system, though highly exploitative, ironically had been providing them protection of patronage from their masters, *the dhaniamas.* With the advent of commercialization of agriculture and market economy, the age old personal relationship of *hali pratha* has been substituted gradually by contractual and impersonal relations between the *dhaniamas,* the landlords and the *halis,* the agricultural labourers. With that the nature of labour market too has changed and situation of availability of large labour supply had intensified the competition for work and that has resulted into decline of wage rates for *halpati* agricultural labourers. The overall condition of *halpati* labourers has deteriorated and their pauperization has further intensified. They have been aware of their misery and wretched conditions and there were few sporadic instances of protests, but they could not put up an organized front against tyranny of exploitative forces because long years of their pauperization and associated submissiveness, ignorance, illiteracy had proved to be major obstacles. Gandhian workers and organization such as 'Halpati Sewa Sangh' has been working for their welfare, but it would never initiate or launch any action or programme that conscentisizes the *halpati* agricultural labourers for their rights and against exploitative practices of higher caste landlords.

In the last segment of this chapter, the encroachment on agricultural and other land of public utilities in the name of development projects in the present globalization era, the present Government of Gujarat (GoG) being its major proponent, would be covered. The GoG has acquired around 22,550 hectares of land through amendment of land laws for the purpose of expansion of industrial estates, industrial parks, special economic zones (SEZs) and to provide infrastructural facilities. For this intent, first of all the controls on purchase of agriculture land were removed in 1994. Simultaneously, regulations for converting agriculture land to non-agriculture land for industrial purpose were loosened up. In 2005, the government decided to allot the government land which was earmarked for public utility purpose – such as waste as well as grazing land – to 'big industries and individual progressive farmers' to develop these plots of land by using modern technology for productive purpose. They are allotted the land on lease without any rent for the first five years. Not only that but they are even allowed to mortgage the land for borrowing money from the banks. The government also has obtained land for industrial houses, under the Land Acquisition Act 1894, from private farmers under the garb of 'public purpose'. Individual peasants have almost no choice and scope for bargaining to get 'market' price. In Kutch and Saurashtra, several hundred thousand hectares of government and private land have been allotted this way to big industries such as Reliance and Adani (see Shah and others, 2008). Not major protest or struggle has so far been reported against GoG's this policy measures and approach. On the contrary, as one of the senior officials responsible for SEZ implementation has claimed in Gujarat, no 'Nandigram' could take place. However, a very recent event has proved that people are not going to accept this sort of infringement by an authoritarian state government which is obsessive and hell-bent on making the state a replica of a model state of globalization regime quite passively and silently.

Mahuva is a part of Bhavnagar district in Saurashtra region of the state and it has tracts of one among the most fertile land strips in the state (Reproduced from internet communication by Anand Mazgaonkar and others as well as Indian express report, date February 21, 2010). Dissimilar to most parts of the state and especially the Saurashtra region, the farmers of Mahuva tract cultivate three crops during an agricultural year and even exports produces such as mangoes, coconuts as well as other fruits. Apart from that the area also locates many dehydrating plants and cotton gins that have been providing means of livelihood to not less than 10,000 people. The state government in its zealous drive for industrialization and globalization and for that purpose inviting global and out-state investors to Gujarat has earmarked this agriculturally fertile strips of land as the 'Silver Corridor' for the purpose of industrial development. In a major shocking decision, which is the main reason for present agitation and outburst of the people, the GoG has sanctioned allotment of 288 hectares of land for the cement plant to be established by the known Nirma group of industries. In addition, the government has also allocated another 3,000 hectares of land on lease to Nirma for carrying out limestone mining for manufacturing cement. In all, the investment would be of the scale of ₹ 2,500 crore and it is claimed that this staggering amount of investment for the set of above mentioned enterprises would provide livelihood to around 420 persons. As A. Mazgaonkar and others have rightly observed,

> The cement plant will devastate land owners, rob farmers and farm labourers of their livelihoods, pollute the air and destroy the pristine coastal and inland ecology. It was only in the last few years that the Government invested tens of millions of public money to construct structures for water conservation and prevention of salinity ingress in this area.
>
> (Mazgaonkar and others, internet communication)

The above quotation shows sheer thoughtlessness on the part of the state government in its obsession for a particular paradigm of development in the present context. The proposed project is likely to have a devastating effect on the lives of some 50,000 people in the region. As the local Member of Legislature (MLA), Mr Kanubhai Kalsaria, who is from the ruling BJP and who is leading the agitation against the proposed plant, informed the *Indian Express* (February 21, 2010), the acquired land also includes a water-body spread over 100 hectares and two dams are coming up in the area which would provide irrigation facility to this area of fertile land. Obviously, people of this sub-region have been protesting over this project for quite some time which has compelled the GoG to form a committee to look into the matter. But it turned out to be a ploy of eyewash. Without once visiting the Mahuva region or hearing people's voice, the committee has given a nod to the government's sanction for the project. People's resistance and protest have been met with high-handedness by using brutal police force. When the leadership sought permission to take out a peaceful rally, the permission was not granted. Despite that the protest march was held on February 20, in a peaceful manner in which eight to 10 thousand people took part and yet the police canned the rally and some 10 persons got injured. The very next day, the MLA and his wife were attacked by a gang of ruffians and security personnel of the company, and both were hospitalized. On February 25, another march was planned from Sabarmati Ashram, Ahmedabad to Gandhinagar, but the government arrested the leaders in the morning and the march just could not place. The authoritarian and undemocratic attitude of the GoG has come to its fore when it deliberately obstructed, Dr Kalsaria, the ruling party's MLA attending Gujarat Vidhansabha and raised the issue.

To conclude, the nature and issues pertaining to agrarian problems have changed over a period of time and the characteristics of the response of the affected peasants to them, hence, would also require careful observation. With reference to post-independent India, of the five major prototypes of agrarian struggles that David Hardiman has typified, mainly two, struggle against the landlords and against the state and its agencies, mainly forest department, have largely been witnessed in the post-independent era, if the case of Gujarat is taken into consideration. In most of the cases, the struggle contains three actors: peasants waging battle for their land-related rights against alliance of the state and the capital that may be in the form of landlords (as in most cases) or as seen in recent times in the form of large industrial groups. However, each case needs to be examined carefully with regard to the complexities involved. For instance, the land reform measures in Saurashtra region has created a situation of intense social tension and strife involving all the three major actors; the state, the landlords and the tenants. But in this case, since the state was determined to implement the reforms because it wanted to serve class interest of its ally, the capitalists, the opposition from *jamindars* or landlords was tamed diplomatically mainly through negotiation and dialogue. The 1950s and 60s witnessed a long-drawn struggle in the Pardi area of the southern-most part of Gujarat. Again it was a tripartite battle involving the then Bombay (and afterwards Gujarat) state, the landlords and the poor landless Adivasis. The Adivasis under the leadership of socialist non-Adivasis leaders were demanding that most of the land of the Pardi region that was growing only grass for commercial purpose by high-caste Hindu and Parsi landlords should be brought under cultivation of various crops and also conferring tenancy right to tribals. The Congress Government took the side of landlords for the political consideration of not to let the Praja Samajwadi Party (PSP) making inroads into their political bastion. The movement could achieve its objective of bringing grassland under crop-cultivation when the political permutation changed with most of the socialists joining the Congress in the newly formed Gujarat state, however, the issue of tenancy right of Adivasis was ignored as the Congress – landlords alliance remained intact. The Pardi Satyagraha was initiated and led by non-Adivasi, high-caste leaders, though it must be noted that the committed leadership which was inspired by the radical ideology consciously and sincerely made efforts not only to involve the Adivasis and to have their active participation in the movement, but to give them the reins of the various events in the struggle. The Bharuch district of Gujarat presented altogether a different scenario. The Adivasis of Valia region in that southern Gujarat district waged a fierce battle against the state as well as the Hindu-caste landlords for tenancy rights and had to pay a heavy price in the form of lives of many of the Adivasi leaders. The struggle later has transformed into addressing a vital political issue of tribal identity, nevertheless land-related issue had worked as a catalyst and still has remained one of the core issues of the larger spectrum of politics under the rubric of identity. This has been one of the agrarian struggles that has been initiated and fought under the Adivasi leadership. The Adivasis of the Dangs district too have to strive hard against the state, both in post-independence era and post-independence period, for their rights over forest-produce and tilling rights of forest land. The movement led by left-inclined leadership was crushed by labelling the leaders as 'Naxalites'. The Dalits in Central Gujarat too had to face wrath of higher caste landlords when they tried to take advantage of various government scheme with the help of some welfare-oriented activists. The most vital issues of forest-dwellers, mainly Adivasis, with regard to the right over forest produce, minimum wages for forest labour and right of tilling forest land have been addressed assertively and in an organized and well thought-out planned manner by 'Disha' and its off-shoot umbrella organization 'Eklavya', and after a prolonged struggle of about 20 years this intensive as well as extensive organizational efforts have achieved significantly by legalizing the forest-land rights of forest-dwellers through an enactment. But, the struggle pertaining to land rights of the people, particularly, the deprived groups, is far from over. In the globalization era, the state, more so in the case of the GoG, is obsessively keen to make the state a highly industrialized state. It has been inviting investments from all over the world by declaring very many policy inducements, infringing land-related rights of the farmers. The large capitalist land-owners who are already into the commercial agriculture would conveniently and merrily shift and divert their tract of interest and join the band-wagon of globalization and industrial development. But, the marginal and small farmers who are dependent on agriculture for subsistence would be facing tough hardships and suppression as the recent Mahuva episode has suggested. It presents a new challenge in terms of the agrarian scenario. At the same time, the age-old problems of Adivasis and other forest-dwellers pertaining to rights over forest-land as well as oppression of deprived agrarian groups by dominant land-owning class would not disappear from social scene as the recent event of Surendranagar district in Saurashtra region indicates (from the report in *Indian Express,* February 19, 2010). In the village called Zinzuwada, the dominant caste group Darbar has forced 187 families of the Maldharis, a pastoral community, to leave the village. This pastoral community sustains themselves through their livestock and hence depends on the village wasteland for grazing. The Darbars even did not allow that and started harassing them by seizing Maldharis' livestock and demanding money for releasing them. The Darbars were even sexually harassing the women. The Maldharis had no option but to leave the village.

It should be mentioned in the end that in Gujarat which is more known for its commerce as well as *mahajan* tradition and culture, and also for peaceful and Gandhian method of negotiation-conciliation approach in reaching solutions in conflict situation of any nature, militant and assertive kinds of agrarian struggles have taken place at many places addressing issues and problems concerning deprived and suppressed groups such as forest-dwellers, Adivasis and Dalits, and which have been driven often by radical ideology. More importantly, these struggles have certainly not only given voice to these depressed and underprivileged groups but these groups have emerged as socially and politically conscious groups with distinct identity and they have raised concerted voice in an assertive manner against the dominant social groups, the state and overall development paradigm. Often, a critical observation has been levelled that in most cases the Adivasis and forest-dwellers have been provided leadership from out-siders, i.e., non-Adivasis. But then, these groups are living quite a vulnerable and strenuous life and on the other hand, the state and the dominant groups are too strong with all the means at their disposal to oppress and harass the deprived groups. And as the case-studies of the above mentioned struggles indicate the leadership, be it in the form of political party with radical ideology such as PSP (in the Pardi Satyagraha) or an organization such as 'Disha', by and large, has steered the movement with conviction and sincerity by keeping in focus the interest and rights of the under-privileged groups. Not only that these leaders have dared and challenged the authority and dominant groups unflinchingly.

Note

1. The narration of this struggle is based on H. Desai and K. Desai, 1997 and K. Desai, 2002.

References

Barrier, N.G. "The Punjab Disturbance of 1907: The Response of the British Government in India to Agrarian Unrest", in *Peasant Resistance in India 1858–1914*, Ed. David, Hardiman, Oxford University Press, Delhi, 1992.

Breman, Jan. "Mobilization of Landless Labourers: Halpatis of South Gujarat", in *Agrarian Struggles in India After Independence*, Ed. A.R. Desai, Oxford University Press, Delhi, 1986.

Chaudhari, Vikram. "Ganotdharo ane Kotla Mehta" (in Gujarati), in *Arthat*, Vol. 25, No. 4, October–November–December 2006.

Desai, A.R. (Ed.). *Agrarian Struggles in India After Independence*, Oxford University Press, Delhi, 1986.

Desai, Hakumat and Kiran Desai. *The Pardi Annakheda Satyagraha: Adivasi Assertion For Rights*, Centre for Social Studies, Surat, 1997.

Desai, Kiran and Nikhil Raj. *Child Labour in Diamond Industry of Surat*, V.V. Giri National Labour Institute, Noida, 2001.

Desai, Kiran. "Land Reforms Through People's Movements", in *Land Reforms in India: Performance and Challenges in Gujarat and Maharashtra,* Eds. G. Shah and D.C. Sah, Sage Publications, New Delhi, 2002.

Dhanagare, D.N. *Peasant Movements in India: 1920–1950,* Oxford University Press, Delhi, 1983.

Engelshoven, Miranda. "Diamonds and Patels: A Report on the Diamond Industry of Surat", *The Worlds of Indian Industrial labour,* Eds. J.P. Parry, J. Breman and K. Kapadia, Sage Publications, New Delhi, 1999.

Engineer, Irfan. "Struggles of Dangi Adivasis for Livelihood and Land", in *Land Reforms in India: Performance and Challenges in Gujarat and Maharashtra,* Eds. G. Shah and D.C. Sah, Sage Publications, New Delhi, 2002.

Gandhi, Mohandas, Karamchand. *Hind Swaraj (in Gujarati),* Navjivan Prakashan Mandir, Ahmedabad, 1995 (reprinted edition).

Guha, Ranjit. *Elementary Aspects of Peasant Insurgency in Colonial India,* Oxford University Press, Delhi, 1983.

Hardiman, David (Ed.). *Peasant Resistance in India 1858–1914,* Oxford University Press, Delhi, 1992.

Hardiman, David. *Feeding the Baniya: Peasants and Usurers in Western India,* Oxford University Press, Delhi, 1996.

Hardiman, David. *Peasant Nationalists of Gujarat: Kheda District 1917–1934,* Oxford University Press, Delhi, 1981.

Hardiman, David. *The Coming of the Devi: Adivasi Assertion in Western India,* Oxford University Press, Delhi, 1987.

Jani, Indukumar. *Be Daykano Safal Sangharsh: 'Jungle-Jamin Name Karo'.* Harsha Prakashan, Ahmedabad, 2009.

Lobo, Lancy and Jayanti, Mecwan. *Shoshan ane Atankni Aagman Adivasio (in Gujarati),* Centre for Culture and Development, Vadodara, 2003.

Parulekar, Godavari. *Manav Jage Che Jyare (*in Gujarati), R.R. Sheth Publication, Bombay, 1976.

Pinto, Stany. "Land Alienation and Consciousness Among the Vasavas of South Gujarat" (An unpublished Ph. D. thesis), Centre for Social Studies, Surat, 1999.

Shah, Ghanshyam, Hemantkumar Shah and Kiran Desai. "Globalization, Gujarat State and Welfare for Poor" (An unpublished report), Centre for Social Studies, Surat, 2008.

Shah, Ghanshyam. "Caste and Land Reforms in Gujarat", in *Land Reforms in India: Performance and Challenges in Gujarat and Maharashtra,* Eds. G. Shah and D.C. Sah, Sage Publications, New Delhi, 2002.

Shah, Ghanshyam. "Land Rights: Struggles of Adivasis and Dalits" (A chapter of an unpublished report), 2010.

Shah, Ghanshyam. "Unrest Among the Adivasis and Their Struggles", in *The Other Gujarat: Social Transformations Among Weaker Sections,* Ed. Takashi, Shinoda, Popular Prakashan, Mumbai, 2002.

Section III
Marginalized Sections

6 Dalit Movements in Gujarat

From 'Imitation' to 'Transformation'[1]

Arjun Patel

Studies on Dalit Movements[2]

Like in other parts of India, the Dalits of Gujarat have also launched movements from time to time on various issues. However because of absence of accounts of these Dalit movements[3] in languages other than Gujarati, it is believed that there are no progressive movements in Gujarat.

A few[4] good works are available related to Dalits of Gujarat, in vernacular language. For instance, the study done by Jyotikar (1991) is informative. It gives an account of the history of Ambedkarite movement in Gujarat.[5] Urmila Patel (1983) has extensively described the practice of untouchability toward the Dalits of Gujarat. She covered issues such as untouchability, its nature, the social life, education, politicization, social mobility, etc. Similar work was done by well-known historian Makarand Mehta (1995). He examined the situation of Dalits in 19th and 20th century of Gujarat. His study covered some of the important collective efforts made by Dalits of Gujarat for assertion of their rights and a few attempts made by them in the form of satyagrahas launched (1) in 1938, for the entry into hotels, (2) in 1947, for the entry into motor bus, and (3) in 1948 for the entry into temples. He addressed the theme of social change among the Dalits of Gujarat in the 19th century and the Dalit upliftment programmes led by Maharaja Sayaji Rao Gayakwad, Gandhi and Ambedkar. Lobo (1991) in his study, carried out in Central Gujarat examined the issues and process of conversion among the Dalits of Gujarat and the status of those who were converted into Christianity. It gives sociological insights into the nature of social mobility through religious conversion.

In addition, studies done by Desai (1976), and Ghanshyam Shah (2001) were also useful for understanding the status of untouchability in Gujarat. A booklet by Arjun Patel (2005) pertaining to Dalit identity in Gujarat brought out the structural conditions under which the identity of the Dalits emerged and how it has changed with the changing times. In an interesting paper published by him (2002), the nature of Dalit–non-Dalit conflict in Gujarat was explained. Recently, Y.A. Parmar (1987) examined the successful upward social mobility among the Mayahvanshis of Surat city and described the 'sanskritization' process among the Dheds of Gujarat, who tried to upgrade their social status through a change of caste name. This process was according to him started after availing the benefits of the new opportunities during the British era. Bose (1981) analysed the upward mobility of the Dalits of Gujarat and concluded that anti-reservation agitation was used against the Dalits to check their upward mobility. Likewise, literature is available on the efforts of Maharaja Sayaji Rao Gayakwad for the upliftment of the Antyaja of various prants of the then Vadodara state.

These sources are valuable to understand the Dalit situation in Gujarat and indicate that from time to time, the Dalits of Gujarat have made collective efforts for bringing change in their existing social condition, although using different ideologies and approaches. But, no significant attempt was made by the sociologists to understand in a full-fledged way the Dalit movement in Gujarat. Though references are available for at least the last two centuries. Here, an attempt is made to collate the scattered published and unpublished materials available in the later part of the 19th century onwards on the subject and to highlight the patterns emerging out of it.

The article is divided into three sections; the first section broadly introduces the issue of Dalits and the second section describes various important Dalit movements that have taken place in Gujarat and the third section gives concluding remarks.

Dalits in Gujarat

The section briefly covers the demographic profile, structural positions and plight of Dalits, and their assertion for their rights.

The total population of Dalits in Gujarat according to the 2001 Census is 35.92 lakhs. It constitutes 7.1 per cent of the total population of the state. In all, there are 30 sub-groups among the Dalits of Gujarat. Among them, the Mahyavansi constitute the highest percentage (43.2%) of the total Dalit population. Next come the sub-groups such as Bhambi (29%), Bhangi (11.3%), Meghval (4.9%), Senva (3%), Garoda (1.9%) and Nadia (1.3%).

According to the 2001 Census, a significant percentage (39.3) of Dalits in Gujarat live in urban areas. The sex ratio of Dalit population in the state is 925 for 1,000 male which is below the national average (936) for all the Dalits, but higher than overall the sex ratio (927) for the country.

According to the 2001 Census, 70.5 per cent of the Dalit population in Gujarat is literate. This is higher than the aggregate national figure for Dalits (54.7%).

Generally, the word 'Dalit' is used to refer those groups defined as scheduled castes (SCs) by the Indian Constitution. They were known by various terminologies in the religious texts of ancient India such as *Raxasha, Deetia, Asur, Chandal, Pancham, Atishudra, Antyaj* or *Namo-Shudra.* Gandhi gave them the name 'Harijan',[6] i.e., 'children of God'. Here, we prefer to identify all these groups as Dalits; means 'the oppressed'. However, the exact word for SCs that was used by those who were engaged in uplifting them, e.g., Sayaji Rao was word Antyaj, Gandhians have refereed them as Harijan, etc.

Dalits are a part of the Hindu social system, which is governed by the powerful and age old 'varna' mechanism evolved by the Brahmins, who are supposed to be outsiders to this country.[7] The varna system divided the Hindu society into four social divisions: Brahmins, Kshatriyas, Vaishyas and Shudras. The Dalits are not included in the four-fold varna model.[8]

In the Hindu social structure, Dalits occupy the lowest rank. The condition of Dalits is very precarious. They are treated as outsiders of the Varna system. Therefore, they are referred to as *'Avarna'.* However, in the recent days, the situation has reversed. The Hindu upper caste who branded Dalits as untouchables or as outsiders of the varna system came forward to assimilate them as a part of the Hindu society.[9] Without doubt, Dalits have remained very much oppressed in all the spheres; including social, cultural, economic and political (for more details see Ghurye, 1960; Mehta, 1981; Bombay Gazetteer, 1901; Forbes, 1973; Patel, 1983; Jyotikar, 1991; Patel, 2005). They were exploited and subjugated for centuries. In the Hindu social system, they were treated as 'untouchables'. Their mere touch, and in a few places even their shadows or voices were enough to pollute the so-called upper caste Hindus.[10] However, in independent India, constitutionally, at least on paper, they are no more termed as untouchables. But many empirical studies conducted at various parts of India, including Gujarat[11] show that they are still living with the stigma of untouchability. Recently, *The Times of India* has published a series of reports (on February 7, 8, 9, 10, 2010) which show the pathetic condition of Dalits in Gujarat with regard to temple entry, being served at tea shop, untouchability practice in schools and treatment meted toward Dalit sarpanchas as at Gram Sabha and Gram Panchayat meetings.

Like in other parts of India, Dalits of Gujarat suffered from inferior status. Due to untouchability, they were restricted to enter private as well as in public spaces. Forbes (1973) in his book narrated the plight of Dalits of the 18th century in Gujarat. At that time, he was serving as a chartered officer in Dabhoi of Vadodara district. He described how Dalits were treated in-humanly by the Hindu upper castes. They were restricted from entering the village through the main gate. A similar tradition was found in the adjoining town of Shinor. He observed that Dalits of Kheda district had to tie a broom at their backs so that their foot-steps get erased and thus save 'Savarna' from pollution. Similarly, Parmar (1987) mentioned that the Dheds of Surat had to tie a broom behind the waist and hang the *Kuladi* (an earthen vessel) round their neck to catch their spit. The untouchables were not allowed to stay in the upper caste locality.[12] Of course, due to the 'graded inequality'[13] the feelings of hierarchy were also found among various sub-groups of untouchables. Various Caste Panchayats of Dalits passed resolutions for maintaining such internal differences among them. This can be observed from their occupational distribution and special privileges and rights endowed to certain castes.[14]

In 1801, Sinor was under the region of Sayaji Rao Gayakwad. On December 26, 1801, a senior officer from Vadodara instructed the concerned official working at the lower level at a local place to not use the services of a Bhangi for lifting mattresses as they were going to be used by the upper caste officials. The senior official warned the lower official that how can the Hindu religion remain intact when you are using the untouchables in lifting the mattresses which are going to used by the upper caste?

New dimensions in the history of Gujarat have started taking place since the arrival of the British and more so since the 19th century, with the introduction of education, industrialization, opening of new avenues of work, construction of railways, innovations in media, etc. Public transportation system, the press, schools, etc., brought the issue of caste discrimination to the surface (Mehta, 1981). It had created upheavals in the Indian society and made an impact on the age-old relations between Dalits and non-Dalits.

Dalit Movements in Gujarat

Various kinds of collective efforts were initiated for the liberation of the Dalits of Gujarat, which were focused to bring changes in their social, economic, cultural and political spheres, by using various strategies and programmes such as Satyagraha, agitation, protest, strike, etc. The leadership for them was provided by both; Dalit and non-Dalit leaders. In all, eight types of Dalit movements can be identified in Gujarat. They are:

1. through upward mobility
2. by Maharaja Sayaji Rao Gayakwad
3. through Gandhian approach
4. by Ambedkarites
5. through religious conversion
6. through literature
7. through Phule–Ambedkari ideology
8. through Indian Constitution

Dalit Liberation through Upward Mobility

The condition of the untouchables started changing with the arrival of the British. The British introduced certain fundamental rights such as education, voting, free access to the public places, opportunities for employments, etc. The untouchables who benefited from this started claiming for their legitimate rights such as equality and due share in the benefit of development. This remained as a constant conflict between the Hindus and the Dalits as the former were placed in a higher position in the caste hierarchy, whereas the latter were placed at the lowest. The Dalits were asking for their due share and the upper castes Hindus were rejecting as it would question their dominance.

Parmar (1987) has examined the process of upward mobility of the schedule caste people who traditionally occupied the lowest position in the later part of the 19th century onwards. He narrated the process of how the Mahyavanshis came into contact with the Europeans, the Christian Missionaries, Parsis and Muslims that have helped them in acquiring new occupational opportunities and education. The internal and external forces also contributed in the creation of social awakening among Mahyavanshis. They were benefited by the urban industrial growth, constitutional provisions and special programmes that have boosted their development.

According to Parmar (1987), the Mahyavanshis and other SCs suffered from socio-religious discrimination at the hands of Savarnas. They were ill-treated since centuries. Traditionally, they were put at the lowest rung of the social pyramid. They were known as 'Dheds', which is a derogatory term used by the Savarnas to remind them of their degraded status and thereby keep them psychologically/emotionally subdued and maintain hegemony over them. They were forced to wear different clothes. They were forced to hang clay utensils (locally called Kuladi) around their necks to spit and had to trail thorns behind them to wipe out their foot prints.

Traditionally, the Mahyavanshis were engaged in clean as well unclean activities which were low and carried no social prestige.[15] They were debarred from acquiring education in the early part of the 19th century.

According to Parmar (1987), during the 17th, 18th and 19th centuries, the trade of Surat attracted various communities such as Hindus, Muslims, Parsis, Arabs, Persians, Jews, Armenians, Spanish, Dutch, French, Portuguese, Danes, Swedish and Christian missionaries. They provided the 'untouchables' with benefits of new occupational and educational opportunities created due to trade. These communities employed the untouchables in their private and domestic services which proved to enhance their betterment and advancement. They got social acceptability and thereby enjoyed prestige and power in the society. Besides, railways, steam factories and military services provided new employment opportunities for the Mahyavanshis. Thus, they got an opportunity to engage themselves not only in better paid jobs, but also in jobs holding high prestige and which were less labour intensive. As a result, they got a chance to go to various places such as Bombay, Poona, Karachi, Britain and Johannesburg in search of better employment.

Likewise, the Mahyavanshis took benefits of the education given by the Christian Missionaries and public schools even though it was resisted by the upper caste people. It helped them in creating a new 'educated group' among the Mahyavanshis. They tried to reform the traditional socio-religious practices which had downgraded their community.

They started demanding change in their traditional caste name from 'Dhed to Mahyavanshi'. For this, they launched a movement known as the 'Majavat Rajput Movement' in 1900. Within a short period of time, this movement spread out in the entire region between Bombay and Ahmedabad.

Parmar (1987) has vividly brought out how the Dheds through this movement started claiming that they originally belonged to Mayavat Rajput lineage of the Kshatriyas. They have organized various meetings and sabhas at various places. Alongside, they published in caste magazines, brought out pamphlets and handbills which supported their claim that Mahyavanshis are descendants of Rajputs and by passing several resolutions and submitted memorandums to the then government demanding for their reorganization as Mahyavanshis.

The educated leaders of Mahyavanshis have pressurized the government to officially register the new name Mahyavanshi by using some or the other tricks and techniques. Ultimately, they succeeded in getting a new name registered in 1939 in the erstwhile Bombay state. On December 25, 1939, the government of Bombay declared that the word 'Dhed' had been discontinued from all government correspondence and instead the word Mahyavanshi was to be used. Parmar (1987) pointed out this achievement was a result of their collective and concentrated efforts.

Similar types of efforts for changing the existing caste names were made by the other sub-castes of SCs such as 'Khalpa', 'Garoda' and Bhangi' to 'Rohit', 'Guru' and 'Rishi', etc., in that order by neo-educated persons in the respective castes during the 20th century.

Dalit Liberation by Maharaja Sayaji Rao Gayakwad

Like in other states in India, the condition of untouchables of Vadodara state during 18–19th century was pathetic. The then kings of Vadodara were wedded to the idea of 'Gauo-Brahmin Pratipalak' i.e., King as the protector of cow and Brahmin, as both were considered holy. There is enough evidence which shows the discriminatory and prejudicial attitudes towards the untouchables.

Maharaja Sayaji Rao Gayakwad (henceforth Sayaji Rao) has tried to change the situation of Antyaj by initiating State policy and programmes in their favour. He has taken various measurers in the spheres of social, economic, educational, political and cultural to improve their lot. He applied secular means to change the condition and mainly adopted welfare approach. It has created far-reaching changes for the long run. Of course, he failed to address the Brahminical structure of which the Antyaj have become victims. In fact, he has tried to bring changes without disturbing the Brahminical Social Structure. In other words, he does not want to bring radical changes, but aspire for positional changes of the Antyaj.

The Sayaji Rao rule began in 1780 in Vadodara. Sayaji Rao II became the prince in 1819, while Sayaji Rao III become Prince of Vadodara at the age of 12 on May 27, 1875. He was an adopted son. Like Chhatrapati Sahuji Maharaj of Kolhapur, Sayaji Rao III of Vadodara also made efforts for the welfare of the untouchables years before similar activities were initiated by Gandhi and Ambedkar.

Sayaji Rao III was the first Gujarati prince to have reacted positively towards the problems of untouchables and the tribals. He took up the issue in a young age of 20 when no one else would have dared to do so.

Like others in Maharashtra[16], earlier to him Sayaji Rao III (1862–1939) was the first who initiated activities to uplift untouchables and tribals. His approach toward 'untouchables' was different from the earlier rulers. In those days no one[17] dared to initiate the efforts to uplift the untouchables in Gujarat. Whereas, Sayaji Rao showed courage for taking initiatives for the welfare of the untouchables. He was very much influenced by the individual freedom and liberal ideology of the Western countries.

Among the many imitation taken for the upliftment of untouchables by Sayaji Rao, educational activities were eye-catching. He realized the importance of education for the development of any group of people. He consciously tried to break away the caste rigidity. He aimed at the upliftment of the downtrodden people, particularly 'untouchables' and tribals.

At the end of 1893, Sayaji Rao started four residential schools for the untouchables; which were located at Vadodara, Amreli, Patan and Navsari. In these residential schools, food and clothing were provided free of cost. He started a school for the Bhangis in the year 1898. In the year 1901, Sayaji Rao passed a law for imparting free and compulsory education to all.

In the later part of the 19th century, he started 15 schools among which one was exclusively for females. The number of schools and students increased by 10 times during a period of 40 years between 1900 to 1940.

He started one Sanskrit school in 1913 to train the Gardoa (one sub-group of untouchables) in Sanskrit. He provided for hostel facility and scholarship.

In the Gayakwadi state of Vadodara, the numbers of untouchable students were 1,926 in the year 1900–01 and it increased to 20,873 by the year 1938–39.

In fact, he often published advertisements in local newspaper encouraging untouchables to be educated. They were given higher posts. Up to 1935, there was not a single untouchable officer in Vadodara State. A delegation of ' untouchables' met with Sayaji Rao in 1936 and presented their case before the him that there were 15–17 untouchable graduates, but they remained unemployed. Sayaji Rao being unaware of this immediately called his personal secretary and ordered to give them jobs. He announced a garden party and invited 900 persons. In the party, he announced scholarships for untouchable students to study abroad. He appointed untouchables in various departments of government. The upper castes became very much annoyed by these moves. Sayaji Rao was condemned by 'Savarnas' because these moves were directly assaulting on their personal interests. They felt that if the untouchables got educated they would ask for higher wages on the jobs. But they were not successful in preventing Sayaji Rao for carrying out such activities.

Sayaji Rao had firmly believed that the untouchables will not be able to live a life of dignity, unless they become economically independent. So, he took steps to empower them on the economic front. He gave impetus to weaving, making items of leather, etc. He encouraged cooperative societies for 'Chamars' and 'Vankars'. While giving renovation funds for repairing wells, lakes (talav) or community platforms in the village, Sayaji Rao left instruction that no one should stop the untouchables from their use. He was quite worried about the inhuman behavior of the upper caste people.[18] Sayaji Rao also published a Gazette allowing temple entry to untouchables. He declared untouchability as a cognizable offence. Sayaji Rao made provision for reservation in jobs as early as the beginning of the 20th century. In 1902, he gave priority to the untouchables in jobs and reserved jobs in Municipal Corporation. He also made regulated money-lending activities among the untouchables. In those days, the upper-caste money-lenders used to cheat the illiterate, poor indebtors. Maharaja also gave political representation to the untouchables.[19] This is how Sayaji Rao Gayakwad made efforts to bring social justice to the untouchables of his time.

In 1911, Sayaji Rao gave permission to 'untouchables' for reading the newspapers and books in the Central Library of Vadodara.

Though Maharaja Sayaji Rao has been to foreign countries, he also felt that it was important to visit the rural areas. In the year 1882, he first visited the Kheda Prant of Vadodara state. He published a notification stating that any person could meet him directly, if he/she wished to present their personal problems. At the time of his visit to rural areas, he met the common people directly and freely mingled with them. He often took meals with them on their farms or in their houses in order to discuss their problems. He implemented many new things which he learnt from his visits to foreign countries.

Along with the school, Sayaji Rao also started a hospital for the 'untouchables' and gave all the facilities to them free of cost. He introduced an examination for the appointment of Hindu purohits (priests) and made legal provision that any person, irrespective of his caste could appear for this examination. To eradicate the discrimination based on castes, Sayaji Rao Gayakwad stopped the 'Purana'-based rituals which promoted the differences based on caste. These were radical steps in those days.

Sayaji Rao was quite upset about the untouchability in the Hindu religion. Setting an example, he openly dined with the untouchables.[20] He arranged a series of lectures for the upliftment of the untouchables. He worked for the untouchables not only in Vadodara but also in other states.

Sayaji Rao also promoted agriculture, as he firmly believed that it was one of the foundation of social progress. That is why he encouraged[21] farmers for the adoption of the latest methods of agriculture.

Since the 19th century, the condition of untouchables started improving rapidly.

Many organizations and renowned people were impressed by the activities initiated by Sayaji Rao for the untouchables. Due to these activities, a few Dalits were freed from the traditional clutches of the upper castes. As noted earlier, some of them independently started constructive activities for the untouchables.

Sayaji Rao heavily criticized the hypocritical behavior of the upper caste Hindus regarding their stand on casteism. It has resulted in envy[22] of the upper caste Hindus towards him. He openly criticized the Hindu upper castes that they disliked the racial and discriminatory attitude of the British towards them, but they conveniently forgot that when they themselves behaved similarly towards their people, the untouchables. Sayaji Rao appealed to the upper caste people for self-introspection and showed his readiness to take the leadership for the cause of untouchables.

However, the upper castes were confident that Gayakwad would never succeed in his mission of mixing untouchables with the upper castes. But due to the consistence efforts from Maharaja, new leadership emerged among the Dalits.

Dalit Liberation through Gandhian Approach

At the end of the 19th century and in the beginning of the 20th century, it was said that the condition of the untouchables was quite miserable in all the spheres, be it social, economic, education, political or cultural. Before the arrival of Gandhi from South Africa in 1915, except Sayaji Rao Gayakwad and Christian missionaries no one took interest in the welfare of the untouchables. During the British era due to some policy-related changes the inter-relations between the untouchables and non-untouchables began to change. After the arrival of Gandhi from South Africa, he decided to work towards India's independence. In order to achieve his target, he needed support from all the sections of society. So he started work to among the untouchables.

In 1917, at the beginning of the Gandhian era in Gujarat, the first political conference was held in which some of the resolutions related to social reforms were passed. But this conference did not pass any resolution related to the upliftment of the most oppressed sections of the society. Thereafter, Gandhi realized the importance of untouchables in the independence movement. So, Gandhians started addressing the issue of Dalit.

Due to the efforts of Mama Saheb Phadke and Thakkarbapa, they decided to organize meetings in the locality of Bhangis for establishing direct contact with them. However, up to the second decade of the 20th century, the Dalits were not given entry into school. During 1917, Thakkarbapa received a complaint that the Savarnas had dropped the idea of co-education with the untouchables. So, he decided to start a separate school for the untouchables from a donation by a mill owner of Ahmedabad. This is how constructive works were started by the Gandhians. As part of this initiative, Dalits were given education, although this was not easy. For example, on November 1915, the fundamentalists harassed Indulal Yagnik and Dadubhai Amin at the time of the conference of untouchables held at Nadiad.

Gandhians have also taken up the issue of removal of untouchability. When Gandhi was in South Africa he received humiliating treatment from the British authority on the basis of racism. He decided to fight against such racism and launched Satyagraha against the British authority in South Africa. Similar kind of discrimination based on caste was prevalent in India in those days. Gandhi, came back to India in 1915, surprisingly he had taken a different view[23] and applied an altogether different approach for removal of untouchability.[24] He mooted the idea of 'change of heart' for solving it, and declared to solve the problems of caste discrimination through peaceful action and persuasion. He introduced the concept of 'Seva' to his followers.[25] Yet, he was a supporter of the Varna system. He was of the opinion that Bhangis had to earn their livelihood through sweeping work. Of course he believed that there should not be any occupations based on differentiation. The status of Bhangis should also be equivalent to that of Brahmins.

In order to get the support of the untouchables and establishing his leadership over the untouchables, Gandhi started the 'Gujarat Harijan Sevak Sangh' (GHSS) on October 13, 1932[26], headed mostly by Baniyas and Brahmins.[27] He Inspired the Harijans to join the freedom struggle and work through GHSS. This is how he institutionalized the grass-roots activities for untouchables throughout Gujarat. He often attacked the ills of untouchability and made an appeal to the non-Harijans that they should cleanse their heart from the sin of untouchability. It was said that he became one with the Harijans in appearances as well as in their life-style.[28]

Gandhi persuaded Harijans not to adopt extreme attitudes towards the Hindus and their institutions. He emphatically stated that no Harijan should go on a fast or against anybody. He advised them to observe what the Hindu castes were doing for the removal of untouchability which separated them from the rest of Hindus.

In spite of all such efforts, Markarand Mehta (1981: 126) concluded that despite such strong network, Gandhi did not succeed in developing and building self-respect and self-esteem among the untouchables. Not only that, he held Gandhi responsible for the under-development of independent leadership among the Harijans.[29]

Ambedkarites' Efforts for Dalit Liberation

To maintain the hegemonic position of the upper castes over the untouchables, the latter were consciously deprived of certain basic human rights which anybody can enjoy as a citizen. Free entry of the untouchables was prohibited at public places such as temples, bathing ghats, water tanks, public wells, schools, panchayats, etc. To establish the human rights of the untouchables, Ambedkar launched a few Satyagrahas such as temple entry Satyagraha of Kalaram temple in Nasik, Water Satyagraha at Mahad, etc. All the Satyagrahas were launched with a view to make the upper castes realize that like anybody else the lower castes also should have free accesses to public facilities. In a way it was a challenge to the monopoly of the upper castes and an attempt to assert their rights as citizens.

A few of the Dalits from Gujarat who migrated to Bombay to earn a livelihood were quite influenced by the Ambedkarite ideology. Solanki (1876–1953) was the first Gujarati Dalit to get a matriculation degree from Mumbai presidency in 1894. He undertook activities for Dalit upliftment among the Gujarati Mahyavanshi Samaj in Bombay. Solanki came into contact with Ambedkar and took active role for the upliftment of Dalits in Gujarat throughout his life. Likewise, many Dalits engaged with the activities aimed at the development of Dalits. Chhatrasingh Lalji Untekar of village Untadi in Valsad district, Chhabildas Sukhabhai Masekar of Valsad, etc., were influenced by the Ambedkarites movement and they started their activities in Gujarat.

In Gujarat, the Ambedkarites started their activities from 1920s. They formed 'Bahiskrut Hitkarini Sabha' in the year 1924. Three Gujaratis were included in the Governing Board. Some of the Dalits who identified themselves as Gandhians were also influenced by Ambedkar.

The approach of Ambedkar for liberation of Dalits was different from that of the Gandhians. Ambedkar saw that the Dalit problem was a 'political one' and required secular means to solve it. Dr Ambedkar started his own political party called 'All India Scheduled Caste Federation' (AISCF) on July 18–19, 1942 at Nagpur. Dalit representatives from all over India had participated in this meeting. P.M. Patasi, a member of District Local Board, Gangaram Pitambari Burdas, Karsanbhai M. Leuva, Revabhai Bhudarbhai from Surat participated in this meeting. Influenced by this, the Dalits of Gujarat started their independent political platform.

On December 1942 the Gujarat branch of the AISCF was established, while its systematic structure evolved in 1944. Revabhai Bhudarbhai Parmar was appointed as President of the Federation. From 1943 onwards, planned activities of Ambedkarities started taking place under the banner of AISCF.

Ahmedabad was the central point of the Ambedkarite activities. Mehsana and Kheda were the adjoining districts of Ahmedabad. Mehsana was very orthodox with regard to the practice of untouchability. Many Dalits had migrated to Ahmedabad from Mehsana for their livelihood and were working in the cotton mills. Mehsana district was a part of the Gayakwad state of Vadodara. Where the activities of Dalit upliftment were much pronounced, the Dalits of this state took advantage of the benefits of education and became aware of their condition.

Kalol was the centre of the cotton mills. There were three mills where the Dalits from the surrounding villages worked for their livelihood. Some settled in Kalol. But they found it difficult to commute to their native places frequently as their villages were not connected through trains and they were not allowed to sit in the motor buses due to the stigma of untouchability. Under these circumstances, these Dalits organized themselves under the AISCF and fought for the right to travel by motor buses. They launched a Satyagraha in 1943 under the leadership of Govindji Samaji Parmar and finally succeeded. Some Savarna youths of Sardhav village threatened to burn the Dalit locality, but the Dalits were not discouraged. The Congress Dalit activists extended their cooperation in the motor-Satyagraha. Viraji Manaji was injured seriously during the Satyagraha as a result of which he died a few days later. Jogendranath Mandal wrote a letter to Sayaji Rao and the officers of Vadodara state who immediately rushed to the place of the incident.

Though Ambedkarite activities in Gujarat did not become popular for a variety of reasons, it can be a topic for further research.

But certainly it has provide different approach to the Dalit movement than the Gandhians.

Ambedkarist also exposed Gandhian attitude towards crucial issues such as temple entry to the Dalits. The then government passed a law allowing untouchables, entry to the temples. It was opposed by the Gandhians. They propagated that though the government had passed a law, it would not be in the interests of Harijan's self-respect to enter the temples only on the basis of a law. Thus, the Gandhians made a categorical statement that for the sake of establishing one's (Harijan's) rights no Harijan should enter the temple by themselves.[30]

According to Gandhi, those Dalits who were after the temple entry issue were not true devotees as they had no concern for God. They were running after their rights and hence away from their 'religion'. He advised Harijans to have patience by saying that if the upper caste understood the needs of the Harijans, they would themselves invite them into temples. According to him, the society should realize this issue and take lead for inviting the Harijans into temples. He asked Harijans to bring home Ganga's holy water and bathe at home with it. The Harijans were asked not to make any efforts for entering the temple. But this call of Gandhi did not work because, as Makrand Mehta (1995) rightly observed, for untouchables, the fundamental question was of their human and civic rights which were closely associated with their self-respect and dignity rather than their religious identity.

The worrisome thing that happened in the movement relating to temple entry of the untouchables was that without prior consultation of the Congress and Majoor Mahajan, the Vankars (one of the sub-groups of Dalits) working as labourers in the cotton mills declared their support to the temple entry Satyagraha of Harijan through a strike. The behavior of the workers angered the Gandhian activists. The leaders of Majoor Mahajan took up this issue and tried to explain to the Dalit workers that both the issues, i.e., temple entry and strikes are different from each other. Dalit Satyagrahis were quite clear in their stand and stood up firmly for their self-respect and continued strike (Mehta, 1995: 218).

In fact, the Gandhians could give no satisfactory answer about the agitation of the Harijans. But due to the persistent efforts of the Gandhian leaders, a resolution was passed in one of the meetings that the workers have not behaved in a 'good manner' in the temple and hence they lost much rather than gained. A request was also made to withdraw the strike. Gandhi sent a massage from Delhi saying, 'Harijan, you remain as true children of Hari'. Thus, Gandhi appealed to the Harijan workers not to go on strike and avoid conflicts as he wanted to avoid confrontation among various groups of Hindus.

On the other hand, to settle this controversy, the Gandhians tried to persuade Sadhu-Sants (sages), Acharyas (religious teachers) and trustees of the temples to allow Harijans in to the temple. Ravi Shankar Maharaj was given the responsibility for persuading the Harijans to quit the demand for temple entry and to end the strike. Vallabhbhai Patel,[31] understood very well the depth of the problem and considering the situation, took an aggressive stand towards the temple authorities and explained to them that there was no way out except letting the Harijans in and no Gandhian can interfere with this right of the Harijans.

Similarly, the Dalits also tried to assert their civic rights which they got from British. For instance, in 1937, B.D. Kher, CM of Mumbai Prant and also President of 'Maharashtra Harijan Sevak Sangh', passed cognizable law which allowed the Harijans to enter in all the hotels. Some of the Harijans mobilized the Harijans on this issue and thereby asserted[32] their rights. At that time also, some of the Gandhians tried to persuade the Harijans not to make this an issue.

For instance, Muldas Veesya, President of Maharashtra Dalit (Harijan) Samaj, made an appeal that the attitude of the Harijans after entering the hotels should be very polite and systematic.[33] Recalling the cultural tradition of the Harijans, he said that Harijan Sanskriti always inspired them to go for food prepared at home rather than food prepared in the hotel. But Harijans, particularly those who were influenced by the Ambedkarite thoughts started asserting their rights for the hotel entry. The impact of this incidence was observed in many cities of Gujarat such as Surat, Rajkot, Dholka, Viramgam, etc.

There were occasions of tension and even fighting among the Gandhian Dalits and Ambedkarite Dalits, and also between their organizations. 'Gujarat Varnashram Swaraj Sangh' called a meeting and passed a resolution strongly criticizing the order of Bombay government that allowed the untouchables into the hotels. They found this law hurting the interests of the Hindu religion. The orthodox upper castes opposed the law by saying that there could be no improvement if the Harijans and Savarnas started eating together. They asked, 'what about our civil liberties?' According to them, this law resulted in creating enmities between the two communities (Mehta, 1995: 151). The agitation for hotel entry did not last longer than about two months, but it certainly created havoc in the Gujarat Society.

Thus, the Gandhians approached remained peaceful. They preached to the Harijans to live in harmony with the upper castes. Mehta (1995: 70) observed that they were giving much emphasis on purity and religious matters. Not only that, they also tired to persuade the lower castes of the Hindu society saying that they should not blame the upper castes for their misery. They should remain within the Hindu fold.[34] It seems for Gandhian, the unity of Hindu was the main concern. Why Gandhi's approach remained different compared to the movement he laid in South Africa for the rights of Blacks from the case of rights of Harijan in India, is a matter of inquiry.

Dalit Liberation through Religious Conversion

Religion is an important aspect of one's life because it governs the minds of people. The Hindu religion sanctioned the discriminatory behavior of the upper caste because of which the Dalits launched a movement. The aim of the Dalit movement was to achieve equality.

The Dalits born with the stigma of untouchability remain with it till death. No one has any control on his/her birth in a particular caste. But according to Ambedkar, they certainly have a choice to remain Hindu or not. Dr Ambedkar certainly gave a chance in advance to the Hindus to change their attitudes towards the untouchables in Yevala conference held on October 13, 1935. Giving a warning, he declared that a change of religion was the only option left for the Dalits, if the non-Dalits did not change their attitudes towards Dalits. He declared that he would not die as a Hindu. The Dalits spent a lot of resources to get due respect from the Hindu fold. But by and large, some of the sections of Dalits realized that it was futile to fight for a respectable and independent position by remaining in the Hindu fold.

The Hindus at large did not take Ambedkar's warning seriously. At last after 35 years, Ambedkar and lakhs of his Dalit followers left Hinduism and embraced Buddhism. They decided not to take part in the Hindu religious festivals, *ratha* (chariot) processions and similar occasions of worships. They took 22 oaths, one of them rejects Rama and Krishna as their Gods.

For Ambedkar, there was no option left for liberation of the Dalits except through religious conversion. He came to this conclusion after struggling for more than two decades for the basic human rights of the untouchables. However, it is to be noted that the appeal for conversion was not equally accepted throughout India. Compared to Maharashtra, the untouchables of Gujarat accepted[35] less the appeals of Ambedkar to convert from Hinduism to Buddhism. The reasons for this need further investigation.

One of the reasons may be that they are again given a low status. This is the crux of all their problems. Unless and until the caste system is abolished not only on paper but also from the mindset of the Hindus, the problems of the Dalits will remain the same. This condition was not acceptable to the orthodox Hindus because they did not want to lose their hegemony through which they have survived through centuries. They wanted to retain it forever. Lancy Lobo (1991) studied the condition of the converted Christians from untouchable classes. He found that the Christianity was not able to save the convert from the sufferings of the untouchability. It was observed that though the Christian faith teaches equality of all human beings, yet the Dalit converts to Christianity remained more or less in the same social condition as the Hindu Dalits. Christianity failed to give them equal status.

Conversion[36] though raised the general social status of the Dalits did not solve the problems of Dalits. Studies show that the Dalits were unable to change their status even after the change of religion. This is also true of Gujarat. The society needs overall changes. It is understood that unless and until this is a cultural change, mere change of religion is not going to solve their problem.

The case is similar in other parts of India as well. In South India, the untouchables called Pallas, Pariahs, Malas, Madigas, etc., who have embraced Christianity have had same kind of experience. It is found that even among Christians, the relationship between the upper-caste Christian and lower-class Christian has not changed. Also, the attitude of the converted Hindu upper castes and converted Hindu lower castes has remained the same. Thus, without a change in the attitudes social emancipation is not possible.

It was believed that with the increase of urbanization and education, untouchability will go. But in reality it has not happened so. Untouchability continued to exist. The attitude of the upper castes towards the Dalits has not changed. The educated urban Dalit were also facing the problem of untouchability and discrimination. It was thought that the problem of untouchability would be abolished by renouncing Hinduism. But it has also not come true. Inequality and injustice still remained. The Dalits were living in abject poverty. Their lives are miserable and they believe that Buddhism is the only religion which has the potential to liberate the Dalits. To some of the Dalits, self-respect was more important than material gains. Their struggle was not just for their economic development but also for their honour and prestige.

Dalit Liberation through Literature

Literature can also play important role in maintaining or breaking social order. The Dalits were considered as Shudras and were denied basic education since thousands of years. Obviously, the monopoly of the literature in India remained with the upper caste writers who used literature for maintaining the BSO[37] (Brahminical Social Order).

However, some of the people of downtrodden castes who happened to get the opportunity for having education after the arrival of British, started raising their voice through various forms of literature for their emancipation from the clutches of the oppressive caste system. Mahatama Jyotiba Phule for the first time in modern India started challenging the Lalit (of upper caste) literature.

Dalit literature movement became popular as Dalit Panther Movement (DPM). It is basically a violent struggle of the Dalits to challenge the hegemony of the savarnas by creating their own literature called Dalit literature. It was written with an aim to create radical awareness among the Dalits about their problems. Like in other spheres, the non-Dalit writers dominate the field of literature. The non-Dalits who belonged to the exploited classes wrote about the misery and welfare of the Dalits. But these writings were challenged by Dalit writers educated as a result of the British initiatives.

In Maharashtra, Dalit literature became more popular after 1975. Today, the situation is that no literacy conference concludes without making a reference about Dalit literature. In Maharashtra, the Dalit literature which began at the time of Jyotiba Phule got a spurt during the time of Ambedkar. The DPM movement caught momentum in Gujarat, and during the last two decades it has became more prominent in Gujarat. The Western Indian Dalit literature particularly of Maharashtra has influenced much of the Gujarati Dalit literature.

In the first quarter of the 19th century, the Dalits of Gujarat became active in Ambedkarite Movement. Though compared to Maharashtra, the DPM is new to Gujarat, it succeeded in raising the consciousness among the Dalits and gave a jolt to the mainstream of Gujarati literature. The DPM has emerged as a movement of literature through which educated Ambedkarite Dalit writers have started challenging the hegemonic position of the upper castes. Dalit literature is a distinct literature compared to the usual traditional literature. It has consciously maintained the distinction between the established Brahminical literature and literature based on communist ideology. In the Dalit literature, the misery and pain of the Dalit was given the central place. Without much bothering about the form of the literature, the Dalit writers have described the concert realities of their life. Of course, it was criticized heavily, particularly during the initial phases on the ground of its form. Now, the criticism is not so contentious. Upper caste writers have also accepted[38] it.

One can see the clear impact of writings of Ambedkar on Dalit literature. It also reflected Dalit problems, issues, challenges and aspiration for their emancipation. Dalit literature mainly covered topics related to blind faith, varna vyavashta, inhumanity, injustice, atrocities and the forces which work against the betterment of Dalits and caste system. The Marathi and Gujarati Dalit literature revolved around these topics.[39]

Dalit literature has emerged out of the inequality based on varna, caste, etc. Dalit literature aims to achieve self-esteem through self-consciousness and self-awareness. It is a struggle for evolving one's identity. It is also a quest for the emancipation from the oppressive social system. In some Dalit stories, the exploitation of women became the reason for the rebel/revolt.[40] In Hindi literature also, the conflict between the landlord and labour was the theme in the context of the poverty, exploitation and class inequality. Unity and resistance for injustice, which emerged out of such a situation is seen as the sign of consciousness and steps towards liberation. Various kinds of the protests and agonies were created out of the social reality. The relation of Dalit, who became victim of age-old social system is quite obvious. Dalit literature is not written for the sake of writer's self-fulfillment. Instead, certain type of social change is expected from this literature.

Dalit Liberation through Phule–Ambedkar's Ideology

Unlike Maharashtra, the spread of Phule–Ambedkarite's ideology was very less in Gujarat in those days. Up to 1990s – many of the Bahujans of Gujarat were unaware of the works of Phule. Of course, the picture has changed now,[41] particularly after 80s. However, it is not without problems. Over a period of time, it has got divided into various fractions. However because of the spread of BAMCEF (Backward and Minority Community Employment Federation) and BSP (Bahujan Samaj Party), Dalits and other backward castes and communities became increasingly familiar with their problems with reference to the BSO.

Some of them became followers of this ideology and worked day and night to change the BSO under which their forefathers were subjugated and exploited for generations. The BAMCEF and BSP have been trying hard to inculcate the Phule–Ambedkar's ideology among the SCs, Scheduled Castes (STs), Other Backward Castes (OBCs) and the minorities, though it was not easy thanks to the history of Gujarati culture, influences of Gandhi and Congress, Mahajan tradition, graded inequality in the caste system, slow spread of Phule – Ambedkar's thoughts, etc. Unlike in Maharashtra, the upper-caste intellectuals and the enlightened men who identified themselves as 'progressive' somehow kept themselves aloof from the 'Bahujan movement' or 'Bahujan ideology'. Often, they criticized the leaders of BAMCEF and BSP. They hardly took the name of Ambedkar or Phule.

As mentioned earlier, sections of Dalits have realized that without bringing a change in the system, their problems are not going to be solved. Hence, they opted for bringing about a change of the BSO. It was realized by Dalit activists that an alternative ideology was necessary to counter the existing established ideology. The Dalits put forward the 'Phule–Ambedkar ideology' against the 'Manuvadi ideology'. They are busy evolving social polarization among the SCs, STs, OBCs and minorities, who together constitute 85 per cent of the population and are the victims of BSO.

Evidently, the pace of social change is slow. The Dalits are also aware of the strength of the ruling class. They have realized ways to overthrow the BSO by using democratic means and democratic institutions. Unlike the Naxalites or Maoists, they do not want to take to arms for achieving their cause. They have realized the strength of voting power of 'Bahujans' (SCs, STs, OBCs and minorities) in the democratic set-up and through democratic process by using the Constitution of India have started spreading awareness among the educated sections of the Bahujans.

Since 1970s, national-level and state-level conferences are being organized regularly by the BAMCEF. The usual topics at the conferences are the negative impact of government policies, the need for organizational efforts, and creating awareness about their Mahapurush[42] who have fought against the Brahminical social system. They also published various periodicals such as *Mulnivasi Bharat, Bahujan Ka Bahujan Bharat, OBC Awaz, Kahani, Bahujan Navjagruti,* etc. The Dalits had realized that seven per cent Dalits will not produce effective results in the political arena. So, they have made a broad base of the victimized social groups of the Brahminical social order. Thus, the Dalits changed the strategy for their liberation movement. They expanded the category from Dalit to Bahujan. Now, they feel that the term Bahujan also has some limitations. Therefore, they tried to expand these categories to Sarvajan. They have spread the slogan of 'Sarvajan Hitai Sarvajan Sukhay.' Through this strategy, they have captured the political power of Uttar Pradesh, which is considered as one of the important states on the Indian political map. They are trying to spread out their geographical and social base throughout India. In Gujarat also, constant efforts are made to spread the social and geographical network of Bahujan Samaj through BAMCEF and BSP.

Now, Dalits do not want to keep their trust in Savarns for their own development. A section of Dalits feel that they themselves will have to come forward for solving their problems on their own. They are moving ahead along these lines. Since last two decades, constant efforts have been made for spreading the Phule–Ambedkar's ideology. For this, they are have been conscientization not only the Dalits of various parts of India but also of abroad. Efforts are also being made to incorporate the OBCs, STs and minorities. Today, the Dalit activists claim that they have made an equally powerful social organization which is capable of fighting RSS (Rashtriya Swayam Sevak Sangh) which strives to maintaining the BSO. The organizations of Dalits are powerful because they are cadre-based. The Dalits are capable of showing their strength to the Brahminical forces who have kept them under subjugation in the fold of Hindutva.

The Dalits have been organizing themselves under the banner of 'Mulnivasi'. It is also criticized, particularly by the Savarna intellectuals that certain Dalit elites are promoting their interests in the name of Mulnivasis, but hardly anybody listens to them. To counter the Bahujan formula, the Brahmins under the RSS banner and the political wing of BJP tried to counter the Bahujan force. Thus at present two types of parallel ideological battles are going on in India including Gujarat. This process is fundamentally different from the earlier one. In the Hindutva politics, the leadership remained in the hands of upper castes, while in the Bahujan Politics, the leadership came to the hands of the Bahujan people. That is the difference.

Today's Dalit movement of Gujarat is qualitatively different for the following reasons: (1) They are searching their role in history. They realized that the struggle against Brahminism is quite old. The present efforts are continuation of the efforts of their forefathers. (2) There is a certain approach to the movement. The Phule–Ambedkar's ideology is in the hearts of their movement. Their movement is wedded to certain ideology. They are clear about their ethos and objectives. It is a goal-oriented movement and hence the possibilities of success are more. (3) The Dalits have not remained confined the movement to seven per cent of themselves. They have included 85 per cent of the population of SCs, STs, OBCs and minorities. (4) They are focused about their enemy. They are launching the movement of 85 per cent vs. 15 per cent population. Geographically, they are spreading their movement to all-India level. The day-to-day happenings and the state policy level implications are being continuously analysed in a Phule – Ambedkar's perspective with certain examples and logic. These are some of the reasons to get the cooperation of the local people.

Due to all these, the level of consciousness among the Dalits has gone up. While in the year 1990, hardly anybody knew about the name of Mahatama Jyotiba Phule;[43] now talking about Phule and his mission is common through out Gujarat. Many of the Dalits of Gujarat are now aware of the name of their Mahapurush, particularly Jyotiba Phule, Sahuji Maharaj, Narayan Guru, Ramaswami Periyar, Dr Ambedkar, Birsa Munda, etc., upto 1995, no one was ready to take note of Brahminism but now-a-days even the upper caste people have became aware of the Bahujan movement. This is how the Dalits are making their attempts to evolve their own distinct independent movement. It is hoped that the Bahujan movement will bring desirable results in the coming days.

'Movement' and 'Counter-Movement'

Both the types of efforts – movement and counter-movements – are found among the Dalits of Gujarat. The upper castes want to keep their hegemony intact. They do not want the Dalits to be fully independent and separate. So they tried to save the situation in their favour. *Swadhayay Parivar*[44] is trying hard to co-opt the Dalits and the other backward sections to the Brahminical fold. They use various techniques to rekindle Brahminism in the 21st century. Phule – Ambedkarite Dalits believe that Swadhayay Parivar is trying to justify the 'varna' system. They banned the book written by the supremo of Swadhay Parivar, Pandurang Shastri on Sanskruti *Chintan* as *Vikruti Chintan*. They believed that Pandurang Shastri is polluting the thoughts of the backward classes to protect the BSO by justifying the varna system.

A group of Dalit activists are of the opinion that the Dalits are making futile attempts to merge in to the mainstream by joining Swadhayay Parivar, while the opponent group believes that the psychology of the Dalits needs be considered to understand their action. They made a counter-argument that by joining Swadhayay Parivar, the Dalits have send a signal that they want to avoid conflict. But this view is countered by the Dalits that those who are joining Swadhay Parivar are not completely aware about the hidden agenda of the Pandurang Shastri.

Like Swadhayay, the activities and the network of Swaminarayan sect is also very powerful; particularly among the middle castes and higher middle castes. The influence of Saibaba, Jalarambapa, Sitarambapa, etc., is also very much there. The Kathakars such as Moraribapu, Praful Shukla, Sidhansu Maharaj, etc., are working hard to spread the Brahminical ideology through the medium of Ramayana, Mahabharata and Gita. Religious activities in Gujarat are in full swing and are directly or indirectly preparing ground for spreading the ideology of Hindutva. The BJP, a political wing of RSS, basically a Brahminical social organization remained successful to counter the awareness that emerged out of the KHAM[45] (Kshatriya, Harijan, Adivasi and Muslim) alliance around the mid-1980s in Gujarat.

Dalit Liberation through Indian Constitution

Indian Constitution prepared under the leadership of Dr Babasaheb Ambedkar played a significant role in changing the age-old restrictions imposed on Dalits through Brahminical customs and regulations.

Before going into the details of the role played by Indian constitution in uplifting the condition of Dalits in the structural context, let us have a brief idea about the conditions of Dalits under the Brahminical custom, in the guise of Hindu religion. Hindu religion is embodied with inequality and injustice to the untouchables. The Dalits cannot expect social justice from Hinduism. The Varna system has got legitimatization from the Hindu Shastras. Purusha Shukta has given explanation of how the social classes have emerged. The unequal social classes in India got sanction from the Hindu religious texts. The texts gave superior power and prestige to the dwijas compared to the Shudras and Atishudras. The Brahmins and the upper classes have maintained the system of Chaturvarna – a system based on inequality and gave them a higher rank and thus a greater opportunity to dominate and exploit others.

A Shudra was not supposed to build a house of his choice. They were not supposed to wear certain types of Dhotis.[46]

In Gujarat, an untouchable had to keep the horns of an animal at their well so that new comers to the village could remain well informed that they were not supposed to drink water from these wells and thus avoid from being polluted. Also, as mentioned earlier, free movement of Dalits was also restricted.

One of the visible element of the Indian caste system was that the punishment was not decided on the basis of the nature of the crime but on the basis of the caste/varna of the offender. If persons were Brahmins then they were given very less punishment even for the most serious crime. But it was reverse in the case of Shudras. Thus, even for a very minor offence they were given severe punishment.

As was done in the casse of Shudras, the Brahminical system kept the whole of the women folk under subjugation. They were denied education and property rights. They did not have freedom and always had to live under the dominance of the male members throughout their lives. They were not treated as human beings. The condition of the Dalit women was most pitiable. Shudra and Atishudra women were doubly exploited. They were kept at the bottom of the Brahminical system and at the same time they were also kept under the patriarchal system.

As per the Brahminical social system, there existed restrictions on choosing one's occupation as per one's will. One had no option but to accept the occupation of his father. This means a son of a Chamar could never become an advocate or a doctor under the Brahminical system. The lucrative occupations were thus held by the higher castes while the lower castes had to perform the non-lucrative occupations. They had to perform the work which required high physical labour. Priesthood was the monopoly of the Brahmins. Of course there were instances where a brahmin could adopt the occupation of his liking if he did not want to perform his traditional one, but this freedom was not granted to other castes. To keep the dominance of the Brahmins intact, they have evolved a system in such a way that the hegemony of the Brahmins will remain unchecked. There were certain rules and regulations of taking food-water and daughters from other castes. A girl from Brahmin caste would marry within the Brahmin community only.[47]

The Indian Constitution that came into existence in 1950 has immensely contributed in breaking the prevailing BSO. The Indian constitution has set up its main agenda in the preamble itself. It aimed to build a society on the basis of equality, freedom and social Justice for all. In all, the Indian constitution has more than 300 articles which were developed on the lines of building a society based on the above ideals.

It is true that the Indian Constitution was not able to change the society altogether. In this regard, the Indian constitution has its own limitations but certainly, it has brought important changes in the Indian society. A close work at the Indian constitution enunciable altogether, hows different principles than those of the of Varna-based principles. For instance, equality before law was denied in the Hindu custom, but it is there in the Indian constitution. The Brahminical customs have not given equal treatment to all. Nevertheless, the Constitution in this sense, from the Bahujan's viewpoint has brought radical changes. It has brought about very fundamental changes in the Indian society and has shaken the Brahminical hegemony.

A national leader of BAMCEF, in one of the national conventions at Pune said that once upon a time their forefathers were not supposed to walk freely on the roads of the Pune city and now their progeny drive a motor car on that road. This change has not come automatically. It happened due to the implementation of the Indian constitution. It is an outcome of the farsightedness of the great leader Dr Ambedkar. He has drafted the Indian constitution in such a way that the Bahujans are experiencing 'revolutionary changes' in the Indian society today. At present, one witnesses a crisis in the Brahminical hegemony that has taken place due to the Indian constitution.[48]

Today, at least theoretically no one can restrict the Dalits to take water from public wells and tanks; they cannot be denied education; they cannot be forced to do menial work, they cannot be denied to possess ornaments, umbrellas, riding on the horse at the time of marriages, walk freely on the roads, etc. All the restrictions imposed by the Brahminical laws and regulations have been wiped out by the weapon of the constitution of India. It has not only brought significant but revolutionary changes in the Indian society.

Concluding Remarks

The above discussion tried to throw light on the Dalit movement with reference to changes that have taken place in the wider society in the position of Dalits in the social structure of Gujarat.

Hardly any attempt is made so far to consolidate various Dalit movements in Gujarat. The above details revealed that the Dalits of Gujarat have raised their voice from time to time and lead movements to protest, assert, agitate, reform and alter the course of various issues. The present chapter made an attempt to collate the scattered information about the Dalit movements in Gujarat and find out the pattern emerged out of it.

Broadly, two types of Dalit movements are found in Gujarat. First, by the Dalits themselves and Second by the non-Dalits. For example, the Gandhian movement, and efforts made by Maharaja Sayaji Rao Gayakwad, were led by the non-Dalits, while Ambedkarite's movement, collective efforts for sanskritization, movement against the untouchability, protest through conversion, etc., were led by the Dalits themselves. Some of these were led by the liberal ideology where as the others were led by radical ideology. Similar is the case with the approach and programmes carried out under these movements.

Many of the Dalit movements are led by still remaining with in the Brahminical social structure. But a few of them are led to challenge the existing structure. The former movements were reformatory or colonial in their nature, while the latter can be termed as of radical type which aimed to bring transformation in the BSO. Thus, both the movements are distinct in their nature and approach. Hence different in their strategies, programmes and ideologies.

Anti-untouchability movement can be divided into two. One is reform movement and another is aimed at creation of alternative structure. Sanskritization movement falls in the former and the religious conversion movement can be placed in the latter. While the reform movement strives to bring changes by remaining in the Hindu social structure, the alternative movement rejected the Hindu Brahminical social structure and tried to bring out alternative cultural environment by converting to other religions. Both the movements have used the political means to achieve their goals.

Gandhi has emphasized the change of heart approach and not the change of system approach for raising the status of the Dalits. Ambedkar was different from Gandhi in his approach. He advocated for secular means to achieve the respectable status for the Dalits in the society. The study of Mahyavanshi shows that once upon time, they were known as Dhed but they have successfully climbed up in the hierarchical position by imitating the life-style of the upper castes and by putting forward strong demands of Rajput origin. Dalit Panther Movement has adopted the more militant way for establishing their identity. A lot of literature was created by the Dalit intellectuals but they miserably failed to create a movement out of it. In post 1970s, a Dalit movement based on Phule–Ambedkarite's ideology has emerged. Like in other parts of India, in Gujarat, Ambedkarite's movement has changed fundamentally of a period of time.

As mentioned in the text, the Ambedkarite's movement which took place in between 20s and 50s, and Ambedkarite's movement started in post-70s were qualitatively different, the early phase of Ambedkarite's movement, the Dalits though they have adopted the agitational stance in the form of launching Satyagraha as a way of protest was not very much against the system as such. Now their focus has changed to changes the system. They started directly attacking the BSO. The movement also expanded to cover SCs, STs, OBCs and minority communities. They have identified their so-called enemy and tried to polarize the victimized class of BSO under the category of 'Mulnivasi'. This is a qualitatively different kind of movement. They used political means to achieve their aim of demolishing the BSO by using the secular means in a democratic way. Stratification based on social, economical, political and cultural spheres comes in the way in polarizing the Bahujan Samaj. What shape it would take in future, only time would tell. Thus, both types of collective efforts for cooption in the BSO and rejection of the BSO are going at present in the Gujarat today. Both have resulted in bringing change in the condition of the Dalits.

Notes

1. It is a qualitative change which involves changes in the position or direction of the system in question.
2. The word Dalit movement is used in this article in a very loose sense. It has not used in a form of textual definition. Here it is used to denote the collective effort made directly or indirectly for liberating the Dalits from the Brahminical social structure by way of welfarism, reformism, radical change and enhancing awareness. Of course, not necessary ideologically about their position in the society by both Dalits and non-Dalit leaders.
3. In the absence of studies, ignorance is prevalent about patterns that exist regarding the Dalit movement in Gujarat. Besides, a few scholars also tend to

believe that there is hardly any movement in Gujarat; this feeling comes out more openly during the communal frenzy witnessed in Gujarat in 2002.

4. There are published and un-published sources which give information about such efforts. Studies done by Desai (1976), Jani Indu Kumar (1976), Masihi and Desai (1980), Shah Vimal (1980), Bose (1981), Urmila Patel (1983), Y.A. Parmar (1987), Jyotikar (1991), Lobo (1991), Metha (1995), Ramesh Chandra Parmar (1996), Makwan (1998), Shah Ghanshyam (2001), Punalekar (2001), Arjun Patel (2005), etc., have explored the topic which will can be covered under the broad theme – 'Dalit situation in Gujarat'.
5. The author has drawn extensively from both published and un-published materials on the subject and also tried to contact the persons aware of the facts about such movements. The study gives an extensive account of the Dalit movement; particularly Ambedkarites movement which took place during the period 1920–1970. His study covers the condition of the Dalits in the 20th century. The study also covers the activities of Sayaji Rao Gayakwad and Gandhi for the upliftment of the Dalits of Gujarat.
6. The word Harijan has remained very controversial, as it is objected by some of the prominent Dalit leaders as the word Harijan is also used to refer those children born to Devdasis (the women devoted to services of god) through illegitimate sexual contact hence identified as a derogatory term.
7. A great deal of controversies are going on about the origin of Brahmins. Four major views regarding the origin of Brahmins are prevalent. One group believes that Brahmins are not the original residents of this country. They came to India from foreign countries. The second group believes that like other castes, Brahmins are also the original residents of this country. The third group is of the opinion that none of the groups living in India are indigenous and all are foreigners to this country, though they do believe that some groups have settled earlier than the others. The fourth view upholds that Brahmins also originally belong to this country but in history they have been out of the country and back again. Of course there is a broad agreement that the Brahmins are late comers to this country than many of the tribals and OBCs.
8. Dr Ambedkar (1988: 125–149) explained who were the untouchables and how they came to become Shudras. He also explained in detail how the untouchables were kept outside the Varna system.
9. It seems that this has happened mainly in reference to the changing times. In contemporary India, politics based on Hindutva is very powerful and the advocates of the Hindutva are engaged in spreading their net to incorporate as many groups as possible in its fold. Secondly, the Hindu fundamentalists might have realized that if they do not incorporate the so-called *Avarna* in to their fold the latter might convert to other religions. This would not be in their favour.
10. For more details of the nature of discrimination of the untouchables in various parts of India, refer to G.S. Ghurye 1957: p. 1–27.
11. For more details about the untouchability in Gujarat see the works of Desai IP, Patel Urmila, Shah Ghanshyam, Parmar Y.A., Jyotikar P., etc.

12. This was not wiped out completely at the initial decades of the 21st century. Even in Surat, Dalit professors were denied accommodation in the apartments to stay along with the upper castes.
13. According to the Ambedkar the principle of 'graded inequality' was the heart of the BSO. In this scheme, each group felt that though it was lower than other groups it was at the same time higher in rank compared to certain other groups. This was an in-built mechanism to keep the BSO intact automatically.
14. For instance, the Dheds (Dalit) had monopoly over meat and leather of dead animals such as cows, buffalos, etc., but the Bhangis only were allowed to take the skin of dead animals such as sheep, goat, etc.
15. Traditionally, the untouchables were associated with unclean activities such as removing the dead cattle and skinning them, removing the dead cats and dogs and cleaning the latrines, streets and roads. They also used to consume the meat of dead animals and engaged in 'Veth' (forced labour without remuneration). They also used to go to provide the 'datan' (stick of fresh babul used as tooth brush) to Savarnas house and in return they used to get left-over food from them. In 1918, the caste panchayat of the Mahyavanshis passed a resolution that no caste member should either carry night soil on their head or pull a hand cart full of night soil. They were requested to do away with other type of low occupations.
16. Jyotiba Phule first started a school for the Dalits in 1852 at Pune. After that Babu Sashiddar Banerjee started a second school for the untouchables in West Bengal in 1865 and Sayaji Rao was third who had started schools for the untouchables in 1883.
17. In those days in Gujarat, many upper caste reformers such as Durgsram Mehtaji, Mahipat Ram, Rup Ram, Narmad, Karsandas Mulji, etc., were influenced by the Western thinking and they were aware of the problem of Dalits, but unlike Mahatama Jyotiba Phule none of them dared to shown, courage to work among the untouchables. They were only sympathizers to this movement.
18. In a circular dated July 12, 1983, he announced that no one could stop the untouchables from using public services. If anybody tried to prevent them, the government would take stern action.
19. Shri Govindbhai Morarjibhai Chunavala is the first MLA from untouchable community in the Gayakwadi assembly. In 1930, he also made a compulsory rule that at least one member of an untouchable community should be nominated in prant panchayat. He also took care so that the untouchable political representatives were treated with dignity. He also made special provisions for the untouchables (Gautam Ramath: 1941)
20. Similar approach was adopted by Chattrapati Sahuji Maharaj of Kolhapur State in Maharashtra. He often used to go to drink tea at the tea-stall of an untouchable. The upper caste officials have also to join willy-nilly.
21. He wrote off the past debts of the farmer and reduced the rate of the land revenue. He often arranged 'Krishi Melas' and demonstrations related to

chemical fertilizers, agricultural implements and improved seeds. He adopted a very practical approach for improving the standard of life of the people of Vadodara state.

22. A Journal 'Buddhi Prakash' published from Ahmedabad wrote that: 'the untouchable should be educated but where do you (addressing Sajayi Rao) want to carry them? Are you going to make them collectors and Mamlatdars?, In the similar manner, 'Praja Bandhu' was against the move of Sayaji Rao for forcing the Savarnas to remove untouchability from their day to day life. The journal rejected the notion saying that those Dalits who got education became capable enough to mix with the higher caste people. It rejected the idea of Sayaji Rao that the upper caste people should move in the area of untouchables.
23. In South Africa, Gandhi took up the issue of discrimination as a question of self-dignity and self-respect for the blacks. Gandhi himself being a black in the eyes of whites (British) became a victim of racism and launched a systematic Satyagraha against this. He got tremendous cooperation from the Indians who had migrated to South Africa for trade and employment and he finally won the battle against the racism.
24. When back to India, freedom movement against the British was going on and he made up his mind to take the leadership of this movement. For this, he wanted to harness mass support of the all the sections of the Indian society to launch a successful freedom struggle movement.
25. When asked for his advice what to do after getting education by a Bhangi youth, instead of change of filthy occupation Gandhi said that one should earn his/her bread by practicing his/her father's age old Varna-based occupation.
26. Poona Pact was signed in 1932. Ambedkar, who strongly criticized the attitudes of the upper caste towards the untouchables and put the case of untouchable strongly at the round table conference, convinced parishad for the separate electoral of the untouchables. Gandhi also claimed that he was the true leader of the Harijan. To counter the claim of Ambedkar, Gandhi promised that he would wipe-out the stigma of untouchables in the coming 10 years, i.e., by 1942. GHSS was subsequently started in this backdrop. One has to find out to what extent GHSS has succeeded in its commitment.
27. The leadership of GHSS groups was justified by Gandhi by emphasizing that it was the moral duty of the upper castes, as their fore fathers have forced the Dalits to live in an in-human condition. They have to fulfill their moral obligations (Prayaschit). Gandhi instructed the leaders of the GHSS groups to take up the cause of the untouchables to atone for the deeds of their forefathers who had forced them to live under inhuman conditions.
28. In 1921, he had taken an oath from the volunteers of non-cooperative movement that they would remove untouchability from their individual lives. He adopted one of the daughters of a Harijan and voluntarily accepted to live with Harijans.
29. The questions can be raised here that whether freedom of Dalits was the priority of Gandhi? Did Gandhi really want to solve the problems of

untouchable or want to save Hindu Social Order or both? Why Gandhi took different approaches for solving the similar kind of problems. Such questions need further probing in order to know the actual reality.

30. Even Gandhi had exactly taken this type of stand on one occasion. Gandhi in one of his letters which he had written just three days before his assassination revealed that he did not understand the insistence of Harijan for entry into temples.
31. He was quite aware about the strength of Ambedkar. So, he did not want to take the confrontation further and took aggressive stand against the governing body of Swaminarayan temple, who vehemently opposed temple entry of Harijans. He explained the authority that there was no alternative except to open the doors of the temple. According to him, it would be wise if the temple authorities gave temple entry to the Harijan. Otherwise, Dr Ambedkar threatened to mobilize the Harijans on this issue and forcibly enter in to the temple.
32. He advised the Dalits to go into the hotels with clean clothes and behave very affectionately and non-violently in any provocative situation. He also tried to persuade the Dalits to enter hotels only in an exceptional situation.
34. For instance, when Mama Saheb Fadke had gone for inspection in one of the schools, where he advised the Dalits that they should not make a mistake by blaming and holding the upper castes responsible for their own conditions as justice was available in God's home. He elaborated that the upper castes remained up mainly because of their forgiving nature. They have not left their holy beliefs and dignity even though they suffered from a number of droughts, whereas the untouchables consumed meat and liquor. The Gandhians advised the Dalits to stick to the Hindu religion.
35. In Gujarat, compared to other parts, conversion found more in central Gujarat and North Gujarat. Why it has become successful in certain places and proved unsuccessful in the other places of Gujarat? This question needs investigation.
36. Conversion is a burning issue these days, particularly for the tribals. The Hindu saints tried to reconvert the tribals who left the Hindu religion and embraced Christianity. But the central question is that where do they place them? Whether they place them with Brahmin, whether they place them with Baniyas or whether they place them as Kshatriyas?
37. Ambedkarites believed that the great epics such as Ramayan, Mahabharata, Gita, Purans, Vedas, Ramcharit Manas, Smruties, etc., were all written in the interest of the Brahmins and other upper castes. The literature greatly influenced the then society.
38. One of the reasons for giving acceptance was passing the challenge to an individual and not social system as such. Hence there was not much threat to the Brahminical Social Order.
39. Dalit novels such as Panther, Akrosh, Garud, Kalo Suraj, Dalit Bandhu, Ajampo, Mukti Nayak, Disha, Dalit Mukti, Dalit Mitra, Abhuday, Naya Marg, Tamnna, Pragati, Jyot, Taras, Akshy and Aganiyat, Vyathana Vitak,

Malak, Ghidh, Neluyu, Priyatma Part 1 & 2, Naklank, Khumbhi, Pratiksha, Shul, Mul, Dhul, Talap, Tirad, Choki, etc., are some of the noteworthy work in Gujarati literature.

40. In the story of *Thali* written by Mohan Parmar, the Harijan woman named Ravi has become sexual victim of the Darbar (lower rank Rajput) Mansingh. She is fed up with the atrocities and one day she goes with the sickle to kill Mansingh but her thinking about her child and family prevents her to do so. She changes her mind and offers Mansingh to marry her and start a family life. This phenomenon also challenged the social status of a Darbar. In other story, *Lakha* of Madhukant Kalpit Ramtadaye tries to rape a Dalit woman named Kali. And Kali attacks him with a sickle for her self-defense. In the story *Vantod* written by Shri Bhi. N. Vankar, Jivali who became a victim of the teasing rebels with a sickle. Thus, in this story, one can see both; the social reality and women's militancy against their exploitation.
41. BAMCEF, registered in 1978, stood second in rank in Gujarat after Maharashtra in terms of the activities and fund collection. Activity of BAMCEF also spread in the Hindi belt and even in South India. The branches of BAMCEF are found in most of the districts in Gujarat. More than 2,000 activists work for BAMCEF in the state. Today one will find a branch not only at the district level unit but also at the tehshil level. BAMCEF being actively engaged in establishing nationwide network for spreading the ideology of Phule and Ambedkar and are trying to make strong the 'Bahujan Samaj'.
42. Of the various saints and Gurus, the Mahapurush of Modern India, Particulars after 19th Century prominent among them are Mahatma Jyotiba Phule, Chatrupati Sayaji Maharaj, Rama Swami, Periar Naikar, Shri Narayana Guru, Birsa Munda, Savitribai Phule, Baba Saheb Ambedkar and Kahshi Ram.
43. The author got a phone (in the year 1990) call from Surat Radio Station inquiring about confirmation of sex of Mahatma Jyotiba Phule on the eve of centenary year. Because in Gujarat word 'Ba' added with name means female (e.g., Kasturba). This much ignorance was prevalent 21 years ago, but now the situation has changed remarkably in Gujarat.
44. It is a well-organized activity started by Pandurang Athavale. It is well received, particularly among OBCs of Gujarat. Dalits and tribals of Gujarat also attracted by this activity.
45. This alliance was a part of the strategy of Congress to win the election in nineties. The master mind of these alliance was of Madhavsing Solanki and Zinabhai Darji. Both were Congress men and very influential leader at the top level.
46. In south, the Shanars and the Izavas were not allowed to build a house beyond one story. There was also restriction on what sorts of material should be used in the house. The Sanaras of Madras were not supposed to carry umbrella in their hands. They were not allowed to wear shoes. They were not allowed to wear golden ornaments and were not allowed to keep a cow. Their language was of a lower standard. Wilson (1877: 79) noted that in South certain women were not allowed to cover the upper portion of their chest.

The Shudras were not allowed to keep the name of their child as per their choice. They were not given services by the priests, barbers, etc. The Brahmin doctor, who was considered to be a modern man, tied a cloth while checking the heartbeat of the Shudra patient. The untouchables were supposed to stay at the outskirts of the village. Even today in many villages, one will find caste-wise hamlets. Ghurye (1960: 10)had noted how village localities segregated on the basis of caste in various parts of India. In Punjab, an untouchable had to keep a broom in his hand to identify himself. While moving out, an untouchable had to speak loudly to intimate the upper castes that an untouchable was passing through this road so that could keep distance to avoid pollution.

47. In Gujarat Baniya caste, a trading community has sub-caste divisions such as Shrimali, Porvad, Modh, etc. Again this division get divided in to groups such as Dasa Porvad and Visa Porvad. Again, these groups are divided into sub-groups such as Dasa porvad of Surat and Dasa porvad of Mumbai. A Dasa porvad of Surat is not supposed to take the bride from the Dasa porvad of Mumbai. These restrictions are still there in even the 21st century.
48. Let us see a few of the articles of the Indian constitution as examples which have hit the BSO. Article 14 gives right to equality. Article 15 prohibits discrimination on the basis of religion, caste, colour, sex or the place of birth. Article 16 gives equal opportunity of employment in the public services. Article 15(4) and 16(4) aims at giving social justice to the backward castes. Article 17 abolishes untouchability. Article 14, 15(1), 16(1), 15(4), 16(4),38,39,46 and 335 are with regard to development of backward classes. There are many such articles which have nullified the Brahminical provisions based on Shastras. All these articles have demolished the Brahminical written and unwritten laws and rules and regulation, and customs and so-called moral values.

References

Ambedkar, Babasaheb, *Dr Ambedkar Sampurna Vadmay,* Vol.13, Dr Ambedkar Pratishthan Kalyan Mantralay, New Delhi, 1988, .

Bose, Pradip Kumar, "Social Mobility and Caste Violence: A Study of Gujarat Riots", *Economic and Political Weekly,* Vol. 16, No. 16, April 18. Also reproduced in *Caste, Caste Conflict and Reservations (1985),* Ajanta Publications, New Delhi, 1981.

Campbell, Jemes M., *History of Gujarat: Ancient, Medieval, Modern,* Vintage Books, Gurgaon, 1989.

Conversion, Emigration and Social Mobility of an Ex-Scheduled Caste from Central Gujarat, Social Action Trust, New Delhi, October–December, Vol. 39, No. 4.

Desai, Harshad and Chandu Maheriya, *Sambardathi Swamannagar,* Centre for Social Studies, Surat, 1995.

Desai, I.P., *Untouchability in Rural Gujarat,* Popular Prakashan, Bombay, 1976.

Enthoven, R.E., *The Tribes and Castes of Bombay,* Cosmo Publication, Delhi, 1920.

Forbes, Alexander Kinloch, *Hindu Annals of Western India, with Particular reference to Gujarat,* Heritage Publishers, Delhi, 1973.

Gazetteer of the Bombay Presidency, Gujarat (1877), Surat and Broach, Vol. 2, Bombay: Government Central Press.

Ghurye, G.S., *Caste and Class in India,* Popular Book Depot, Bombay, 1960.

Jani, Indukumar, *Atyachar ane Alprishyatana Be Pad Vachche Pisata Dalito,* Khet Bhavan, Ahmedabad, 1976, .

Jyotikar, P.G., *Gujaratni Ambedkar Chanvanno Itihash – 1920 thi 1970,* Dr Babasaheb Ambedkar Janmshatabdi Ujavni Samiti, Gandhinagar, Gujarat Rajya, 1991.

Lobo, Lancy, *Religious Conversion and Social Mobility: A Case Study of the Vadodara in Central Gujarat,* Surat: Centre for Social Studies, Surat, 1991.

Mackwan, Martin and Harshad Desai, *Gujaratma Dalito Par Atyachar: Ek Dastavej ane Tena Lekhajokha,* Centre for Social Studies, Surat, 1998.

Masihi, Edwin J. and Dhiru B. Desai, *Dalit Panther Movement in Gujarat.* Shah Vimal, Removal of Untouchability (Proceeding of a seminar), Gujarat University, Ahmedabad, 1980.

Mehta, Makarand, *Samajik Parivartan Ane Gujaratna Asprushiya, Arthat,* October, 1981, Vol.1, No. 1.

Mehta, Makarand, *Hindu Varna Vyavastha, Samaj Parivartan Ane Gujaratna Dalit,* Ami Publication, Ahmedabad, 1995.

Parmar, Rameshchandra, *Hathma Zadu Mathe Melu,* Centre for Social Studies, Surat, 1996.

Parmar, Y.A., *The Mahyavanshi: The Success Story of a Scheduled Caste,* Mittal Publication, Delhi, 1987.

Patel, Arjun, *Dalit Atyachar Ange Savedhanic Jogvayio Ane Teno Amal,* Seminar Paper, Centre for Social Studies, Surat, 2002.

Patel, Arjun, Maharaja Sayajirao's Approach to Dalit Liberation in Gujarat. Paper presented at the National Seminar on 'Stationing Dalit Movement: Past, Present and Future at History', Mumbai University, 2004.

Patel, Arjun, *Gujaratma Dalit Asmita: Udbhav Ghadtar Ane Sanvardhanni Prakriya,* Centre for Social Studies, Surat, 2005.

Patel, B.B., *Workers of Closed Textile Mills,* Oxford and IBH Publishing Co. Pvt. Ltd., New Delhi, 1988.

Patel, Urmila, *Gujaratna Vikasta Samudayo,* Mangal Prabhat, Ahmedabad, 1983.

Punalekar, S.P., "Dalit Literature and Dalit Identity", in Ghanshyam Shah (ed.), *Dalit Identity and Politics,* Delhi: Sage Publications, Delhi, 2001.

Shah, Ghanshyam, "Untouchability in Rural Gujarat: Revisited in Dalits and the State", by Shah, Ghanshyam, *Dalit and the State,* Centre for Rural Studies, LBSNAA, Mussoorie, 2001.

Shah, Ghanshyam, "Anti-Untouchability Movements", in *Caste, Caste-Conflict and Reservations,* Ajanta Publications, Delhi, 1985.

Shah, Vimal, *Removal of Untouchability* (Proceeding of a seminar), Gujarat University, Ahmedabad, 1980.

Shah, Punalekar and P.K. Bose, "Anti-Reservation Agitation and Structure of Gujarat Society", in *Caste, Caste-Conflict and Reservations,* Ajanta Publications, New Delhi, 1981.

Shinoda, Takashi, "The Structure of Stagnancy: Sweepers in Ahmedabad District", by Shah, Ghanshyam, *Dalit and the State,* Centre for Rural Studies, LBSNAA, Mussoorie, 2001.

Wilson, John, *Indian Caste,* Vol. 1 and 2, Times of India, Bombay; William Blackwood and Sons, Edinburg and London, 1877.

7 Hindutva's Foot Soldiers: Dalits, Adivasis?

Ram Puniyani

The recent Gujarat genocide of Muslims brought to fore a tragic realization of our polity. Apart from the 'success' of the Sangh Parivar in 'efficiently' coordinating this carnage and ensuring that the possibilities of rehabilitation are stifled, the factor most worrisome has been the participation of poor Dalits and Adivasis as the foot soldiers of Hindutva, doing the dirty job for the project of Hindu Rashtra. While the core leadership was with the mobile wielding supporters of Sangh Parivar, a major share of violence and looting was perpetrated through the recruitment of the subaltern sections. It is these sections that did the major part of actual implementation of the street violence. How could the major victims of Hindutva politics be mobilized for the service of RSS project of 'Hindu Rashtra in One State', in the laboratory of Hindutva politics? How could the scum of the earth, the broken people, the poor and pauperized be indoctrinated to undertake the ghastly acts unleashed against the minority community?

Recent Happenings

The mobilization of Dalits for Kar Seva and the subsequent campaigns for Ram Mandir have been very intense. Many of them were sponsored to visit Ayodhya as Ram Sevaks also. In the anti-Muslim pogrom, they could be coopted because of various reasons. To begin with, Gujarat textile industry, which was the flagship of the industrial status of Gujarat and was foremost among the textile trade, has been on the decline resulting in job losses for a huge section of the population.

Recruiting these sections in the violence was the major part of the strategy of the organization of the genocide by the Sangh Parivar. The closure of the textile mills in the 1980s and 1990s resulted in loss of more than 100,000 jobs, and collapse of a whole social infrastructure and culture. It also resulted in pauperization and destitution among Ahmedabad's working class. For sociologist Jan Breman (2002), it comes as no surprise that the front organizations of the Sangh Parivar were able to mobilize the lumpenized subaltern castes to assist in the genocide unleashed by them. More so, they were given the signals that there will be no reprisals due to taking part in the pogrom and the assurance that the loot will belong to them.

Similarly, Adivasis have been involved in a large number to indulge in the violence and looting against the Muslims. Interestingly, the victims of the violence do not hold Adivasis responsible for the attacks on them. They are saying that Adivasis were mobilized by allurement, threat and payment to do what they did against the minorities. Also, Adivasis in particular were more involved in looting than any other type of crime during these riots. As a run up to the genocide, the Adivasi psyche was carefully cultivated in the direction of anti-Muslim sentiments. The Hindu-Bania money-lenders were made to reduce the rates of interest from 120 per cent to 80 per cent or so, in order to project that Bohra money-lenders at 120 per cent are exploiting them.

The Backdrop: Gujarat in 70s and 80s

Gujarat's socio-economic development explains a number of factors which led to the present genocide, and involvement of subalterns as the foot soldiers. It is interesting that Gujarat has not seen any major reform movement in the past many decades. The neighbouring Maharashtra saw non-Brahmin movement right since the 20s and this movement assisted the process of social transformation towards the democratic civil society. Gujarat overall was the house of Right wing politics and conservative social forces dominated the scene. It is here that the Swatantra party (the one supporting big capital and opposed to public sector) had a major base; it is here that there were not many major leaders from Dalit movement and from communist movement. The hold of Right wing politics was threatened by the KHAM (Kshatriya, Harijan, Adivasi, Muslim) combination in late 70s. The upper caste struck back in the form of anti-reservation riots. Achyut Yagnik (Yagnik, 2002) points out that the educated middle classes, mainly the Brahmins, Banias and

Patidars sharply reacted to this by starting agitation an against the reservation system. The clashes between Savarnas and the Dalits in the industrial periphery of Ahmedabad gradually degenerated into caste war that spread to the towns in 18 out of the then 19 districts. In many villages dominated by land-owning Patidars in North and Central Gujarat, Dalit *bastis* were burnt.

Caste tension resurfaced in 1985 in the second anti-reservation agitation. The BJP leadership drawn mainly from upper caste realized the need to expand their social base to achieve electoral success. They coopted the Dalit OBCs in to their gambit by different Yatras, etc. Advani's Rath Yatra saw pitched battles between Dalits and Muslims. Yagnik further states that RSS 'successfully' created a rift between the 'Hindu Adivasis' and 'Christian Adivasis'. In absence of deeper social reforms, the modern institutions and values of liberty, equality and fraternity remained weak and Hindutva, by default, provided the much needed identity to the Dalit OBCs. This process saw its heightened expression in the wake of Mandal Commission implementation. Vajpayee formulated this response of the Sangh Parivar to Mandal Commission succinctly. He stated that we have brought Kamandal (religion-based issues) in response to Mandal (symbolizing the aspirations of Dalit-OBCs).

As a matter of fact, Gujarat is the 'model' base of the Sangh Parivar. It is not for nothing that it was chosen as the laboratory of Hindu Rashtra. The regrouping of social layers in Gujarat has been taking place since the last three decades in an intense fashion. Along with urbanization, there has been a parallel process in which the rich peasants of Gujarat have achieved an enhanced social status. This Patidar caste (cash-crop farmers) has been upgraded by a process of religious maneuvering. The polarization of the middle class (Brahmin, Bania) and Patidar occurred around 1980, around the issue of reservations for the lower castes. In 1980, Gujarat witnessed an extreme form of caste violence directed against the lower castes. The first major move of Hindutva base was to oppose the affirmative action for the Dalits. It got manifested in anti-reservation riots during the early 80s. It was argued that the Dalits have been pampered. Due to this, the children with real merit are suffering in jobs and in admissions in professional colleges. This anti-Dalit riot was the alarm bell of the times to come.

These anti-reservation agitations played a key role in consolidating the base of upper castes and upwardly mobile middle classes. The Sangh Parivar stood by to support these upper-caste onslaughts. By using clever strategies, Sangh Parivar was also able to give an upwardly mobile channel to a section of Dalits who were aspiring for a better place within the Hindu society. In Gujarat, one can clearly see the social functionality of creating the 'other' (Muslim). Here, earlier the ultimate object of hate was the Dalit, by a clever manoeuvre, the Muslim was substituted for that, the Dalit was unleashed upon the 'other', an atmosphere of terror was created, which helped to maintain a 'status quo' of the social hierarchy.

The long-term goal of this politics is to push back the process of social transformation towards the pre-modern hierarchies. Various yatras and campaigns of VHP gave cohesion to this social base. The Sangh Parivar's ideological manipulation of the situation played a major role. It operated on two levels. At ideological level, it regarded all those who are not Muslims and Christians as Hindus. This negative definition was given a further twist by asserting that Hindus worship cow, Ram, Vedas, Gita and Acharyas. So in turn, all Adivasis and Dalits have to adopt these symbols and ideologies. This move gave a new identity to large a section of subalterns. The large proliferation of different Vanvasi Kalyan Ashrams, Shishu Mandirs and other institutions occupied the cultural space lying vacant due to the absence of major reform movements. The major challenge, as Shah (2002) rightly points out, for the proponents of Hindutva is to build unity among all Hindus without disturbing dominance of the upper castes and class. Hindu Mahasabha had launched the Bharat Hindu Milan Mandir in 1920s and they have been more active in Gujarat since 1970s. Besides undertaking activities to unite various sects and organizing religious festivals, they take up welfare and relief measures for the poor. The main thrust of these organizations is to build unity and harmony among the upper and lower castes.

It is in this context that the anti-Christian missionary campaign was brought in. The argument that all those living in this country are Hindus was taken to the practical logic. The ones converting to 'other', 'foreign' religions were supposed to be doing so under the allurement of the money or other favours. Hinduism was projected as superior to other faiths as it neither does, nor believes in conversions. Here, two birds are killed with one stone. Hinduism, i.e., Brahmanism, cannot undertake conversions in the real sense, as it is an exclusive club. The lower castes do like to convert to escape the social injustice imposed by the upper caste, practising Brahminical ideology. The argument is cleverly twisted and the 'elite exclusivism' is presented as the virtue. So, all those who convert are supposed to have succumbed to the guile or intimidation of the 'foreign religion' so they need to be 'reconverted back' to Hinduism by newly developed rituals. Also, they have to be taught to throw away their old gods and taught the virtues of Ram, Gita and Acharyas. And in this direction, the Christian missionaries need to be taught a lesson, few Bibles to be burnt, Nuns and Fathers beaten up, etc.

Gujarat has seen all this more than the other places of India where the religious fascism of Sangh Parivar is stalking the streets.

Cultural Onslaught of Hindutva

While Gujarat has been the major field of operation, other parts of India have been witnessing a similar process. In different states, the local cultural metaphors are being substituted by the newly manufactured ones. In his exhaustive appraisal of Surat riots of 1992, Irfan Engineer (1993) points out that the propaganda of the BJP has communalized the young in Surat epically those belonging to Machhi, Kharva, Rana, Ghanchi, and traditional OBC communities. According to Engineer, earlier they used to be strong supporters of the Congress, but have now moved away from it. These communities have prospered in the recent years and are looking for new power equations and broader identities. They are shedding their old customs and *kuldevis*, and have begun adopting the customs of upper castes. The BJP has 'successfully' responded to their aspirations by giving them a broader identity through its Hindutva campaign. Also, its propaganda has given this identity a nationalistic and patriotic color. A reform movement to give up certain rituals preceded the desire for a broader identity and subsequent communalization in these communities. Education is also on the rise among them. Simultaneously, their economic base has widened as they have moved into new areas, instead of confining themselves to their original professions. They are also looking for a wider political role for themselves. While the old political equations and arrangements in the Congress provided them with only limited opportunities, BJP as a rising force is providing them new opportunities and greater participation.

The propagation of Hindutva through *Vinayaka* idols is one of the common features. In most of the southern states, the VHP and other affiliates of the Sangh Parivar have been promoting the Brahminical rituals and are Brahminizing the existing rituals and practices. Many an accurate sociological studies have shown the tactics adopted by Sangh Parivar in culturally coopting the subalterns in to the gambit of the Brahminical culture. The Sangh Parivar has also used different social facilities such as night schools and youth camps to subsume the Dalit identity into a pan-Hindu identity. Many a Dalits have subordinated their caste identity and claimed themselves as Hindus (Anandhi, 1995). The degeneration of Dravida Munetra movement into the AIDMK and the capitulation of present DMK to the Brahminizing influence need no recounting. The upwardly mobile aspirations of sections of Dalits have given Sanskritization process a boost.

This onslaught has operated at three levels. At the level of ideology it has been saying that it does not believe in caste system. Further, the origin of caste system itself has been shifted from the original codes of Manu to the influence of 'Foreign' religions! As per this, the invading Muslim kings wanted to convert all and sundry by force. And those who defied this had to face lots of ignominies and had to take resort in jungles and thereby became untouchables. Also it has been propounded that ideas of Ambedkar and RSS on caste system are similar. Here in a clever move, the polar opposite nature of both these is hidden from the people. Dr Ambedkar burns Manusmriti and presides over the drafting of the Indian Constitution. The RSS upholds Manusmriti and asks for rejection of the Indian Constitution.

At social level long ago, Hindu Mahasabha founded Bharat Sevashram and Hindu Milan Mandir. Lately, RSS has founded many an organizations for Dalits. The core philosophy around which these operate states that the caste struggle is not desirable and what we need is caste harmony, Samajik Samrasata (social assimilation). This has trapped many middle sections of Dalits who have derived benefits of the reservation and other social avenues. These organizations floated by the RSS have given a broad Hindu identity to the section of Dalits, who have accepted it as an avenue for upward mobility. The plethora of these organizations apart from organizing Hinduized versions of popular festivals also arrange the programmes of inter-dining (Ram Khichadi) to make their social presence felt among the Dalit sections of society. The tendency to blindly worship Phule and Ambedkar has been taken full advantage of by Brahminizing them. Sangh Parivar has no problems in worshipping these major contributors to Dalit movement so far as their teachings are kept under wraps.

Dalit Movement

Parts of the reason due to which these strategies have succeeded are the fragmentation of the Dalit movement. Phule identified both the aspects of need of Dalits, the material and the ones related to Dalit self-respect. His depiction of peasant as a 'Shudra and peasant both' contains the deep understanding of the social situation of the exploited sections. His contribution Shetkaryache Asaud (cultivators whipcord) is a good example of his grasp on the situation of Dalits. Similarly, Dr Ambedkar also recognized the need to base the Dalit movement on the material and identity issues. That is why he could find the Independent Labour Party even when talking of Mahad movement for access to public water and Kalaram Temple agitation to get social equality. Later, Dadsaheb Giakawad's agitation for land rights had the germ of this integrated need in it. In early 70s, while Dalit Panthers did come out with brilliant manifesto, even before it could be translated into some agitations most of the leaders of the movement found themselves in the lap of established leadership of upper caste-class parties. The emergence of Kanshi Ram on the horizon of Dalit politics was full of great promise but his lack of assessment of the fascist nature of Sangh Parivar and its difference from other parties resulted in its opportunist alliance with the party of Hindutva. The intense fragmentation of Dalit leadership in a way is a reflection of the lopsided approach to the problems of Dalits. Last few decades have seen an exclusive focus on issues related to Dalit identity at the cost of their material issues. The Phule–Ambedkar approach of synthesizing both these has been forgotten. This may be one of the main reasons for not being able to give a unified direction to the Dalit masses. In the resulting vacuum, the Hindutva ideology has occupied the space and the consequent subordination to Hindutva politics and readiness to act as foot soldiers of the Sangh Parivar's agenda of Hindu Rashtra is there for all to see.

Aims of Hindutva

Hindutva is the politics of the Hindu elite, propagator of Brahminical values in the modern garb, preserving the birth-based hierarchies of caste and gender. In present parlance, it is a counter-reaction to the process of social transformation which occurred during the last century, more particularly after independence. The process, by which, the pre-modern hierarchies have been shaken to some extent. It is politically comparable to fascism and fundamentalism. Fascists did this in the name of race while Hindutva does it in the name of Hindu religion, trying to hide the Brahminical content of its current versions. It got boost and power mainly due to the upper-caste reaction to the assertion of the Dalits for their rights. It is a counter-reaction of the upper caste-class to thwart the process of social transformation towards liberty, equality and fraternity. It's clever use of cultural mechanisms has given it 'success' in parts to make 'use' of the subalterns for their dirty jobs.

Future Directions

Gujarat is the most heightened expression of the state of affairs prevalent in the country. While the balance of forces may be different in different places, the broad contours are similar. At many places, the Dalit–Bahujan–Adivasis have better organizations and perspectives, but the overall lack of direction leads to it subjugation to Sangh Parivar in critical times. The decline of left politics and progressive culture has stifled the space and left a vacuum which has been occupied by the new Brahminical symbolisms. Even existing progressive institutions have been Brahminized to some extent. Global support to the retrograde culture and imposition of the lopsided globalization has also some role to play in today's pathetic situation. All said and done what we can work on is the development of proper programme for the realization of the twin-track agenda, material and identity, through different mechanisms, agitations and struggles. Also, a need for broad democratic platform for the defense of our constitution, democratic ethos and pluralism is long overdue. The fragmentation of Dalit leadership and its underestimation of the threats to the Indian democracy from Sangh Parivar by other section of Dalit leadership are contributing immensely to the 'success' of Hindutva politics. Gujarat is probably the last and final call for coming together to take up the basic issues of Dalit, Adivasi, minorities, women and workers. It is already a bit late to evolve a common front, tomorrow will be too late.

References

Anandhi, S., *Contending Identities*, ISI, Delhi, 1995.

Breman, Jan, "Communal Resurgence as a Social Resurgence of Darwinism", *Economic and Political Weekly*, 20–26 April, 2002.

Engineer, Irfan, *Surat Riots, Investigation and Analysis.* Center for Study of Society and Secularism, 1993, pp. 2–3.

Shah, Ghanshyam, "Caste, Hindutva and Hideousness", *Economic and Political Weekly*, April 15, 2002, p. 1391.

Yagnik, Achyut, "The Pathology of Gujarat", *Seminar*, New Delhi, May 2002.

8 Communal Violence and Women in the Context of Gujarat

Sarbani Banerjee Belur

India has been famously known as the largest democracy in the world depicting diversified coalition of people from different cultures, languages and religions living together. However, in the recent times with the rise of communal riots in the country, we can no longer deem India as a secular state. The onus of such radical differences and rifts points to the fact that the political structure of the country and the secular governance has strayed away from its defined path. Secularism was both a deep-rooted ideology among the various political leaders of the freedom struggle as well as a much needed edifice due to the pluralistic composition of the country. In retrospect, however, the partition of India was predominantly marked by the distinction based on religion. This period was marked by communal strafes and violence. Both men and women have been the sufferers. While families were displaced and dispersed by migration caused due to partition, women were sexually assaulted, raped and kidnapped.

Post-partition India declared itself a secular state and the Constitution of India was promulgated in 1950. The Constitution of India was drafted and promulgated keeping in view the secular needs of the Indian democracy. The Constitution endowed the citizens of India with their fundamental rights as well as reflected on the citizenship much more than the religious ethos. It committed itself to religious freedom and constituted protection of minorities. Women were treated as equal citizens of the country at par with men. Articles 14 and 15 of the Constitution have guaranteed freedom and equality to women irrespective of their caste, class, race and religion. However, socio-political changes in the Indian society since post-partition have distorted the social relations within the society. Distinction based on religious identity gained predominance and worked as a foundation to the divide between the Hindus and the Muslims. Religious identity draws itself from the assumption of one's own religion being superior to other religions, and thus displays a formidable amount of cultural difference, cultural resistance and hence a need for a separate identity. However, these differences are in most cases made up of stereotypes and distortion of history as well as division of history into different periods when Muslims were conquerors (Puniyani, 2005; Brass, 2004; Engineer, 2002, 1991)

Communal conflicts based on one's communal identity have not been uncommon in India since post-partition. Communal identity arises from the division on the basis of religion which eventually culminates into antagonistic collectivity. Communal conflicts have erupted time and again and in most of the cases it works as a defensive reaction to the 'other'. The 'other' could be a dominant religion or forces of social change. In the various communal conflicts in India – most of it – being between the Hindus and Muslims, the construction of the 'other' is based on Muslims as being foreigners and the aggression of Islam. While religious conflagrations are quoted by and have mostly been an important causative factor of communal violence, Imtiaz Ahmad (2004) analyses this conflict as an extension of the wider social conflict due to economic prosperity of the Muslims. Varshney (2002) argues that the conflict between the Hindus and Muslims is an outcome of the absence of civic ties across communities. Civic ties in the form of civic networks can be associational forms and everyday forms. The examples of associational networks are business associations, professional organizations, sports clubs, while everyday forms of network are Hindu-Muslim families visiting each other, eating together, joint participation in festivals. He asserts that this type of communal conflict based on religion is more of an urban phenomena as such networks are absent.

Communal politics does not concern only the patriarchal and the political powers. It has always played a major role in determining the rights and limits of women (Patel, 2009). While the patriarchal powers perceive women as the bearer of their identity and honour, the political powers are discriminatory towards women.

Social Organization of Gender

Gujarat violence has been widely termed as a 'gendered violence'. The media reports discussed 'women's bodies have been the battleground in Gujarat violence'. Women's gender positions in the 'manly' patriarchal society have classified women as the 'weaker sex'. Women and their sexuality have always been treated as the symbol of culture, honour of the community and nation. Sarkar (2002: 2872–76) notes that 'there is a dark sexual obsession about the allegedly ultra-virile Muslim male bodies and over-fertile Muslim female ones'. In communal violences, mass use of rape is the most widely used form of sexual violence inflicted upon women. Agnes (2002), Sarkar (2002) and Nussbaum (2005) argues that by the mass use of rape, a community can be collectively dishonoured. During communal conflicts, women of the minority community are thus the worst victims and bear the brunts of violence in the form of rapes, kidnaps and other forms of sexual violence. The reason pertains largely to the fact that dishonour to the women equates itself to the dishonour to the race or the community (Bhasin and Menon, 1998). Nussbaum (2004) and Sarkar (2002) argue about women's bodies signifying the nation and creation of virulent masculinity that reasoned with the indomitable torture which was perpetrated on the Muslim women. According to Nussbaum (2004), 'if the female body symbolizes the nation, then in the struggle of two emerging nations the possession and impregnation of women is a potent weapon in consolidating power'. This suggests that the violation of the honour of men is more important than the integrity of women. On the same lines as Nussbaum and Sarkar, Ahmed (2002) draw similarities between the Gujarat violence of 2002 with that which took place in the year 1969. Ahmed's (2002) article suggests, in both the instances, the collective violence used sexual subjugation of the female body as a weapon to humiliate the Muslim community.

Hence, communal violence in our society tend to leave permanent scars in the psyche of women of different communities, different religious backgrounds which in the long run prevents women's united efforts to achieve gender justice both in the personal and public domains (Patel, 2009).

The Gujarat violence elicited strong condemnation both at the national level as well as internationally. Human Rights Watch (2002) mentioned that over 2000 Muslims have been killed in the Gujarat violence. This violence has clearly resulted in the further ghettoization of the Muslims who have been a minority community in the Indian context. Robinson (2010) in her study looks at ways by which ghettoization of Muslims have affected their everyday lives and how it has confined the women survivors of the violence to specific neighbourhoods. Furthermore, these women in spite of the sexual violence they have undergone are reluctant to fight for their own justice. The attack on women in the Gujarat violence was pre-planned, organized and carried out with a specific aim to malign and humiliate the Muslim community in particular (Sarkar, 2002).

This article is a review of literature based on the available vast collection of studies and committee reports that seeks to understand and argue the sexual violence that women have undergone in the horrendous episode of communal violence in Gujarat. The first report which will be reviewed is a fact-finding report by a women's panel sponsored by Citizen's Initiative, Ahmedabad (2002). This report focuses on how has the Gujarat massacre affected minority women. The second report which we focus on is a feminist analysis of the genocide in Gujarat. The resultant of the collective feminist solidarity was International Initiative for Justice in Gujarat (2003). Out of the numerous fact-finding reports that were published in the aftermath of the Gujarat violence, only International Initiative for Justice in Gujarat focused specifically on women. As there was a failure of the national legal system, internationalizing the issue of violence against minority women seemed to provide the only hope. The third being the Communalism Combat report (Setalvad and Anand, 2002). This report goes beyond a detailed documentation of the Gujarat violence and exposes a well-planned conspiracy against the Muslim community. Unlike the Citizen's Initiative report and the International Initiative for Justice report, the Communalism Combat report focuses on the political scenario behind the Gujarat violence. Though it does not focus directly on the sexual violence faced by women, however, it does give us a chronology of events in various places that led to the brutal violence against women, men and children of the Muslim community. The fourth report which investigated the Gujarat violence of 2002 was the Human Rights Watch report. This report focused on the attacks on women by interviewing various residents who were eyewitness to the sexual assaults.

All the fact-finding committee reports aims at giving a macro-view of the situation in Gujarat as well as a close up of the atrocities faced by the women especially. Findings indicate that the Gujarat violence was both state-sponsored and state-condoned, while the Gujarat government characterized it as a spontaneous reaction to the Godhra incident. The ruling political parties of the state worked in close cooperation with the administrative machinery of the state, e.g., the police to plan and organize the violence. The various fact-finding committees that were set up addressed to the immediate need of the Muslim women who suffered in the ongoing communal violence. There was a complete breakdown of the state machinery which is revealed by the fact that National Commission of Women, the apex body for protection of women's rights guaranteed under the Constitution of India had not visited the state at the time of the ongoing communal violence. While the Women's Panel report sponsored by Citizen's Initiative, Ahmedabad brought out evidence and sufferings of the Muslim women as the communal violence was ongoing, the International Initiative for Justice in Gujarat worked towards drawing international attention to the very concrete impact of the violence on the lives of ordinary Muslim citizens of Gujarat. The Citizen's Initiative, Ahmedabad (2002) fact-finding report panel was conducted under conditions of continuing violence and curfew in many parts of Gujarat. The basic objective of these teams was to assess and determine the impact of the communal violence on the lives of the minority women in Gujarat. The reports were based primarily on the testimonies of the sufferings and traumas which the survivors underwent as well as the make believe experiences of the team members themselves which corroborate the facts. The main findings of the reports are the compelling evidence of the most extreme form of sexual violence against minority women. All these reports referred to rape and sexual assault as a weapon to dishonour, humiliate and subjugate the Muslim community. Three specific features of the crimes faced by women were brutality, the extreme sexual violence and their collective nature. There were mass-rapes, gang rapes, forced nudity, insertion of sharp objects in female genitals, cutting of breasts, slitting the stomach and reproductive organs. Women who were gang raped during the Gujarat carnage reported their attackers as saying: "use her as much as you want now, we won't get her tomorrow" (IIJ 2003: 34). The report also finds evidence supported by the testimonies of the women themselves and the survivors of the communal violence that pregnant women were specifically targeted. Pregnant women were hit on their stomachs with sticks and their stomachs slit open. That terrible day, I was hiding with some others on the roof of my house. From there, I saw my dearest friend Kauser Bano raped, her unborn baby slashed out from her womb before being tossed into the fire to be roasted alive. Thereafter, she too was brutally cut up and torched (Communalism Combat Report 2002: witness: Amina Aapa, interviewed at Relief Camp on March 4 and March 22). Fact-finding by a women's panel sponsored by Citizen's Initiative, Ahmedabad (2002) documented the activists, experiences of dealing with rape survivors in Shah-E-Alam relief camp, Ahmedabad. … women arrived stark naked at the camp. Some could barely walk because of torn genitals as a result of gang rapes. … her body covered with bites and nail marks. Husband of an 18 year-old woman and a resident of Gulmarg Society mentioned that she was pregnant and it was the ninth month of the pregnancy. Her house was attacked by a large mob. Her womb was cut open with a sharp weapon and the unborn baby was taken out and both mother and the child were burnt dead.

There is evidence of state and police complicity in perpetuating crimes against women. A complete breakdown of the state machinery seen as the failure of the state to protect its citizens from acts of violence reveal a much deeper cause of the communal violence. The reports also mention of widespread abdication of duties by the law enforcement machinery at all levels. There was no deployment of Mahila police in areas where women were brutalized and police complicity in these crimes is evident as women were denied the right to file FIR. In instances when the FIR was registered, the gruesomeness of the crime was either understated or the facts were obscured. The victims being illiterate would sign on the FIR without verifying the facts. In most of the cases, the police refused to name the accused in the FIR and group FIRs were filed which were later found out to be false FIRs. The IIJ report (2003) elaborates on how the affected people identified many individuals who had attacked but their names did not appear in the FIRs. I lost seven members of my family but not in a single FIR have they written the names of those that have died (Saleem, AA4 area, Ahmedabad, IIJ report 2003). It is because of the discrepancies in the registration of First Information Report and the shame associated with rape which prevented women from registering an FIR. Thus, there has been no official figures on the number of women who were subjected to sexual crime.

Several accounts speak of policemen actively aiding, abetting and in some cases leading the mobs. In other cases, the police turned deaf ear to cries of help and instead asked to fend for themselves. … we lost all hope when the police came with the crowd. When we pleaded with the police that they were meant to protect everyone, they told us to fight them with whatever strength we had (Citizens Initiative 2002).

Testimonies bring forth the fact that even minor girls were brutally raped. Medical relief to the injured and rape victims which is the foremost during such widespread violence was almost non-existent. The International Initiative for Justice Report states that though some doctors in public and private hospitals were trying to help the victims, but various testimonies of victims as well as on the spot report suggest the contrary.

Medical examinations and records of injuries were not maintained and doctors did not help in ways they could have, to record the violence and strengthen the cases of people who sought help. VHP and Bajrang Dal activists were present in many hospitals, at times in police uniforms, thus discouraging dying declarations and statement of injury (IIJ 2003). The International Initiative for Justice reports that the polarization induced and abetted by the state machinery had resulted in the ghettoization even of medical facilities. As an aftermath of the violence, many of the hospitals that were in the Muslim areas have shut down and moved elsewhere. One 40-bed hospital that was running in a Muslim area has moved to a Hindu area. Medical facilities have been re-organized along religious lines.

Testimonies reviewed in International Initiative for Justice also throw light on the gross irregularities in the medical records of the dead and the injured women. The medical records did not mention sexual violence and abuse, inspite of the women coming to the hospital in conditions that indicated sexual abuse. It is for this reason that the nature and extent of sexual violence faced by women in the Gujarat violence is difficult to assess. It has also made it almost impossible to pinpoint on individuals and organizations for perpetrating and inflicting violence of such horrendous nature.

The reports also mention that the health services failed to acknowledge the seriousness of the psychological trauma and did not adequately address post-traumatic stress disorder. There has also been evidence of pregnancy outcomes being affected by sexual and other kinds of violence. Women reported premature deliveries, miscarriages and abortions.

The role of media and vernacular press in the form of provocative language used in 'Sandesh' newspaper, rumours, false stories about Hindu and Adivasi women being raped perpetuated more violence. There have also been reports of fabricated stories of sexual violence of Hindu women and images of brutalized women's bodies that provoked violence against women of the Muslim community.

Plight of Women Affected by the Communal Violence

The state continues to be complicit in the ongoing violence against the Muslim community in Gujarat. The continuing impact of violence is still visible in the form of long term physical, psychological, economic and social consequences for women. The pervasive fear of being sexually assaulted still looms large in the minds of many women in Gujarat today. Muslims have been deprived of their citizenship rights in terms of school facilities, healthcare and housing. Displaced Muslims have begun living together often in the outskirts of the city in the so-called ghettoized clusters. This living in clusters enables them strength in numbers rather being physically isolated.

The International Initiative for Justice reports the mental health consequences on the women who have faced sexual violence. In most cases, women have been silent about the sexual violence/rape that has been inflicted on them. This is largely because of the shame, dishonour of the very act as well as the need to be a part of one's own community and not being alienated or ostracized from it. The repressed silence of their own pain together with being a witness to the innumerable gruesome acts has set in trauma among these women. There has been evidence of the survivors of sexual violence having little access to counseling and information related to their sexual and reproductive health.

Apart from the mental trauma, women survivors of the Gujarat violence face economic destitution as they have lost their family bread-winner. In most of the cases, families have been displaced and rehabilitated in the various relief camps. In other cases, those who have managed to return to their homes have done so under conditions of 'compromise' (IIJ 2003). The most important 'compromise' condition by which the Muslims are allowed to enter their original villages and neighbourhoods is the withdrawal of all legal cases against Hindus.

The International Initiative for Justice report also looks into the high incidence rates of early marriages among young girls from the Muslim community. The cause of these early marriages are the persistent threat of another communal violence and the vulnerability of the young girls to sexual attacks.

Is this the new normalcy that face women in Gujarat today?

Communal Violence Bill and its Focus on Women

Based on the recommendations by the various fact-finding committee reports and the International community condemning the Gujarat violence, there was an urgent need to draft law on communal violence in India. Looking at the magnitude of damage both physical and psychological caused by the 2002 Gujarat violence, the communal violence bill was an absolute necessity. The Communal Violence (Prevention, Control and Rehabilitation of victims) Bill was first introduced in the Rajya Sabha on December 5, 2005. The bill was severely criticized and rejected by the civil society at all levels. This bill is of importance in addressing the challenges posed to the secular character of the society and protection of all citizens. The bill has been criticized under the following headings:

1. legislative intent,
2. co-relation between crimes and declaration of disturbed area is false and untenable,
3. undue devolution of executive powers to the government and public servant,
4. failure to create any new offence and add deterrence,

5. no accountability of the state and of public servants,
6. no command responsibility,
7. failure to acknowledge and create offence of gender-based violence, and
8. relief and rehabilitation.

(Anhad, Twocircles.net, Communalism Watch, Counter Currents.org, InfoChange India)

Of the above mentioned headings under which the bill has been criticized, we shall discuss 'failure to acknowledge and create offence of gender-based violence'. According to the critiques, this bill completely ignores the distinction between sexual violence during times of peace and the sexual violence with the intent of destroying the reproductive ability and being genocidal in nature. The violence that was inflicted on women and children in the 2002 Gujarat violence has been discussed widely in the various fact finding committee reports as complying by the legal definition of genocide. To understand crimes against women and children during communal violence, the bill relies only on the crimes specified under the Indian Penal Code 1860, whereas the crimes during communal strifes are of different types. Sexual violence against women needs to be identified as a special form of violence.

Conclusions

Women's testimonies of the role of the state suggest political complicity, pre-planned organization and precision in targeting the Muslim community. After eight long years since the Gujarat violence have taken place and after many committee reports, the plight of the women who have suffered and survived is still a painful saga. Recommendations to the government, the judicial system in India and the civil society of which we are a member have just resulted in a Communal Violence Bill. On one hand, the survivors of the violence faced displacement, on the other there, are no proper rehabilitation schemes by the state government. The continuing impact of the violence is still a dominant part of the society.

References

Agnes, Flavia, "Transgressing Boundaries of Gender and Identity", *Economic and Political Weekly*, Commentary, September, 2002.

Ahmad, Imtiaz, "India and the Muslim World", Commentary, *Economic and Political Weekly*, Vol. 40, No. 9, February 26–March 4, 2005.

Ahmed, Riaz, "Gujarat Violence: Meaning and Implications", *Economic and Political Weekly*, Vol. 37, No. 20, May 18–24, 2002, pp. 1870–1873.

Citizens' Initiative. Survivors Speak: How Has the Gujarat Massacre Affected Minority Women? Fact-finding by a Women's Panel, Ahmedabad, 16, April 2002.

Dayal, John (Ed.), *Gujarat 2002: Untold and Re-told Stories of the Hindutva Lab,* Media House, New Delhi, 2002.

Engineer, Asghar Ali, *Communal Riots in Post-Independence India,* Delhi: Sangam Books, Delhi, 1991.

Engineer, Asghar Ali, "Gujarat Carnage in the Light of History of Communal Violence in India: Lessons from Gujarat", Vikas Adhyayan Kendra, Mumbai, 2002.

Human Rights Watch , "We Have No Orders to Save You", State Participation and Complicity in Communal Violence in Gujarat, 2002.

International Initiative for Justice in Gujarat: Redressing Violence Against Women Committed by State and Non-State Actors. Threatened Existence: A Feminist Analysis of the Genocide in Gujarat. Mumbai: Forum Against Oppression of Women, December 2003.

Nussbaum, Martha C., "Body of the Nation: Why Women Were Mutilated in Gujarat", *Boston Review,* July 29, 2004. www.countercurrents.org/guj-nussbaum290704.htm

Patel, Vibhuti (2009), Fundamentalism, Communalism and Gender Justice, http://www.europe-solidaire.org/spip.php?article13223.

Robinson, Rowena, "Boundary Battles: Muslim Women and Community Identity in the Aftermath of Violence", Women's Studies International Forum, 2010, Vol. 33, pp. 365–373.

Sarkar, Tanika, "Semiotics of Terror: Muslim Women and Children in Hindu Rashtra", *Economic and Political Weekly,* 2002, Vol. 37, No. 28, pp. 2872–2876

Varshney, Ashutosh, *Ethnic Conflict and Civic Life: Hindus and Muslims in India,* Yale University Press, New Haven, 2002.

Section IV
State of Human Rights

9 Gujarat Minorities

A Struggle for Justice

Fr. Cedric Prakash S.J.

A large section of Hindus consider the Upanishads as one of their sacred scriptures. In these scriptures is a very powerful prayer wherein the devotee pleads with God to …

> Lead me O Lord
> from darkness to light,
> Lead me O Lord
> from untruth to truth,
> Lead me O Lord
> from death to immortality.

This constant desire and search for truth became the cornerstone of Mahatma Gandhi's campaign to provide for India freedom from colonial rule. He called it *Satyagraha* (meaning holding firmly to truth), and he based it on the doctrine of *Ahimsa* (meaning non-violence). These two principles, namely *Satyagraha* and *Ahimsa*, which in latter years epitomized Gandhi, were the ultimate weapons in the pursuit of India's freedom. That India achieved freedom by using these values is well-documented but the fact that more than 62 years after independence, the country has not been able to mainstream these values, is the unfortunate reality that can be seen in the brutal and fragmented world that so many Indians live in today.

For Mahatma Gandhi, Gujarat was 'home'. It was here that he established his famous Ashram on the banks of the river Sabarmati in Ahmedabad. It was from the walls of this Ashram that Hindus, Muslims and Christians sang together the celebrated hymn, 'Ishwar Allah tero naam, sabko sanmati de Bhagwan' (Bless us Lord, with the wisdom to understand that You can be called God or Allah). This hymn was a call to transcend the narrowness of one's own religion and embrace and respect the other and his/her religion. It was a legacy given by the Father of the Nation, which we should be proud of and which we should have mainstreamed.

Mahatma Gandhi also held in very high esteem, John Henry Cardinal Newman, who some years earlier, in his search for truth, wrote the immortal poem, 'Lead kindly light amidst the encircling gloom ...'. Gandhi had it translated into Gujarati and it became one of the favourite hymns of the Ashram. Gandhi was a man totally committed to peace, but who realized that real 'peace' can be achieved only when 'truth' prevails.

On May 1, 2010, the Gujarat Government loudly trumpeted a 'Swarnim' (Golden) year of the State since its birth in 1960. The tragic irony is that there is really nothing much to celebrate and in fact, the vast majority of the people – be it the Adivasis, the Dalits, the minorities, the women and children, the millions who struggle to eke out a living – are at the receiving end of the vicious policies and poor administration by this government which spends most of its time, money and energy on false propaganda.

This chapter intends to focus on the 'minority bashing' which the authorities love to indulge in and the struggles that the minorities face in their search for justice.

Gujarat Carnage 2002

In order to understand what is happening to the minorities of Gujarat, one would need to situate the reality in the carnage of 2002.

On November 21, 2002, the Concerned Citizens' Tribunal consisting of several eminent citizens and headed by Justice V. Krishna Iyer (a former Judge of the Supreme Court of India), made public a report entitled CRIME AGAINST HUMANITY, based on the Gujarat carnage which began on February 27–28, 2002. This report was written on the basis of more than 2000 oral and written testimonies, both individual and collective, from victim survivors and also from independent Human Rights Groups, Women's Groups, NGOs, academics and others.

The Tribunal, in its findings and recommendations, clearly indicts the Government of Gujarat and holds them responsible for the unfettered violence, murder, arson and looting that took place in Gujarat that year. This violence (though not an 'action-reaction' syndrome) followed the burning of the S6 compartment of the Sabarmati Express Train at Godhra (in eastern Gujarat) and the death of 59 people.

What took place in Gujarat has been recorded in studies, analyses and reports by fact-finding teams, human rights groups, statutory bodies such as the National Human Rights Commission, the media and many others (both in India and abroad). It is not necessary to get into the nitty-gritty details of the carnage which are both, gory and horrendous.

The major trends that emerged from each of these reports and that corroborate the findings of the Citizens' Tribunal are:

- What took place in Gujarat was not merely communal violence or riots; it was a genocide, a carnage, an ethnic cleansing that was designed to ostracize or wipe out a whole community.
- The carnage was well-planned and well-executed. It was not a 'spontaneous' reaction as it was made out to be. The preparations must have taken several months. A year earlier, a widely circulated Gujarati daily had listed several hotels run by the Chilya community which had non-Islamic names. During the carnage, most of their hotels were razed to the ground. A meticulous census was conducted on the Muslims and Christians of Gujarat in 1999. The data helped rampaging mobs know exactly whom to attack and where.
- The carnage was meant to break the backbone of the Muslim community's economy. It succeeded to a great extent in doing this.
- The middle-class (including several well-to-do and educated women) were blatantly involved in the violence; there were very few people who were willing to come out and take a stand to prevent what was happening.
- In some areas, Adivasis and Dalits were used very effectively in the arson and looting of Muslim homes and establishments.
- It was a state-sponsored genocide. The Citizens' Tribunal has clearly indicted in addition to the Chief Minister and politicians, several high-ranking bureaucrats and police officials. The Sangh Parivar was given a free hand to do what they wanted. The police were apparently given clear instructions not to take any action. There is also evidence to show that some were encouraged to join in the violence – which they did, with ruthless finesse. State Ministers and leaders of 'the Parivar' (like the mafioso) were seen leading the mobs. (The 'Tehelka Sting Operation' which was made public in October 2007 provides ample evidence to substantiate this fact.)

A Historical Perspective

In order to have a better understanding of what has been happening in Gujarat, one would need to go back to March 1998, when the Hindu nationalist BJP (Bharatiya Janata Party) won a two-third majority in Gujarat. It was the very first state in the country that gave them such a massive mandate with unqualified support. The build up to this victory was gradual but efficiently planned; that Gujarat was bound to become the laboratory for the Hindutva ideology was clear as daylight.

The Bombay bomb blasts in 1993, in a way put the brakes on the aggressive posturing by the Hindu fundamentalists. In some ways, this also helped the Muslims of Gujarat who for some years had been at the receiving end of the agenda of right-wing Hindus. The Muslims of Gujarat seemed to be in a better position to counteract any attack by the Hindutva elements within the government. Governance or the needs of the people was never the top priority (and never will be), so these Hindu fundamentalists found another soft target, namely the Christians to consolidate their position in Gujarat. From March 1998 onwards, Christians and their institutions were attacked with frightening regularity. A huge church which was under construction was pulled down in Ahmedabad city by the Sangh Parivar mob. Several other churches all over the Dangs and other parts of South Gujarat were attacked or burnt in December 1998 and January 1999.

On December 4, 1998, more than 35,000 Christians marched on the streets of Ahmedabad in a protest rally against the attacks on Christians in Gujarat and other parts of India. For the first time, the fundamentalist elements were put on the defensive though that did not stop them from going on a rampage a few weeks later. An anti-constitutional census was taken of the Christians and Muslims in 1999 and despite a *suo moto* by Justice Calla of the Gujarat High Court, the collection of data continued unabashedly.

After a hue and cry nationally and internationally, the attacks on the Christians gradually subsided. However, this posturing had already translated into very important parliamentary seats in the general elections of 1999. (This Christian bashing still continues as was seen in February 2006, when a huge Hindu revival programme called the Shabri Kumbh Mela was organized by some fundamentalist groups in the Dangs and was aimed solely against the Christians. The famous *kathakar* Morari Bapu and the Chief Minister of Gujarat spewed venom at the Christians and their activities during this gathering.)

As February 2003 (the original month for state elections) approached, the BJP definitely needed an agenda. All bye-elections and other local elections held in 2000 and 2001 saw them losing miserably in most constituencies both in Gujarat and elsewhere. The attack on the

World Trade Centre in New York on September 11, 2001 was just the 'appropriate opening' for the sinister designs of the Sangh Parivar. But they still were not sure whether attacking the Muslims in any way would help or would meet with further reprisals. It was the 'Godhra incident' that provided the trigger. When the state elections which were pre-poned and held in December 2002, the 'Hindutva wave', gave the BJP a comfortable two-third majority.

The ruling political class never intended that peace and normalcy return to the state. For instance, on May 1, 2006, the Dargah of Rashiduddin Chisthi in the Fatehpura area of Baroda was razed to the ground, sparking off another round of communal violence which claimed six lives, and left many others injured and homeless. The Dargah (which is the tomb) of this revered saint, was frequented by both Muslims and Hindus alike and was believed to be more than 200 years old. This insensitive act and many such others, by a callous administration is a clear indicator of how one religion can be pitted against another even when efforts are being made at the grassroots to restore communal harmony.

As the next state elections drew near towards the end of 2007, expectations were high for a change of guard. There were several indications to show that the ordinary citizen was fed-up with the communal and insensitive government. Several efforts were made at every level of the society to make the ordinary person aware of the atrocities being inflicted on the minorities with the help of government machinery. As things turned out, whilst the BJP did fractionally lose some of their seats and a large percentage of the vote share, they still won and were able to once again form the government in the state.

The election results of December 2007 were a major setback for all those trying to establish a society that is more humane, just, tolerant and peaceful. It is also a clear indication that 'communalism' has been mainstreamed and institutionalized in Gujarat.

The results of the parliamentary election of May 2009 (as also in 2004) has provided a glimmer hope for the future of Gujarat, as the BJP was not able to 'take over' by getting all the seats from Gujarat to parliament. In spite of their loud boasts, they managed to get just one more seat (in comparison to 2004) making their parliamentary representation just 15 out of a total state strength of 26.

The Gujarat Reality in 2010

Today, more than eight years after the Gujarat carnage, minority bashing seems to have become institutionalized in the state of Gujarat. This takes place in both subtle and direct ways. Some ways by which it has been happening are given below:

Ghettoization of the Muslims

Ghettoization of a community is an important strategy in ensuring their alienation. The Muslims in several cities, towns and villages of the state of Gujarat have been confined to ghettoes. In Ahmedabad, most of them are restricted to an area called Juhapura (also known derogatively as mini-Pakistan) or to some parts of the Eastern side of the city. Many of these areas do not have basic infrastructure and facilities and the government does nothing to remedy the situation. For example, in Juhapura, there is just one nationalized bank which started a little over a year ago for a population which is perhaps more than 4,00,000. This means that the Muslims who live here have to travel distances to avail banking facilities or find more innovative ways for a banking system. In most parts of the up-market western side of the city, a Muslim will not be able to buy a house or own a shop to carry on his legitimate business. Some Cooperative Housing Societies have even amended their bye-laws to ensure that flats are not sold to Muslims.

Fake Encounter Killings

The Gujarat Police seem to be having a free hand to mercilessly kill Muslim youth in cold blood. Stories are concocted of how the accused Muslim youth had plans to 'assassinate' the Chief Minister of the state. There is also the even more 'hard-to-believe' story of how while the alleged sequence of the crime was enacted, the accused 'tried to pull out the gun from the holster of a standing policeman or tried to escape', leaving the police with no alternative but to shoot dead the accused. In 2007, some senior IPS officers were finally arrested for stage managing such encounters. The arrest of more officers in the Sohrabuddin case (Sohrabuddin and his wife Kauserbi were killed in a fake encounter in November 2005) continues as late as May 2010.

Constant Intimidation and Harassment of the Christians

As mentioned earlier, Christians were the target of plenty of bashing in 1998 and 1999. After the community brought this matter to the national and international fora, there was an immediate halt on these direct attacks. However, again in 2006 (as mentioned above), in a state-organized programme, in the Dangs district of Gujarat, Morari Bapu and the Gujarat Chief Minister were vitriolic in their attacks on the Christian community. The Christians, who constitute a minuscule 0.53 per cent of the state's population, continue to be the object of constant intimidation and harassment from the authorities. There are constant enquiries on 'foreign funding', on whether the Christians have foreigners among them, on the type of activities they engage in to empower the Adivasis and Dalits, etc. Since January 2010, there have been at least 60 official enquiries on Christian institutions which are unconstitutional in nature. Every year before Christmas, the Sangh Parivar has been organizing *ghar vapasi* programmes in areas which have a sizeable section of Christians.

Manipulation of the Judiciary

The Hindu fundamentalists and the state government have absolutely no problem in tampering with the judiciary in order to benefit their majoritarian agenda. There are several public prosecutors appointed by the government for the legal proceedings post the Gujarat carnage, who have primary membership in the RSS/VHP. It is therefore, not without reason that even the Supreme Court of India has had very little faith in the Gujarat Judiciary and had to move cases out of Gujarat. On March 5, 2010, the Chief Justice of Gujarat very categorically stated, 'We are concerned about the future of the Gujarat judiciary, where money has become the main source and where you can buy anybody with the power of money'. He was clearly asserting that the judiciary here is corrupt!

The Freedom of Religion Act

In March 2003, the Gujarat Government unanimously passed its draconian Freedom of Religion Act which prohibits anyone from changing his/her faith unless one has the permission of the civil authority. For five years, the government did not have the courage to frame the rules which are needed to govern such an act. It finally did so in 2008. The Act is clearly directed against the minorities because the government has a misplaced fear that more and more Adivasis and Dalits of the state will want to embrace either Islam or Christianity. In the same vein, the anti-cow slaughter Law of Gujarat which was amended not long ago, was clearly aimed at destroying the livelihood of several Muslims.

Manipulations in Education

Fascist forces have always tried to manipulate the educational system in order to brainwash students from a very early age. Several of the textbooks produced by the Gujarat State Schools Textbook Board reflect a strong anti-minority bias. In one edition, it was categorically stated that Christians and Muslims 'were foreigners in India'. This statement has since been removed after an outcry by academics and human rights activists. However, several other biases against minorities continue to be reflected. In August 2006, at an examination of the Gujarat Public Service Commission for Medical Officers, almost 15 of the 100 questions had statements directed against Muslims and Christians.

Sidelining those who Stand up for the Minorities

Through its various policies and its posturing, the Gujarat Government, very blatantly sidelines or opposes anyone who takes up for the cause of minorities. One has only to look at the way human rights and other social activists have been intimidated in the past years to understand this. These people are subject to constant interrogations, searches and even threats. Newspapers which take up the cause of the minorities are denied government advertisements in their publications. Movies such as 'Parzania' and 'Firaaq' which tried to highlight the situation of minorities in the state were not allowed to be screened. The message is clear, 'stand up for the minorities and you will be made to shut down'.

Posturings of a Hindu Rashtra

When the government neglects or ignores the fact that the Mughals contributed very positively to the growth of the state and constantly postures on a Hindu Rashtra, it will definitely result in a greater sense of insecurity within the minority community. In several parts of Gujarat, huge billboards at the entrance of a town or a village proclaim the area as a Hindu Rashtra. Such acts are directly violative of the Indian Constitution. Yet, they seem to have the sanction of the state authorities.

Communalizing Trivial Incidents

There have been several incidents over the last few years which were very insignificant and non-communal in nature. However, the active involvement of some of the right-wing Hindu forces ensure that such incidents turn into communal riots and most of the times, the minority community is at the receiving end. That several of these 'communal' incidents take place just before a major Muslim festival cannot be put down to mere 'coincidence'. The pattern with which they recur clearly indicates that they are part of a subterfuge to disrupt the forthcoming festivities.

Co-option of Some Minorities

The 'divide and rule' policy is a time-tested strategy of fascist forces used by the Gujarat Government to its great advantage. This government has left no stone unturned to get some people from the minority community to sing their paeans. Recently, the Chief Minister of Gujarat had a photo opportunity with some members of the Vohra community while they heaped praises on him. On April 2010, when a German parliamentary delegation visited Gujarat, to assess for themselves the situation of minorities in the state, a group of rich

Muslim businessmen, had no problems in condemning this visit. These Muslim businessmen are the very same who have no qualms in seeking for themselves and for their profits, German and other European business partners.

Our Response so Far

When the rule of the majority indulges in 'minority bashing', there is always the danger of taking recourse to 'minority-ism' or just to give up because one is either afraid or feels that the only way out is to succumb, because the perpetrators are too powerful to take on. What then does one do in order to strike a balance, yet assert one's identity as a citizen guaranteed by the constitutional rights and freedoms of the country?

Our response together with several other like-minded individuals and groups has been manifold. These include the following interventions:

To Speak Truth to Power

In a state which is supposedly avowed to Gandhi's principles of *Satyagraha* and *Ahimsa*, our ability to speak truth to power has always been and will continue to be the basic response against any injustice to minorities or any other section of the society. We tell it as it is. We let others know the stark truth without any sugar coating. We leave no room for diplomatic niceties because in such situations, sweet talk only de-focuses from the ground reality. Taking on a government which not only encourages, but also indulges in ostracizing of its own citizens, is fraught with problems. We have highlighted some of these above. However, our experience over the years has demonstrated that inspite of the intrinsic difficulties it does help in keeping the ground situation on the radar, and it also in some ways helps to put the government on the spot.

To Document, Study and Analyse the Situation

One is unable to 'speak truth to power' if one does not consistently document the day-to-day reality within the state. The strategies of those in power are varied. They often use very subtle and indirect means in their offenses. It is therefore imperative for us to be in touch with the situation as it exists. Checking out what the media says about what is happening, studying and analysing the situation regularly and communicating this to the public in general is an important part of our efforts to ensure justice for the minorities. Dossiers which highlight the struggles of the minorities and other victimized groups and translations of relevant publications and other materials into the vernacular help in the wider dissemination of our concerns and concerted response.

To Engage in Advocacy

One of the big drawbacks in the wake of the Gujarat carnage 2002 was that there was never a people's movement to counter the onslaught on the minorities. Further, what is well-documented is that even some from the middle class indulged in the riots and other forms of violence. In the absence of a strong civil society movement, the only alternative has been to engage with the media, with the legal system and with the concerned individuals and groups. This has not been easy, especially since the government has on its side the powerful industrial lobby and other vested interests. In some ways however, breakthroughs have been made with the establishment of the Special Investigation Team (SIT) by the Supreme Court of India, and the fact that they have at least interrogated some of those in power for their involvement or complicity in the violence of 2002. There are several other legal interventions which include a group of citizens challenging the Freedom of Religion Act in the High Court of Gujarat. All this would not have been possible, were it not for a consistent campaign by individuals and groups across the board.

To Mainstream Constitutional Rights and Freedoms

In Gujarat, a section of society has literally been 'getting away with murder'. This is obvious from the recent arrests of certain powerful police officers. The rule of law would never have been sabotaged if citizens knew of their rights and freedoms which are guaranteed by the Constitution. It has been a long struggle to make people aware of this. In a system which has been endemically corrupt and has always sided with the powerful, the victim has very little chance for justice. The easier way is to opt out. Our efforts and that of several others have been to educate various sections of the society on the fundamentals of our Constitution in order to preserve the wealth of a vibrant democracy.

To Network

The story of the response to the Gujarat carnage is that of the strength of a section of society in constant touch with one another, supporting each other's initiatives and networking on critical issues. This show of solidarity has gone a long way in highlighting the plight of the minorities and other victimized groups. Networking with others is never easy. It has the usual difficulties of leadership, visibility, one-upmanship, etc. There is also the fact that some, for various reasons, do not want to go the whole way. Government and other vested interests also indulge in a tactical 'divide and rule', coopting some when they are able to perceive initiatives of support. Nonetheless, networking with one another has been one of the key aspects to bring to the fore the situation of the minorities of Gujarat.

Conclusion

The above is an attempt to put in perspective the current situation of the minorities in Gujarat, and some of the responses which are in place. It underscores the connivance of the ruling dispensation in the state with certain groups, to contain the rights and freedoms of its citizens and in particular the minorities.

The situation in Gujarat indicates that untruth, falsehoods and myths have taken the place of truth. Systematic efforts have been made by the majority and in particular those in authority to demonize the minorities and keep them in an environment of fear and insecurity. In such a scenario, it is essential for all to pay heed to Mahatma Gandhi when he asserts that, 'in matters of conscience, the law of majority has no place'.

10 Some Paths to Forgiveness
Religious Conflict and Shared Living in India*

Harsh Mander

People of diverse faiths and cultures have lived together with peace and goodwill for millennia in India. However, when India won freedom in 1947, Hindus, Muslims and Sikhs were embroiled in a feverish bloodbath. This left the country torn into two; a million people were killed, and ten times that number permanently uprooted from the land of their birth.

The people of free India adopted a Constitution which guaranteed to the minorities religious freedom and equal protection under the law. The experience in six decades of freedom has been of a sometimes bitterly contested but still and enduring authentic secular democracy.

However since independence, there also have been thousands of 'communal riots'**, or episodes of mass clashes between people of Hindu and Muslim faith, and pogroms, resulting in the recorded loss, according to one painstaking estimate, of at least 25,628 lives (including 1,005 in police firings).[1] In my interviews with hundreds of survivors of communal violence of the minority Muslim faith, I learnt that the families of most had not suffered for the first time. Each had many agonising tales of losing loved ones, and the looting and torching of their homes in several successive riots. In fact, the saga of their lives seemed like the spaces *between various communal riots,* often starting with the cataclysmic upheavals of 1947. These spaces were almost

---

* Many parts of this article have appeared in my book *Fear and Forgiveness: The Aftermath of Massacre* (Penguin India, 2009).

** The term 'communal riot' connotes in India mass violence between religious communities. Communalism is the ideology that people of different faiths have divergent and conflicting interests.

stolen, tragically fragile, insecure interludes, during which they struggled to lead full and happy lives before being overtaken and destroyed once again by the politics of hate.

Whenever they reflect on and talk of their futures, riots continue to dominate their mindscape. They speak repeatedly of their plans of what they would do for the protection of their families, not *if* a communal riot breaks out again, but *when* it does. (Their plans were usually of finding safety by shifting to Muslim ghettoes and sometimes by arming themselves and very occasionally in fantasies of bloody retributive violence.) On such tragic and hopeless certainties of recurrence of the trauma of periodically repeated profound loss and suffering in violent communal upheavals, no enduring peaceful future can be built. The ideas of forgiveness and reconciliation that this essay explores are a response to the sporadic but repeated hostilities, and this perceived certainty of recurrence.

It is remarkable that despite this recurring communal bloodletting during and after the traumatic partition of the country, there has been no systematic structured official (or even significant non-official) processes of 'truth and reconciliation', to help perpetrators and survivors of hate-violence come together; to see and speak to each other; acknowledge their crimes and failings, their hate and fear, their grievances and suspicions; to seek and offer forgiveness, trust and goodwill; and ultimately help bring closure and eventual healing.

Part of the problem is that the threats and grave peril, both of the on-going communal violence and of subversion of justice to minorities, are not sufficiently acknowledged by the state, political parties and civil society organizations. Even where relations between communities deteriorate, and states are partisan on communal lines – and soft on organizations that are committed to destroy the secular democratic foundations of the nation – many continue to live in dogged denial. Secondly Also, much of the violence and injustice is not overt, it rages unseen in the hearts and minds of people. We attend to it only when violence actually spills on to the streets, when the dust and dirt of our pavements are soaked in human blood, when the bodies of girls and women are violated, and when the smoke of fires of homes and shops rises to the skies, leaving behind the burned rubble of vandalized hopes and dreams. We deliberately overlook the covert violence of everyday. Even the governments, political parties and social organizations in India are today most frequently equivocal, unsteady and reluctant in dealing with the intensely sensitive and potentially divisive issues raised by communalism. They no longer are prepared to stand up to be counted.

However, the Indian people have arguably had more experience than most through centuries of living with diversity[2], therefore even without organized processes of reconciliation, there are usually natural spontaneous processes of reaching out and healing that follow bouts of sectarian violence. In many communal conflagrations that I have witnessed and handled (as a former head of district governments), I have observed that within days of such mass sectarian upheavals, persons of goodwill and compassion reach out from each community and others grasp their outstretched hands gratefully. There are spontaneous individual and collective expressions of remorse and grief at the loss suffered by the other community, and of compassion, through which processes of social and personal healing set in.

But without structured modes of facilitating reconciliation for survivors of the partition violence of 1947, there has not been adequate closure for families that experienced the agony and permanent uprootment from and the loss of their loved ones and homeland. My own parents and their extended families lost their homes amid hate, slaughter and arson in a region of the country that became a part of Pakistan in 1947, and their grief of loss remains dormant more than 60 years later, just below the surface. Perhaps we needed to bring together people who lived with the violence from both sides of the border, to share truth, discover their common burdens of suffering and privation, and thereby find the spaces for individual and collective forgiveness much earlier.

In most cultures, through many phases in human history, warring and bitterly estranged people have from time to time wearied of battles and hate, of destruction and fear, have instead buried their weapons and collectively sought or rediscovered ways of living together with peace, faith and goodwill. In lay terms, reconciliation may be understood as processes by which is achieved the restoration – between members of different racial, ethnic, religious or social groups or classes, who have been divided by mass violence, organized campaigns of hate and distrust or prolonged oppression – of mutual dialogue, understanding, social, cultural and economic interactions, trust and amity. This restoration aspires to achieve levels of shared living and social relations that at least match those that prevailed before the violence or hate campaigns, or to even higher levels that are mutually considered more acceptably just and egalitarian. It involves the expulsion or neutralization of loathing and suspicion that invaded social relations between diverse people, and in the end a genuine meeting again of hearts, individual and collective.

The imperative of reconciliation after conflict is that in its absence, hate is retained and nurtured with stereotypes, myths, selective memory and lies about the demonized 'other', and passed on as a dubious legacy from generation to generation. In recent times, memory has been abused, for instance, to 'fuel the fires of hatred' in Northern Ireland, and in the completely varied recollections of their common history by Albanians and Serbs in Kosovo, and Muslims and Serbs in Bosnia.[3] The misuse of distorted memory of falsehoods and deliberate half-truths has also been used globally most widely in recent times to mount a climate of pervasive distrust against people of Muslim faith, in the so-called global war on terror.

In Ludhiana in Punjab, India, speaking to an audience on the need for reclaiming and defending a secular India, I recall being confronted by an elderly man in the audience who wept painfully, 'my family was uprooted from Pakistan in 1947, and it lost many lives in the hands of the Muslims. What can I tell my children? How do you expect me to tell them to forgive and forget?' I replied that my own family belonged to Rawalpindi and suffered in similar ways. I added: 'but why should Muslim men, women and children today deserve hatred, and even worse retribution, for crimes that other Muslim people may have committed decades ago? And more importantly, why is your memory so selective? If you must recall to your children the crimes suffered by Hindus and Sikhs during partition, should you not recount to them also the fact that their Hindus and Sikhs ancestors committed exactly the same unspeakable atrocities against Muslims on this side of the border?'

The falsehoods and half-truths of memory rob the 'other' of not just equal citizenship, but even elementary humanity. The western Indian state of Gujarat in 2002 witnessed some of the most brutal mass violence after partition, especially targeting women and children, in which women's bodies were used as battlefields. The extraordinary support of many women of the majority Hindu community for these acts of mass sexual violence suggests the potency of the toxins of hate that seeped deep into the souls of even women of the majority religious community, and distorted their perceptions of women of a different faith. They stopped seeing Muslim women in their own likeness, as women and as human. It drove them to regard Muslim women as deserving of the same violence which, if it had been instead targeted towards themselves, would have humiliated and crushed them.

Ideas of reconciliation and forgiveness – as well as justice – are intrinsic in varied but related ways to virtually every major strand of diverse religious and secular convictions that have impinged through the centuries on the consciousness of Indian people. These include various tribal faiths, Buddhist, Jain, Vedic, Islamic, Christian, Parsi, Sikh, reformist Bhakti, Sufi, agnostic, atheistic and sceptical philosophical traditions. It is however beyond the limited scholarship of this chapter to track this edifying, compelling and sophisticated canvas of humanitarian ethical, social and political discourse. I will do no more than to quote Gandhi who, in modern times, is arguably the most credible political practitioner and thinker of the politics of reconciliation. In an inconsolable country grieving bitterly for a million lives extinguished by partition, homes and homelands lost forever and a country dismembered by the divisive politics of hate, Gandhi's last battle before his assassination in January 1948 was for the rights of the Muslim people, and not even those who had chosen secular democratic India as their home, but those who had opted for the religious state of Pakistan. The conviction that drove him all his life was that 'there is no way to peace. Peace is the way.' He spoke of peace as 'a heavy downpour of rain which drenches the soil to fullness, likewise only a profuse shower of love overcomes hatred'. His comments on forgiving and forgetting are illuminating: 'To forgive is not to forget. The merit lies in loving in spite of the vivid knowledge that the one that must be loved is not a friend. There is no merit in loving an enemy when you forget him for a friend.'

I recall a peace activist friend who has devoted the best years of his life to attempt to strengthen Hindu–Muslim unity in India, who in a moment of dark despair said to me, 'I have given up hope that Hindus and Muslims will love each other. Today for me it is enough that they do not kill one another.' Such minimalist reconciliation does not eliminate conflict, but only reduces the resort to individual or collective violations of body and property as the means to resolve this. Reconciliation is deepened when it travels well beyond such a resolve to continue to hate but not destroy, to one that positively builds trust, confidence and eventually empathy between previously embroiled people.[4]

I propose that paths to authentic forgiveness and reconciliation must traverse at least four milestones: acknowledgement, remorse, reparation and justice. The first of these elements, acknowledgement, involves for me a public acceptance – by direct perpetrators, by state authorities, but also by people and organizations who openly or tacitly ratify the violence or were silent or indifferent as it unfolded – that grave and unjust violence and discrimination actually took place, causing unconscionable suffering to those who were targeted by the violence. The second, remorse, is a public expression of collective sincere regret or contrition for the hate, violence, injustice and suffering that transpired.

Reparation for me involves the material elements of reconciliation: at the very minimum, it entails adequate and timely assistance to enable victim survivors to sustainably achieve shelters, livelihoods, common resources, habitats and cultural environments that are at levels at least comparable (and, I believe, better) than what they enjoyed prior to the conflict. This is in conformity with established principles of international law, under which restitution involves 're-establishment of the situation which existed before the wrongful act was committed'.[5] There can be no compensation for loss of loved ones, homes and valued ways of life, since no monetary value in the world can be attached to these deprivations. But reparation should still address, with humility and sensitivity, these losses as well to the extent that is humanly possible, to assist the survivors to keel living. For it to be even more healing, not just the impersonal state but also perpetrators or people who share the identity of the wrong-doers, should be actively mobilized in a process of rebuilding. In the aftermath of the Gujarat 2002 massacre, some Hindu village folk were successfully mobilized in the region surrounding Godhra, the epicentre of the upheaval, to contribute their voluntary labour to rebuilding the destroyed homes of their Muslim neighbours, and this manifestly was intensely healing for the battered survivors.

Justice involves firstly legal justice, the equal application and protection of the law of the land and by institutions of the state, including fair, timely and non-partisan processes of registering police complaints, investigation, arrest, bail, prosecution, trial and appeal. It includes also accountability to people and the legal system of public officials who are charged with preventing and controlling communal violence, reparation and restoring peace. Finally, it involves restoring peace: the establishment of a sustainable environment of harmony and amity founded on legal and social justice, guarantees of non-repetition, freedom from fear and distrust between communities, and strengthening of social, economic and cultural bonds between them.

Those who oppose post-violence human rights struggles often suggest that efforts for legal justice were undertaken long after visible violence had ceased on the streets, only revive enmities and cause further unrest and tensions rather than encourage peace. These threaten the fragile peace that is constructed with so much difficulty in post-conflict societies. This argument reminds me again and again of beliefs that a family in which a woman accepts repeated violence in the hands of her spouse without complaint or resistance is a peaceful one, and a household in which she is encouraged or supported (or instigated?) to be emboldened enough to speak out is one in which the peace and sanctity of family life is being imperilled and destroyed.

Indeed, the pleas for shrouding throbbing pasts in suffocating silence are particularly unjust for women survivors of communal violence. There are even in normal times, enormous conspiracies of silence that surround violence against women, whether in homes, work places or on the streets. In all communal squalls, the bodies of women are specially targeted. Women's bodies are refashioned as the property of the hated 'other' and as symbols of their honour, therefore attacks on these aim to humiliate the men who 'own' them and help break their spirit. Imposed consent for silence as forms of spurious reconciliation are likely to muffle the unhealed agony of women survivors most of all.

It is only when the crimes of the past are acknowledged, and atonement made with public expressions of genuine remorse, when the state, the perpetrator and survivor all join hands to rebuild broken lives, and when justice is done and seen to have been done, is it possible for those who suffer to forgive, to heal, to trust and possibly to even love again.

A survivor of the apartheid in South Africa famously and tellingly reminded members of the Truth and Reconciliation Commission about the enormous imbalances of power that are implicit in alternate notions of reconciliation and justice. 'Reconciliation is only in the vocabulary of those who can afford it', he agonizingly countered them. 'It is non-existent to a person whose self-respect has been stripped away and poverty is a festering wound that consumes his soul'.[6] I have found nothing in what members of the Commission said that adequately responds to his anguished challenge.

In a visit to South Africa, I tiptoed in awe before accounts of the justly celebrated Truth and Reconciliation Commission of South Africa, constituted after the political end of apartheid. It has inspired at least a score of other such commissions in other countries which have attempted to assist their people to deal with a history of strife.[7]

I wondered what lessons we could learn from the experience of the Truth and Reconciliation Commission in India, to bridge the communal chasm that is growing between people of different faiths.

The South African Truth and Reconciliation Commission assured legal amnesty to all perpetrators of atrocities as long as they admit their crimes before the Commission in the glare of a watchful media. It was argued in defence of the South African Commission that this was a major advance from earlier commissions elsewhere, in which amnesty was negotiated behind closed doors, and behind the backs of the victims of these mass hate crimes. However, the truth is that even in South Africa this decision was hastily imposed from 'above', without adequate information, debate, let alone the democratic consent of millions of Black people who had lived with the indignities, injustice and terror of apartheid, even though the decision had absolutely critical bearing on both how they dealt with their past and they built their futures. Hugo van der Merwe, a South African scholar, says that the ANC leadership at that time believed that 'for local dynamics to change, national intervention must first take place. This will then filter down, or create the conditions (and incentives) within which local actors can pursue reconciliation processes'.[8]

Desmond Tutu specifically rejects what he describes as the 'Nuremburg trial paradigm', suggesting the victims (or human rights defenders) should not individually or collectively pursue legal charges against their wrong-doers, nor should the state authorities 'run the gauntlet of the normal judicial process' to bring them to face trial and eventual punishment.[9] He offers some practical arguments, such as that without this agreement, the apartheid leadership would not have agreed to a negotiated settlement, and that anyway the judicial system would have continued to be biased against the victims.

There can be both convincing rationales and debates about the imperatives of compromises that are entered into by political leaderships in historically difficult moments of transition, such as those faced by the post-apartheid South African nation at the time of its rebirth as a democracy in 1992. I can understand (but not necessarily agree) if Tutu and Mandela defend the decision of assured amnesty for truth-tellers who committed unspeakable crimes of apartheid as the only one that was politically feasible at that moment in the South African history, if they admit even the possibility that the decision may have been politically appropriate, but at the same time *ethically* flawed. But my problem is with Tutu's *ethical* (and not political) arguments in defence of this amnesty because these are intended to state moral principles that have much more universal application: briefly that even legally determined and imposed punishment is retribution, which in turn is vengeance, and therefore it is ethically wrong.

Using Nozick's (1981) description of retributive punishment meted out through the legal system as 'punishment inflicted as deserved for a past wrong', Crocker[10] persuasively proposes many ways in which retribution is *not* revenge. Retribution is given for a violation that is a collectively accepted wrong; it is constrained and establishes limits to the punishment that can be meted out to the wrong-doer; it is impersonal, principled and takes no personal satisfaction from the suffering of the person who undergoes punishment. Most importantly in our context of communal riots, it rejects the doctrine of collective guilt that mere membership of an opposing group justifies revenge. I will argue that ethnic conflicts that in India are mainly in the nature of disguised pogroms or genocides, in which there are clear victims and perpetrators, with primary culpability of state and organizations that are dedicated to the manufacture of hatred and the instigation and planning of the sectarian violence. In these circumstances, retributive justice, by challenging impunity, negating counterfeit hierarchies of suffering between communities and re-establishing equality before the law between people of disjoined communities, necessarily paves the way for eventual restorative justice.

The dangers of 'reconciliation' imposed on unequal contenders are further highlighted by Sumanta Banerjee[11] who asks the difficult question whether the advance assurance of amnesty for apartheid crimes was only a fig-leaf to disguise the surrender imposed on the weak to give up their rights forever to secure justice from their powerful oppressors. Banerjee points out the paradox that Winnie Mandela, former wife of legendary ANC leader Nelson Mandela, was jailed for fraud and theft during the apartheid regime period, but 'the Truth and Reconciliation Commission cannot punish even a single White gangster, even if it finds him guilty of murders and other crimes against Blacks, during the apartheid era. Thus, while Winnie Mandela gets imprisoned on charges of fraud, the White racists can get away even with the killing of the famous South African radical leader Steven Biko. Biko's murderers, when brought before the Commission, confessed to the killing in all its gory detail. But when his family tried to institute a case against them, it was denied because if perpetrators of human rights abuses fully disclosed all the crimes that they had committed, they were granted amnesty. She describes this bitterly as a 'novel method indeed to bring about reconciliation between the oppressor and the oppressed – at the cost of justice.' Sumanta Banerjee's even more trenchant criticism is that neither the apartheid regime nor the vast socio-economic disparities were put to trial in the quest for truth. As a result, the leaders of the apartheid regime were never held accountable, and '95 per cent of the economy (continues to be) controlled by the same white settlers who created apartheid.' Data also show that 47.8 per cent of Blacks were unemployed in 2003 compared with only 9.9 per cent of Whites.[12]

The victims of apartheid were thus denied by the democratic leadership of new South Africa the right to bring their oppressors to legal justice. I observed in South Africa strong disagreement and dissatisfaction among many Black South Africans with Mandela's claim of collective forgiveness for the brutal crimes of the recent past. Forgiveness to be authentic and genuinely healing must be the voluntary, informed and empowered choice of the survivors, and cannot be forced on them. If it is, the wounds of apartheid will continue to fester.

This indeed has been the experience also of other amnesty legislation in other countries as well that 'legal forgetting'[13] which is politically imposed from above rankles the survivor and does not bring about any real closure for her, nor for the divided societies of which she is a part. To free offenders from the legal consequences of their actions amounts to trading away justice in return for a kind of unequal peace. This was also the experience of post-World War II amnesty laws passed in France and Holland for people who had collaborated with the Germans, and also in many Latin American countries in the 1980s.[14]

Besides, just truth-telling was explicitly required under the rules of the Truth and Reconciliation Commission for qualifying for amnesty, but no expression of remorse. The Commission also made recommendations for reparations for the victims. I have argued my view that for reconciliation to be authentic, it requires at least four components to be accomplished: acknowledgement, remorse, reparation and justice. The Truth and Reconciliation Commission most powerfully assured only one of these components, namely acknowledgement, and to some extent it organized reparation for some of the victims. The Truth and Reconciliation Commission certainly yielded a great deal of truth, and although it did not require remorse, Desmond Tutu who chaired the Commission, and Fazel Randera, one of the Commissioners whom I met in Johannesburg, affirmed that a great deal of genuine regret was spontaneously forthcoming from those who testified to often chilling crimes before the Commission. But the assurance of amnesty traded away – and many like me believe very cheaply – the requirements of legal justice, although others may persuasively argue that the larger ends of restorative justice were indeed achieved.

There can be little doubt that the statespersonship and magnanimity of the ANC leadership, embodied in the towering and charismatic personality of Nelson Mandela and unique humanitarian enterprises such as the Truth and Reconciliation Commission, helped avert runaway bloodletting of the kind that literally tore the Indian nation apart in 1947 (and subsequently the Pakistani nation in 1971). This in itself is an enormous historic achievement. The Truth and Reconciliation Commission hearings also helped the nation, and particularly its Black populations, to confront and to some degree come to terms with the savage oppression of the nightmarish apartheid decades. In the cathartic hearings of the Commission, frequently did Black survivors display the most extraordinary humanity in forgiving their tormentors. As Tutu repeatedly affirms, there is indeed no future without forgiveness.

However, in my short days in South Africa, I repeatedly encountered a country that remains very deeply fractured on racial and overlapping class lines, as well as gender, between Black African, coloured, Indian and White, men and women. Within these there are further divisions, of ethnic groups within the Blacks, the Indians, and Afrikaaner and British White people. The colour of one's skin remains in South Africa the overwhelming defining feature of one's identify, opportunities and social relations, although there is over the last decade a small but growing Black middle class who are seeking to escape the centuries-old confines of race. The incredibly luxurious suburbs are still populated almost exclusively by White people, whereas in the crowded and deprived shanties, it is rare to encounter anyone other than Black men and women, boys and girls. And within each and between each of these are chilling narratives of rape and sexual violence.

Fazel Randera, a Commissioner of the Truth and Reconciliation Commission, said to me, 'I do believe that building on the Truth and Reconciliation Commission process of staring truth in the eye and actively negotiating the society we wish to build, will help overcome many of the problems that not only we face but the world faces. Even class will eventually be peacefully negotiated away'. I am not persuaded. Inequality, racism, patriarchy and injustice will have to be fought constantly by people's resolute democratic (and I am convinced non-violent) struggles and state action. There are no painless short cuts to equality, equity or justice, not even truth, forgiveness and mercy, even though I deeply believe in all of these.

I am not prevailed upon by the premise of the Truth and Reconciliation Commission that acknowledgement and some reparation are enough for reconciliation to occur, without remorse or justice. Is legal justice intrinsically just retributive (seeking punishing of those who caused others harm), or is it equally or even more importantly an assertion of equal citizenship rights, is a question that we repeatedly return to in this volume. To my mind, reconciliation is a process of building or restoring between estranged members of different racial, ethnic or religious groups, mutual trust, understanding, respect and goodwill. It is necessarily egalitarian, and cannot be founded on a surrender of one's rights, dignity and aspirations from a position of weakness. True forgiveness requires a prior establishment of a situation of sufficient equality of power to enable persons who suffered *not* to forgive if they so choose, and for their choice to have consequences on those whom they elect not to forgive. For this reason, I believe that justice and remorse are both intrinsic to an authentic and enduring process of reconciliation.

I acknowledge that it is unfair to expect that the ravages of centuries of colonial rule and 50 years of legalized racism can disappear with one Commission and a decade and a half of democracy. It did prevent untold bloodshed and sectarian slaughter. But staggering economic and racial inequality persists. South Africa remains hopelessly divided on racial lines, with the privileges or deprivations of class mostly reinforcing those of race and gender. Oppression and injustice not only of the past, but also the present are engines of dangerous anger among young people, reflected in a murky sub-culture of brutalized street violence and crime.

I believe strongly that official or non-official efforts for reconciliation should never be even a well-intentioned apology for impunity for crimes, especially by the state authorities, and others who enjoy power. Legal accountability for atrocities and crimes, especially by authorities, paves the way for the possibilities of genuine reconciliation, although by itself it does not guarantee it. As Tina Rosenberg writes, 'if the victims in a society do not feel that their suffering has been acknowledged, then they ... are not ready to put the past behind them. If they know that the horrible crimes carried out in secret will always remain buried ... then they are not ready for reconciliation'.[15]

The paramount humanitarian and political challenge remains of finding a path that leads to authentic reconciliation between the Hindu and Muslim people of India – when they are estranged by violence or memory – but one that includes acknowledgement, remorse, reparation as well as justice. There are clearly no markers for us to follow.

There is no universal set of magic solutions that would apply equally to heal hurt, anger, betrayal and hostilities that have accumulated and been transmitted through generations in different societies and people. The content of reconciliation – as both process and goal – will inevitably vary in different cultural, historical and political contexts. The historical context of Hindu–Muslim conflicts in India is that these and other diverse communities lived together in relative peace through centuries, and it is largely after 1857 (when Hindu and Muslim soldiers, and kings and queens fought the colonial rulers unitedly shoulder to shoulder, and together chose the last Mughal ruler Bahadur Shah Zafar as the symbol of the insurrection against the British East India Company) that the rifts between the two communities were engineered at least in part as an element of colonial policy.

The responsibilities for preventing and controlling communal violence and ensuring reparation almost exclusively vest with the state. The duties for organizing processes of reconciliation are somewhat more broad-based: these obligations also vest primarily with the state, but people on both sides of the conflict and their own organizations also can contribute a great deal to both the success and the arrest of processes of reconciliation. The role of human rights and the social organizations committed to secular democracy and peace is optional, but if equipped with compatible values and skills, they can vastly facilitate the process.

The greatest hope is that among ordinary people in both communities, there are everyday lived ways of giving and receiving trust and respect. There is the courage and resilience of the survivors, and many acts of compassion by people of the majority community. In the daily lives of affected communities, as they struggle with the timeless challenges of finding food, work and dignity, hatred and fear are manufactured and sustained by organizations and the State, but also simultaneously these are resisted and overcome by ordinary people in the ways that they lead their lives. As Howard Zinn affirms, 'human history is not just a history of cruelty, but also of compassion, sacrifice, courage, kindness. What we choose to emphasise in this complex history will define our lives …' There are indeed the glimmerings of individual resistance, of courage and compassion, of love amid slaughter.

Notes

1. B. Rajeshwari, *Communal Riots in India: A Chronology* (1947–2003), IPCS Research Papers. Institute of Peace and Conflict Studies, New Delhi, 2004.
2. Though the respect for diversity and respect has been present from a long time, Amartya Sen in his seminal book, *The Argumentative Indian* (New Delhi: 2006) traces it for the from the time, in a coherent manner from Asoka's reign (3 B.C.) to the present times.
3. United Nations, Religionan Reconciliation Backgrounder, http://www.tcd.ie/ise//postgraduate/reconcileBACKGROUNDER.pdf
4. David Bloomfield and Teresa Barnes, eds., *Reconciliation After a Violent Conflict: A Handbook*, IDEA, Stockholm, 2003.
5. Stef Vandeginste, "Reparation" in *Reconciliation After a Violent Conflict: A Handbook*, eds. David Bloomfield and Teresa Barnes, IDEA, Stockholm, 2003, p. 145.
6. Luc Huyse, "The Process of Reconciliation" in *Reconciliation After a Violent Conflict: A Handbook*, eds. David Bloomfield and Teresa Barnes, IDEA, Stockholm, 2003, p. 25.

7. United Nations, Religionan Reconciliation Backgrounder, http:// www.tcd.ie/ise//postgraduate/reconcileBACKGROUNDER.pdf
8. Luc Huyse, op. cit.
9. Desmond M. Tutu, 'No Future Without Forgiveness' quoted in *Doubleday,* 1999.
10. David A. Crocker, *Retribution and Reconciliation* http://www.puaf.umd.edu/IPPP/Winter/Spring00/Retribution_and _Reconciliation.
11. Sumantha Banerjee *Reconciliation Without Justice.* http://www. epw.org.in/showArticles.php?root=2003&leaf=05&filename=5822&filetype=html
12. Gelb (2003: 4) quoted in http://www.odi.org.uk/rights/Publications/CurranPiron_PublicPolicy&Exclusion.pdf
13. Luc Huyse, op. cit.
14. Ibid.
15. Cited in *Reconciliation After a Violent Conflict: A Handbook,* eds. David Bloomfield and Teresa Barnes, IDEA, Stockholm, 2003.

11 Hinduized Globalization and Human Rights in Gujarat

Girish Patel

Human Rights in the 20th and 21st Centuries

If the 20th century was regarded as a century of the declaration of human rights, 21st century was heralded as the century of the realization of human rights. However, two trends have emerged on the world's arena. There is growing recognition of the need and importance of human rights both at the international and national levels. The international law of human rights has now found a distinct place, is fast growing and getting more enriched and entrenched. In spite of many attacks on the universality of human rights from different corners and on different ideological or socio-cultural specific grounds, the acceptance of the universal human rights as common standards of humanized state, civilized society and dignified life is increasing in every continent of the world. The oneness, integrality, indivisibility, inter-dependence and inalienability of political and civil rights and economic, social and cultural rights is now more and more acknowledged. Even at national levels, large number of states recognizes human rights, though with one or the other reservation, and many others at least pay hypocritical respect to them. No state openly denies the utility or importance of human rights.

And yet paradoxically, gross denial or violations of human rights are taking place both in the North and the South, in the name of national unity and integrity, reasons of the state, war on terror, economic development, social solidarity or cultural nationalism. After the catastrophic World War II, and particularly after learning about the worst crimes against humanity during the Nazi period, it was expected that the world would not dare to repeat the history, but these expectations were belied. Wars, civil conflicts, genocide, state and non-state terrorism, communal/religious/racial/national violence, hatred, intolerance and hostilities, and flagrant violation of human rights and civil liberties have remained endemic features of the post-World War II society. The first decade of the 21st century turned out to be even worse, marked by both war of terror and war on terror. Life is in danger, liberties are an illusion, fear and insecurity are on every human face and human beings have themselves become the most self-endangered species. India is no exception and Gujarat is the model of both legal and extra-legal excesses, abuses and atrocities in the wake of a novel phenomenon of a combination of militant Hindutva and ruthless globalization

India

The modern Constitution in India imbued with liberal and progressive values was intended to work in an old country with its poverty, backwardness, inequalities, castes and religions, illiteracy and starvation and tradition-bound culture, and aimed at transforming it into a modern, liberal, secular egalitarian, democratic and prosperous India. But the reverse has happened. The traditional socio-economic structure and age-old religious culture overpowered the constitutional system, and used and distorted it to serve and consolidate their vested interests. The three major goals of free India, namely, unity in diversity, poverty removal and economic, development and socio-economic cultural transformation, have undergone a metamorphosis. It was hoped that these three tasks will be undertaken simultaneously and with 'all deliberate speed', as they are interlinked and interdependent. However, these hopes were belied. For some time, the leaders of the freedom movement, understanding and recognizing the sensitive issue of unity and diversity, adopted the approach of mutual accommodation and adjustment among conflicting demands of national unity and regional identities, and operated the political system reasonably well, but soon thereafter, the politics of consensus, compromise, accommodation, mutual understanding and tolerance gave way to the politics of conflicts, confrontation and self-aggrandizement, intolerance and hatred, severely straining the federal system and generating various movements of dissensions, insurgency, secession and autonomy, as in J&K, Punjab, North-East tribal areas, Jharkhand, Telangana, etc. This, in reaction, created a feeling and demand for a strong united India –

centralized militarized and even brutalized – to suppress all such movements with a heavy hand, treating such movements as simply law and order or security problem. The craze of the privileged and dominant class for spectacular and fast economic development along the path of industrialization and westernization led them to emphasize upon growth, efficiency, productivity, maximum and rational exploitation of resources, economy, merits, competitiveness with the result that the rich became richer, resourceful acquired more resources, and poor and backwards became more and more marginalized, particularly the unorganized poor, Dalits, Adivasis. Regional imbalances and economic inequalities created islands of prosperity and the rise of strong ambitious and aggressive middle class in the mid of poverty, deprivation and destitution. Rapid economic development, particularly after 1990, meant rootless, ruthless and voiceless growth, and removal of poverty meant removal of the poor themselves as they are looked upon as obstacles in the path of development. Similarly, social and cultural transformation of the Indian society has been displaced by revivalist religious movements, strengthening of hierarchical structure, politicization of castes for power only and coming to the centre-stage of the militant Hindutva ideology, cultural nationalism, and 'one country, one nation, one culture,' in which all non-Hindus become second-class citizens. This perversion of the basic goals of independent India has created severe strains and stresses in the field of human rights, particularly of those who clamour for social justice, economic equality, democratic participation, cultural freedom, distinct identity and autonomy, rich quality of life for all and harmonious development not only for the present but also for the future. Even though the constitutional structure appears to be intact and people in the mainstream, particularly the resourceful and the powerful, continue to enjoy their freedoms and power, the scenario for human rights for all has changed and is facing very serious threats. The synthesis of Fundamental Rights (Part III) and Directive Principles (Part IV) is accepted as one of the basic, unamendable and indestructible features of our Constitution, but in reality, the accelerating erosion of the former and gross denial of the latter have become the permanent and almost inevitable feature of our society.

Gujarat

The model of development so far adopted and of late pursued vigorously, aggressively and ruthlessly has led to sharp contradictions and bitter conflicts in the society, economy and polity in Gujarat society. Considering the growing modern economy, on the one hand, and the stagnant traditional society, on the other Gujarat can rightly be described as one of the advanced states in India belonging to the poor and backwards (15% STs, 7% SCs, 39% OBCs and 11% Muslims plus women in general and poor of other communities). On the one hand, Gujarat ranks very high in terms of gross domestic product, industrialization, foreign and national investment and urbanization, and possessed one of the most aggressive and fairly resourceful middle class of businessmen and industrialists, professionals and bureaucrats, service class both in public and private sector and rich landed interests. We have heard about the projected and ongoing ₹ 1,00,000 crores worth of new industrial investments from domestic and foreign sources, expecting Gujarat to become 'a little Japan' of India. On the other hand, the rising poverty of the masses mostly backwards, galloping economic inequalities, growth of very rich islands, extravagant and conspicuous consumption on the US lifestyle pattern, gross regional imbalances, more entrenched and politicized stratification, rising unemployment, increasing slums and ghettos, acute water scarcity and heavy pollution and serious health problems are the dominant characteristics of Gujarat. In terms of birth and death rates, infant mortality and maternal mortality, women's education and health, child labour and high rate of dropouts in education and inequitable educational expansion, Gujarat's performance is ordinary, sometimes on par with or sometimes even lower than the national average. Uprooting and marginalization of tribals atrocities against Dalits, violence against women and communal and caste conflicts are the core of Gujarat society. High concentration of industries in certain golden and silver corridors, neglect of many areas and particularly the entire tribal belt are examples of uneven and unjust development. Increasing criminalization of politics and society growing communalization, self-aggrandisement, rat-race in economy, new cult of consumerism and commercialization of everything – from drinking water to women of life-organs – mark the emerging Gujarat. Money by any means, power at any cost and pleasure under all circumstances are the new values. Gujarat is already under all circumstances are the new values. Gujarat is already under the spell of the new economic policy driven by privatization, fast economic and industrial development even by authoritarian measures. With this mindset and lifestyle of the super-rich, rich and upper middle class, fortunate NRIs and increasing craze for America, Gujarat can very well be the 51st State of the USA. There is nothing surprising or shocking about these developments in Gujarat. Right form the beginning the core of Gujarat's society has been dominated socially by Brahmins, Banias/Jains and Patels, and economically by industrialists, traders, businessmen and rich peasantry. They have by and large remained highly conservative – not committed to social justice for the poor and disadvantaged, and under the powerful influence of communalism and casteism. Politically, the left and left of centre or progressive forces have never been strong enough, but only peripheral and marginal. The largely conservative Congress Party and its opposition first from the rightist Swatantra Party of Patels and upper-class Kshatriyas in the first party of the 60s and later on from the Hindu communal party (Jan Sangh and the Bharatiya Janata Party) have controlled Gujarat politics. Though the poor and the backward constitute more than 70 per cent of the Gujarat population, they have never been in the commanding position. An attempt was made after the split of the Congress party around 1969 under the leadership of Indira Gandhi to create an alliance of Kshatriyas, Harijans, Adivasis and Muslims (KHAM), it did not work as the alliance of the poor and the backward was not ideological, but only a vote-catching device. Ultimately, it broke down, inviting a backlash from the dominant castes (particularly the Patels) which retaliated by launching a very powerful anti-reservation agitation in the first part of the 80s. The social fabric was totally disrupted first by the caste-conflicts and then by the communal clashes between Hindus and Muslims. The casteist society became highly communalized also under the almost complete control of the majoritarian Hindu party – the BJP, VHP, BD and RSS. The development model first adopted and pursued by the conservative higher castes/classes and middle class dominated Congress party came to be adopted by the BJP which brought its anti-Muslim and anti-Christian Hindutva ideology into it. The Sangh Parivar let loose its Hindutva forces to strangulate the polity and society, culminating into attacks against Muslims in the name of national security vis-à-vis so-called anti-national Pakistani and pro-Pakistani forces, and against Christians in the name of forcible conversion of Dalits and Adivasis. It ultimately bared its true color in the genocide of the Muslims in 2002 under the reign of Narendra Modi. The present ruling ideology represents the most diabolical combination of Hindu communalism, one man's authoritarianism, ruthless globalized developmentalism, cultural nationalism and fascist programme. The successful alliance of Hindutva and globalization known as the model of 'Hinduized globalization', projected as the model for the whole of India, present very serious threats to the human rights, particularly of the poor and the weak, and human rights movement in Gujarat and in India.

Impact of Major Movements on Human Rights in Gujarat

Though human rights situation in Gujarat up to 1900 was more or less similar to the situation in the country as a whole, there were major movements which have specially impacted the human rights and democratic system in different and sometime opposite ways.

Maha Gujarat Movement

The Maha Gujarat Movement in 1956 for the separate state of Gujarat was the first major threat to the single-party dominant position of the Congress party, bringing the Socialist Party, Communist Party, Jan Sangh, many disgruntled Congress leaders and few independents, and had to face the brutal force of the state in excessive use of police power, and the Preventive Detention Act symbolized by the then Chief Minister Morarji Desai's reply to citizens, complaint against the indiscriminate police firing, killing many people 'bullets of the police are the only answer to the stones of the crowds.' It showed to the people of Gujarat that the state machinery of law and order has continued to remain colonial as it was before independence. It also sowed the seeds for the parochial demand for strong leadership in Gujarat to fight for Gujarat in the Centre, which after 48 years was seen to be mirrored in the rise of Narendra Modi after 2002.

In between the Maha Gujarat Movement (1956–60) and Nav Nirman Movement of 1947, the worst communal riots after 1941, but before 2002 flared up in Ahmedabad and Central Gujarat in 1969, killing more than 1000 people, injuring many more and damaging properties worth crores of rupees. This communal riot in which Muslim were at the receiving end was the product of traditional communal divide, the split in the Congress party, anti-Indira hysteria created in Gujarat, the rise of the right opposition and the aggressive assertion by the Hindu Majority. Though it was not state-sponsored, it did get support and encouragement from the Congress (O) Party in power, the administration and the police. This was the beginning of the politicized Hindu majoritarianism which ultimately culminated in Narendra Modi's programme of 2002.

Navnirman Movement

The Navnirman Movement of the professors, students and the middle class had a complex character. The politicization of higher education by Chimanbhai Patel during the 60s was alienating and enraging the students and professors, people's wrath against corruption, symbolized by the then Chief Minister Chimanbhai Patel, the worsening economic and the rising prices after the Bangladesh war of 1971, violent resentment among the conservative, reactionary and communal forces of the Gujarat society against Indira Gandhi who was denigrated as pro-Muslim and pro-Backwards, and the vested interests opposed to the 'Garibi Hatao' programme of Indira Gandhi. Congress all together was to a larger or smaller degree responsible for the movement marked by people's violence and more ruthless state violence. JP's movement for 'Total Revolution' as the inspirator of the Nav Nirman movement was a myth. The total impact of the movement was largely negative-delegitimation of the political institutions, strengthening of right forces, leading role of the RSS, ABVP and Jan Sangh in the second phase of the movement after the resignation of Chimanbhai Patel, many corrupt Nav Nirman leaders and the rise of some fascist tendencies in the civil society. Certainly it did not turn out to be a progressive and democratic movement.

Anti-Emergency Movement

The next was the traumatic experience of the national emergency declared by Smt Indira Gandhi on June 25, 1975. It saw the overthrowing of all democratic norms and erosion or outright denial or destruction of basic rights, Gujarat having an opposition party Congress (O) along with Chimanbhai Patel's new party was not ready and enthusiastic to apply and accept the Central Government's *fatwa* and dictates. Though large number of opposition leaders and others were detained under the preventive detention law and all kinds of restrictions, including pre-censorship on fundamental, political and civil rights were imposed, the impact of emergency in Gujarat was not harsh and brutal. Under a sympathetic government, a very powerful and broad-based resistance movement was launched. It was in a sense, a mass movement against emergency, destruction of democracy and suppression of basic civil liberties. The people of all views and ideologies from the left to the liberals came together under Jay Prakash-led 'Citizens for Democracy' platform. All India organization known as People's Union for Civil Liberties (PUCL) was very active and resisted the Emergency measures. The Gujarat High Court also showed its real independence and authority by declaring the pre-censorship of a Gandhian biweekly 'Bhoomi Putra' as unconstitutional and also by setting aside the vindictive transfer of Justice S.H. Sheth of Gujarat High Court to Andhra Pradesh on the grounds that it was arbitrary and malafide. This anti-emergency movement proved to be significant in many respects:

(a) It showed the importance of the federal structure as a bulwark against national domination and national repression, proving that federalism is not simply a matter of structure organization of a polity, but provides a safeguard against centralized authoritarianism and a space for democratic movement insulated form central attacks.

(b) Struggle for human rights is also a political struggle, seeking to challenge and change the practices and policies of the state. Any attempt to depoliticize it is bound to fail.

(c) Foreign-funded NGOs cannot generally fit such political democratic movement.

(d) Human rights movement must go to the civil society beyond the established political parties and must be people's movement.

(e) The anti-emergency movement in Gujarat was, unfortunately dominated mainly by conservative forces of the Congress (O) and the Jan Sangh–RSS was more worried about purely civil liberties of the middle class without bothering much for the poor and disadvantaged masses. Another very unfortunate consequence having long-term impact was the legitimization of the Sangh Parivar and its entry into the political mainstream. These Hindutva forces ultimately overshadowed the Congress (O) and Chimanbhai's party.

(f) The repression of the workers and plight of the poor, particularly during the second year of the emergency after the rise of Sanjay Gandhi made all leftists realize that democratic rights and civil liberties are more important for the poor and the weak than for the rich and the powerful, and the former cannot carry on any struggle for socio-economic rights without basic civil liberties. This led us to organize our own human rights organization called 'Lok Adhikar Sangh' to fight both legally and politically for the poor and disadvantaged in Gujarat. Emergency of 1975–77 suspending all democratic norms and principles, and converting the federal state into a highly centralized state using (abusing) all constitutional provisions for taking all authoritarian and repressive measures also proved to be a blessing in disguise. It awakened large sections of the civil society of the dangers of constitutional dictatorship of one person or party and of the need for eternal vigilance for defending the hard-won democratic rights and civil liberties. The post-emergency Janata government also showed that the political parties have not learnt the lessons of the emergency and cannot be relied upon for the protection of the Constitution. Its main contribution was the emergence of a strong nation-wide human rights movement.

Anti-Reservation Agitation

The fourth movement namely the anti-reservation agitation in 1981 was totally a reactionary and regressive movement frontally against the very core of the Indian Constitution. It was in a way the rise of the higher, upper and middle class against the emergence of the backward classes, known as the 'KHAM' (Kshatriyas, Harijans, Adivasis and Muslims) theory of the Congress-I Chief Minister, Madhavsingh Solanki who came to power after the fall of the Janata Party government in Delhi and also in Gujarat. The immediate cause was the enhancement of reservation quota of the other backward classes, called Baxi Commission communities from 10 per cent to 27 per cent, in addition to 15 per cent for STs and 7 per cent for both in education and in public employment. The agitation led mainly by the Patels – the rising dominant castes in Gujarat – particularly in Ahmedabad, North Gujarat and Central Gujarat – turned out to be a very violent and militant attack against the Dalits, Adivasis and other backward classes. The resistance from the latter was not very strong and well-organized. The middle classes from both the Congress and the BJP took leading part. It ultimately led to the resignation of Madhavsingh Solanki and replacement by a Tribal leader Amarsingh Chaudhary – a very weak leader who made all sorts of compromises with the agitating people. This half-hearted experiment of bringing together all backward classes and communities purely out of electoral considerations was bound to fail in the absence of any higher uniting ideological framework. The upward class backlash had disastrous consequences for the struggle for human rights and dignity of the different communities constituting the backward classes/communities including Muslims. On one hand, the Sangh Parivar became more entrenched among the higher/upper and middle classes/castes, particularly Patels. On the other hand, the Hindutva forces realized that the movement will completely alienate the Hindu backward communities. Around 1985, the anti-reservation agitation took a communal turn. This was beneficial to the Hindutva forces which took full advantage of the communal divide to communalize the backward Hindu communities and to alienate the Muslims. Thus started the worst phase of Gujarat politics and society. The Congress party with its adoption of the New Economic Policy and half-hearted secular commitment lost its ground leaving the field open for BJP. The backward communities, instead of being radicalized, came to be sanskritized and politically uplifted by the BJP. The civil society was communalized and polarized, and the higher/upper classes/castes used the backward communities as their fighting squad against Muslims. The Hindutva laboratory materialized into a fully saffronized society. The human rights movement worked for a casteless and secular society with human rights for all, but what we found in Gujarat was the intensified casteism and communalism of the Hindu communities, the Muslims being the worst victims.

The anti-reservation movement did not generate a powerful social justice movement among the backward classes. The Dalits in Gujarat did not come under the influence of Dr Ambedkar and remained passive under the Gandhian influence, the Adivasis saw many scattered resistance movements, but never became radicalized mainly as a result of the influence of the Gandhi's followers, working through Ashrams and also because of the absence of any powerful left movement. The other backward communities forming about 40 per cent of Gujarat's population were highly fragmented into innumerable social/occupational castes/communities ranging from the nomadic/denotified communities to few economically/occupationally entrenched communities. There was never any unifying factor or force among them and they were never Mandalized, like their brethren in UP and Bihar. As a result, they came to be coopted by the Hindutva ideology of the Sangh Parivar as militant appendages of the Hinduized upper/higher/intermediate castes/communities. Thus, the anti-reservation movement of 1981 merged into a much more diabolic movement of the rabid Hindutva forces, combining politics of the BJP, religion of the VHP, cultural nationalism of the RSS and goondaism of the Bajrang Dal. This was nothing but the rise of Hindu fascism in Gujarat reaching its nadir under the authoritarian Chief Minister Narendra Modi from 2001. The Hindu laboratory of Gujarat became virtually a 'Hindu nation' with its latent entrenched varna vyavastha and open anti-Muslim *jihad.*

Movement Against Narmada Bachao Andolan

Along with the slow rise of the Hindutva movement in the 1980s, another very significant storm was rising in the horizon around the Sardar Sarovar Project on the Narmada river. It began first as a simple question of building a dam on the biggest river of Gujarat to solve the water problem, particularly of Saurashta, Kutch and North Gujarat – the major draught-prone areas and as Narmada was a major inter-state river passing through three states, namely, MP, Maharashtra and Gujarat, it took the form of a serious inter-state river dispute, mainly centring around the respective shares of the three states and the height of the Sardar Sarovar dam in Gujarat. It was this issue which ultimately culminated into a major development question for the people of Gujarat themselves, namely, development for whose benefits and at what costs and in what manner. This later on provided fodder to Narendra Modi's

Hinduized globalization *jihad* against the poor and the minorities. The dream of bringing Narmada water to the water-thirsty area of Kutch and north Gujarat was shown to the people of Gujarat long back by Bhaikaka-Bhailalahai Patel, the Chief Engineer of the Sakkar barrage on the Sindhu river before India's Partition in 1947 and every school child was brought up with this dream. After independence and particularly after the formation of the Gujarat state in 1960, it turned into an inter-state conflict. After the failure of many attempts for finding a solution, it was referred to the Inter-State Water Dispute Tribunal in 1967 under the Inter-State Water Disputes Act of 1955.

Till 1979 when the Narmada Award was given by the Tribunal, it remained a regional problem in which people were not very much involved. After the award, real difficulties appeared, particularly various studies required to be undertaken, the problem of the large number of people mostly tribals to be displaced and their rehabilitation, environment problems and the involvement of the World Bank financing the project. For the first time, the project-affected people of Gujarat, Maharashtra and MP started organizing themselves around 1982 onward, giving birth to the Narmada Bachao Andolan (NBA) led by Medha Patkar. The NBA first raised the question of displacement of lakhs of families and their resettlement and rehabilitation, about which no plans were prepared and no information was given to the people. Along with this, several issues came up such as environmental impact, financial burden on Gujarat, costs-benefit analysis, non-participatory decision-making process, total non-transparency, etc. All these forced the NBA to take up the NO DAM stand, asking for the complete review of the Narmada Award. This people's movement disturbed and angered the ruling classes and major beneficiaries of the Project – big landholders, industrialists, contractors, middle class. They started the campaign against the NBA and critics of the project, branding them as anti-development, anti-Gujarat and anti-nationals. The then Chief Minister Chimanbhai Patel, all major political parties, the sectarian groups and other vested-interests created a mass frenzy against the NBA, mainly targeting Medha Patkar, adopting all fascist methods, namely attacking the opponents and critics, banning or disturbing their public meeting, prohibiting all independent debates or discussions, instigating people and mis-information campaign, as if it were a war declared by the state against the invaders of NBA from Maharashtra and MP. All civil liberties and democratic rights of the victims of the so-called development project and their supporters were suppressed and even the basic right of the people of Gujarat to know and to be informed about the costs and benefits of the project was totally denied.

This went parallel to the Saffronization movement of the Hindutva forces. It combined both the forces of communalism and developmentalism under the leadership of the BJP leading to the present day Narendra Modi's model of Hinduized globalization. It proved economic incentives to the religious forces and ideology to the shallow materialistic globalized capitalist model.

Saffronization (Hindutva) Movement

As we have seen earlier, the freedom movement in Gujarat was essentially a nationalist movement under the conservative Congress party and largely a Hindu middle-class movement with Muslim league in opposition and RSS foothold in the urban areas of the north and central Gujarat, dominated by powerful land-holding Patels. For Gujarat, Gandhi having left Gujarat in 1930, Sardar Patel was accepted as the leader and not Pandit Jawaharlal. It was natural that in the light of the history of Gujarat under Hindu, Rajput, Muslim, Mughal, Maratha dynasties, largely urbanized Muslim minority organized under the Muslim League, Hindu–Muslim riots at frequent intervals, and absence of strong left or radical movement among the Dalits, Adivasis and backward classes, the Gujarat society was potentially a fertile ground for the rise of Hindu communalism. The 1941 communal riots, followed by a number of such riots in Ahmedabad and elsewhere, just before independence had a serious impact upon the relations between the major Hindu and Muslim communities. For some period, it remained free from such tension, but with the weakening of the Congress after the exit of Sardar Patel in 1950 and Nehru in 1963, and challenge by more reactionary forces and particularly after the split of the Congress party into Morarji Desai's Congress (O) and Indira Gandhi's Congress (I), the situation worsened, finally leading to the worst communal riots in 1969, in which Muslims were mainly at the receiving end. Though the Congress (O) government under the leadership of Hitendra Desai was not directly involved in anti-Muslim campaign. The urban Hindu middle class turned to be very hostile and highly communalized. The failure of the government and its machinery was clearly brought out in the Jagannath Reddy's Commission Report. With the Nav Nirman Movement of 1974 against Congress (I) Chief Minister Chimanbhai Patel's government, the anti-emergency movement of 1975–77, the anti-reservation agitation in 1981–84 and the emergence of Vishwa Hindu Parishad (VHP) around 1980, and the conversion of the anti-reservation agitation into anti-Muslim riots in 1985, the Hindutva forces started gaining greater and greater strength. The BJP won overwhelmingly in the Ahmedabad Municipal

Corporation elections with all Hindu candidates, embolding the Hindutva forces to use Gujarat as Hindutva laboratory. The BJP first formed a government with Chimanbhai KMPP, and after 1996 it has continued to win absolute majority in the Assembly elections. During this period upto 2002, the BJP under the leadership of Keshubhai Patel tried to implement its Hindutva agenda such as performance of Puja in all government hospitals on Dusshera, compulsory singing of Vande Matram in all schools, two unsuccessful attempts to rename Ahmedabad as Karnavati, permission to government employees to join RSS, rewriting of the textbooks for schools, appointment of Sangh Parivar members or supporters as Vice-Chancellors of the universities, discrimination against Muslims in appointments, persecution of the Christian Missionaries in tribal areas, etc. With the cooption of the Dalits and Adivasis in the name of Ram temple in Ayodhya and the post-Babri Masjid riots, the communal divide between the Hindus and Muslims was intensified and the Sangh Parivar succeeded to a substantial extent in communalizing the polity and civil society of Gujarat. However, the wave of communalization of the Gujarat polity and society could not completely suppress common people's demands for the resolution of their day-to-day socio-economic and political problems. At the fag end of the 20th century, these problems again erupted particularly in the rural areas and the BJP Government under the old leadership of Keshubhai Patel had no answer to their problems and again showed its inaptitude and incompetence in dealing with the challenges thrown up suddenly by the massive earthquake in Kutch and other areas of Gujarat in January 2001. The BJP was losing its popular base in the panchayat elections and even in some by-elections to the Legislative Assembly leading to cry for change of leadership. Ultimately, the BJP national leadership had to give in and send Narendra Modi, a staunch Hindutva soldier, to head the government in Gujarat by the end of 2001. In the beginning, he also faced the same problem of erosion of people's support. But suddenly, the Godhra tragedy occurred on February 26, 2002, in which 56 Hindu Kar Sevaks died of burns during the commotion between the Kar Sevaks coming back to Gujarat from Ayodhya and the agitated Muslims on the Godhra station. Even today, i.e., after eight years and after the Nanavati Commission's first report, the Godhra tragedy still remains a mystery – was it an accident or unplanned commotion on the station or a pre-planned conspiracy by the Godhra Muslims? Whatever it may be, it proved to be a big gift for Modi who seized the opportunity and allowed it, either by design or by omission, to develop into a big massacre of the Muslims in large parts of Gujarat as if it were a 'genocide pogrom'.

Modi overnight became 'Defender of the Hindu Faith' and a Loh Purush who alone can protect and defend the interests of the Hindus in Gujarat. Thus started what is known as Modi's model of governance. He fully exploited the Godhra tragedy by terrorizing and demoralizing the Muslim minority and by frightening and creating a sense of insecurity among the Hindu majority, in the name of 'The sole spokesman of five crore Gujaratis'. His 'Pogrom' was far more effective and sophisticated than of Hitler, consisting of use and abusing of law and Constitution, with the support of the NDA government in New Delhi. Once he consolidated his supremacy both in the BJP and among the Hindu upper, middle and lower-middle classes, he stopped talking of or even mentioning the communal holocaust, as if such an incident had never occurred and turned his attention to what he called 'Vibrant Gujarat' with the ambition of making Gujarat a mini-Japan, to the delight and applaud of the fastest growing middle class in Gujarat. The almost simultaneous rise of the Hindutva movement and globalized capitalist free market ideology turned into two powerful weapons in the hands of megalomaniac Modi to establish himself as both Hindu Samrat and Vikas Purush. At present, Modi is an unchallenged leader of Gujarat with his big circuses, Tamashas, festivals, summits and personal publicity as if he alone counts in Gujarat. The Hindu sects, communal upper/middle class, the NGOs and big industrialists idolize Modi as the supreme leader not only for Gujarat but also for future India. This is Modi's model of development – 'Hinduized globalization', which at one stroke challenges all the values, ideals, principals and institutions of our Constitution, converting 'We, the People of Gujarat' into 'Your Majesty's most Faithful Subjects.'

Human Rights in Gujarat

The history and status of human rights in Gujarat is largely determined by the major movements discussed above. Each has left deep and long-term impact upon one or more of the basic rights guaranteed by the Constitution. Apparently, the constitutional system seems to be working. Elections are regularly held, legislatures are working, the government functions, the administration and police are discharging their duties, civil liberties of Part III of the Constitution are continued to be enjoyed by the established sectors of the people who have either money or power or clout with the ruling elites; those who suffer but do not protest go on living their miserable lives; courts are working, big circuses, festivals, entertainment shows, hotels, multiplex theatres and big malls are prospering. Otherwise also Gujarat from the earlier days was and has remained a reasonably well-governed state and economically also an advanced state. Nowadays, Modi's government is on a gigantic and expensive self-publicity campaign about what Modi boasts 'Vibrant Gujarat' mesmerizing the higher/middle classes.

But all these are formal and peripheral, concealing the harsh and pathetic reality. The constitutional institutions and human rights have suffered big erosion, leaving behind only a skeleton. Modi uses the entire government machinery and public money to project one side of Gujarat as Number 1 State in India, the model of development for the entire nation, pushing back more than 60 per cent of the population of Gujarat as invisible and voiceless humanity. Let us also project against Modi's Vibrant Gujarat, the other Gujarat – the real Gujarat hidden behind the glitz and glamour of globalization.

Democratic Rights and Basic Institutions of the Constitution

(a) The Constitution establishes a democratic republic, guaranteeing equal participation of all citizens in all political institutions without any discrimination and aims to secure an all-inclusive polity. Under the BJP's rule after 1985, this basic feature of the Constitution is undermined by denying any political space to the Muslims constituting more than 11 per cent of Gujarat people. According to the Hindutva ideology, only Hindus constitute the nation and all others: Muslims, Christians, etc., are not part of the nation and have to live in India on sufferance as only second-class citizens. The BJP implemented this ideology by putting up only Hindu candidates in local elections and in assembly and parliamentary elections. Through aggressive majoritarian communalism, the Hindutva forces succeeded in marginalizing the Muslims, as the Muslims do not have any constituency where they have a majority. With no Muslim candidates by the BJP, and hardly any Muslim candidates by the Congress on the grounds of winnability in a communally decided society, the political participation of the Muslims in almost all representative institutions has been rendered nil or very insignificant. It means that the Muslims will have no voices in the Gujarat polity. In Modi's Gujarat, the Muslims are not even second-class citizens, allowed to live on the goodwill of the Hindus.

(b) One of the major pillars of democracy is adult franchise, free and fair elections, and freedom of choice, participation and representation. After the 73rd and 74th Constitutional Amendments in 1992, the panchayats, municipalities and municipal corporations have been given constitutional basis and status, after mandatory provisions for all state legislatures to be included in their legislations, namely regular elections, representations to SCs, STs, OBCs and women, five years term, adult franchise, free and fair elections, election commission, finance commission, etc. Thus, we have now constitutionally guaranteed a four-tier government, namely, panchayats/municipalities, district Panchayats, states, Union of India. They are now no longer merely local authorities with municipal function, but important agencies of development, with Gandhiji's ideal of 'Development from Below'. The BJP Government has tried to undermine this basic principal of democratic decentralization first by introducing 'Samras Yojana' and then 'compulsory voting'. Both these measures show what little respect the BJP governments have towards freedom of vote and to contest?

Samras Yojana: The Government of Gujarat introduced by government resolution January 29, 2001, a Samras Yojana for ensuring 'unanimous' election to Gram Panchayats by offering financial incentives of ₹ 60,000 for villages having less than 5000 population and ₹ 1,00,000 for villages having more than 5000 population. This scheme was strengthened by another government resolution of November 7, 2006 by increasing the amount of financial incentives – ₹ 1,00,000 for villages having 5000 population and ₹ 1,50,000 for bigger villages, and ₹ 1,25,000 and ₹ 1,87,000 for villages having unanimous election second time. It also ensures priority in development is to ensure free and fair elections to panchayats, not to avoid or eliminate elections together. The scheme directly attacks the democratization process at the grass-root level. The government imposes a duty upon all officers to propagate the scheme and to secure as many Samras villages as possible. It also enumerates the disadvantages of not following the scheme, namely, less respect for such villages, ineligibility for Tirth Gram Yojana, government officers hostility, etc. The underlying idea of destroying and discouraging elections as an evil and productive of disharmony, conflicts and bitterness is very dangerous, as if directly attacks the very basis of democracy. A survey 'Sumras and Democratization Process' by Persis Ginwll in 2008 points out that the entire Sumras process is non-representative and non-participatory and a close-door process, entrenching the feudal, upper caste and patriarchal system, highly discriminatory, impose consensus and debunking, and suppressing any dissent in public discourse. It is nothing but corrupt practice by the government and encroachment upon the independent election commission for the Panchayats. Moreover, it meets the needs of neo-liberalism, namely, control of natural and community resources and accusation of lands, independent Panchayats will be an obstacle to it. It wants pliable panchayats to ensure faster and unquestioned decision in favour of projects, secrecy and easy control of resources. It takes away the right of subaltern communities to development of their choice. This suits Modi's 'development model' – authoritarian and 'consersual'.

Compulsory Voting: The Modi government recently enacted law for compulsory voting in local elections, hurriedly passed without any deliberation or discussion. This was purely personal and for political purposes – taking credit for being the first in India to secure 100 per cent democracy. Right to vote is a constitutional right of a citizen flowing from the democratic right of political participation, and cannot be converted into a mandatory legal duty with a threat that if you do not vote, you will have to suffer serious consequences. Modi has no power to snatch away the political power of the political sovereign, namely, 'We the People of India'. Moreover, it shows the usual indifference of the ruling elites to the hardships of the rural labour who have migrated for livelihood, as they will have to explain why they could not vote, leading to harassment and illegal demands of the government and Panchayat officers. It absolves the political parties of their political responsibility to educate the people in democracy. Who are you to compel the people to accept the legitimacy of the system which has failed?

The Samras bribes the citizens to spurn the elections, the compulsory voting forces the citizens to vote, both rendering political parties redundant – 'ideal party-less democracy', in which Modi will be the only politician. This is what Modi and the corporate world would want – irrelevance of the political parties and depoliticizing the governance to be left to experts, advisors, technocrats, managers and entrepreneurs. The Samras Yojana and compulsory voting are the beginning. It is in villages where the people will fight for national resources so desperately wanted by the corporate world. The Samras will ensure so-called 'wise peoples' council which can easily be coopted.

(c) Modi's authoritarian style of governance has destroyed the cabinet system of government – one of the basic features of our Constitution. He alone takes all decisions, and does not care whether the ministers approve or disapprove. Ministers are only show-pieces – his Majesty's most faithful servants. Decision to welcome and allot land to Tata's Nano project was his alone, even without the ministers' knowledge. His government is not even presidential, but simply monarchical.

(d) Similarly, the state legislature has become completely dysfunctional. It is summoned only to comply with the constitutional requirement of the assembly meeting within six months. Its sessions are shorter and shorter only to transact minimum official business, questions put by BJP's MLA's are given to them in advance, bills are passed hurriedly and without any meaningful debate. It has stopped representing the people. Instead, it has become the mouth-piece of Modi. Thus, another basic feature of the Constitution, the parliamentary system of government, has been set at naught.

(e) Narendra Modi has completely depoliticized the governance of the state. Appointments to all public sector undertakings, boards, committees, commissions, etc., are all from bureaucrats, and not even from his party members or MLAs as was the practice earlier. He wants completely subservient officials to toe his line and would not tolerate any other interference. The entire administration is no longer government's administration but Modi's establishment to do his biddings. The police has been totally subordinated to his whims and caprices and is there only to carry out his orders, legal or illegal. For him, even development is purely part of good governance, not self-governance. Recently during the celebrations of the 50th anniversary of Gujarat, the Chief Minister of Haryana commented that this appears to be CM's 50th birthday, not Gujarat's. All these actions on the part of Modi aim at one thing, namely, every political or socio-economic issue should be reduced to question of 'good governance', to be taken care of by Modi and his corporate colleagues. Every political element must be removed form all these issues vitally affecting the people. Modi wants clear road and no interference from any corner. Therefore, he talks of 'good governance', never self-governance. Multidimensional development issues involving conflicting perceptions, priorities and conflicts must not be allowed to take any political colour. They are for him, Chief Executive Offices and his experts, technocrats and advisors. Thus, people whose very future is at stake are only objects of policy, not subjects of policy. This is the most dangerous consequence of Modi's style of governance.

All constitutional institutions have been defined or ridiculed. The National Human Rights Commission was not welcome, and was branded as anti-Gujarat. He abused Lyndl, the Chairman of the Election Commission and even mimicked him in public meetings. He has used the Enquiry Commission for his political purposes, and has seen that the reports, interim or any other, are declared to suit his personal interests.

Civil Liberties – State Terrorism

In the mid of fears of disintegration and balkanization, the framers of the Constitution aimed at the maintaining and strengthening of India's unity and integrity and established a quasi-federal state with strong centralizing tendencies. The nation-building process out of the multitudes of diversities and myriads of loyalties is a very formidable task. We really wanted a truly federal nation, free, equal and vibrating states creating unity and strength from diversity and cooperation. But we moved in the other direction. We have succeeded so far in maintaining a united India, but in the process we have generated two contradictory tendencies. On the one hand, the defence requirements and developmental imperative demanded more concentration of power in the centre and greater integration and centralization of resources. On the other hand, our failures and failings have created various insurgent, secessionist and terrorist movements or movements for greater autonomy, which in turn evoked powerful demands for a strong, unitary, militarized state. The increasing belligerency between India and Pakistan, the Chinese aggression in 1962 and the international situation have compelled India to build up and maintain a larger strong and modern army and now nuclear weapons involving huge expenditure on defence. The failures on the social and economic fronts have created large number of people's movements and struggles increasing more and more the state's dependence upon the military and police forces to deal with what the rulers describe 'law and order' problems. The increasing urbanization and industrialization and the new religion of profit-making and rat race for material, prosperity and loosening of the traditional ties have created grave problems of criminal activities, anti-social offences and economic crimes, increasingly criminalizing society, economy and polity, and inviting ruthless police actions. All these have led to state terrorism, police brutalization and governments' lawlessness, a direct threat to people's elemental rights to life, liberty and security, which have appeared in diverse forms.

Increasing Use of Preventive Detention Laws

It is Article 22 of the Constitution which, right from the beginning, has conferred a constitutional legitimacy and status upon the preventive detention laws which the Centre and the States may enact on various grounds, such as unity, integrity and sovereignty of India, national security, public order, maintenance of essential supplies, etc. Such preventive detention laws both by the Centre and the states have continued to remain on the statute book throughout this period. These laws empower the executive up to the level of the District Magistrate to detain any person on the basis of his or her subjective satisfaction that such person's detention is necessary for national security, public order, etc., this is only 'a suspicion' jurisdiction, without regular trials and without any proof of guilt. Though some procedural safeguards such as furnishing grounds of detention, opportunity to represent, consideration of his case by the Advisory Board consisting of serving or retired High Court judges, maximum limit of detention, etc., have been provided by the Constitution itself, nothing can challenge the 'subjective satisfaction' of the detaining authority. The higher judiciary has upheld their constitutional validity. As a result, such laws have been abused for political purposes or for improper considerations, such as business rivalry, personal vendetta, etc. Though the higher judiciary has evolved certain grounds for challenging the detention, such grounds are on the periphery, and cannot probe into the truth or otherwise of the grounds of detention. Thus, limited scope of judicial review, technical nature of the grounds for quashing the detention order, the number of cases pending in the High Courts and the extreme delay in disposal of cases have successfully served the main purpose of keeping the detenue in jail without any guilt and any regular trial for a long period within the statutorily fixed term, and even for a longer period if another order is passed. The two major central laws, namely the National Security Act, 1980 and the COFEPOSA (...) cover the political/security grounds and national economic grounds. The first is easily abused for suppressing any voice of dissent or protest and particularly for sending behind jail political activists who are organizing the poor and the downtrodden such as Dalits or tribals, e.g., the use of NSA against two activists of Dang tribals Gujarat. Their only crime was that they organized the tribals of the poorest district of Gujarat against the collusive atrocities and tortures by police and forest officials. There release could be secure only after eight months. The second type of such laws, such anti-smuggling laws cover economic offences affecting the national economy. On the one hand, these economic offences do not carry the usual social stigma or patriotic condemnation; on the other hand, the laws are manipulated by the executives/politicians and by trade and industry. One can easily find the difference in attitudes and approaches of those in power towards the two classes of detenues – one fighting for the poor or political purposes, the other working against national economy.

Similarly, various states have enacted more or less drastic preventive detention law either for public order or essential supplies. For example, the state of Gujarat has enacted the Prevention of Anti-Social Activities Act (PASA) for detaining land grabbers, food adulterers, drug peddlers, liquor-den runners and dangerous persons who are habitually engaged in certain classes of offences. The law has been extensively abused for all kinds of purposes, public or private. Money passes both ways for securing release also. The safeguards have no meaning. The Advisory Board consisting of retired High Court judges are found to be more executive minded than the executive itself. The High Court cannot dispose of such cases for long. Thus, for hundreds of people to remain in jail for some time has become a routine. People are detained even when regular offences are registered and they are released on bail or capable of being released on bail, on the ground that these provisions are not sufficient to prevent them from committing offences. Thus, all detention laws particularly the State laws have almost become parallel criminal law without any normal safeguards. They have become such a permeant feature of the India social system that people say that the on real fundamental right guaranteed to and enjoyed by the people is the right to preventive detention. In addition to those, the police has been invoking the provisions of ordinary criminal law for temporary detaining of persons, such as Section 144 and Section 151 of the criminal procedure and Section 68 and Section 69 of the Bombay Police Act. Under Section 151, a police officer knowing of a design to commit any cognizable office may arrest, without orders form the magistrate and without warrant, the person so designing if it appears to such offices that the commission of the offence cannot be otherwise prevented and such a person can be detained for a period not exceeding 24 hours unless his further detention is required or authorized under other law. Day in and day out, the common people continue to suffer at least 24 hours detention. This is a much abuse provision invoked by the police to threaten deter or terrorize people who plan some agitation or priest. Similarly, the police can issue temporary orders under Section 68 and Section 69 of the Bombay police act to the same effect. Prohibitory orders under Section 144 are also often invoked whether the law and order machinery apprehends some movement or protest or struggle by the people. When more than 10,000 people marched to the site of Sardar Sarovar dam on the Narmada river in Gujarat, they were stopped by the police, taken to Rajpipla, 15 km away and detained in the open compound and were asked to go back to their villages at night. When people asked the police whether they were arrested or detained, no satisfactory reply was forthcoming. Finally, they were told that they were detained under Section 68 of the Bombay police act. Nothing was on record. In such cases, the people under police orders had to suffer much, particularly in respect of food and transportation facilities. The more drastic detention laws constitutionally legitimized and ordinary detention orders authorized by ordinary criminal law constitute a normal, recurrent and gross violation of the right to life and personal liberty of the common people particularly those who fight for the poor and thus constitute a serious threat to the democratic rights of the struggling masses.

Anti-Terrorist Acts and Other Repressive Laws

The tribals' insurgency in North-East tribal areas, the secessionist and autonomy movements in Jammu & Kashmir, and terrorist activities by Khalistani organizations in Punjab have led the government to enact anti-democratic, repressive laws conferring almost unbridled powers to the army and the police, such as the Assam Disturbed Areas Act, 1955, the Armed Forces (Assam and Manipur) Special Powers Act, 1958, the Punjab Disturbed Areas Act, 1983, the Armed Forces (Punjab and Chandigarh) Special Powers Act, 1984, etc. The state of Jammu & Kashmir has been practically handed over to the army. Regarding the widespread use and abuse of such laws, the people's union for democratic rights in its report on Nagaland, Mizoram and Manipur observes, 'one cannot remain insensitive to persistent reports of sexual torture, cold blooded murder, the burning of villages and the persecution of whole communities.' This use of the armed forces by the state against its own citizens is not good either for the armed forces or for the people. This is exceptionally so because intervention by the armed forces in the region, to mediate the conflict and maintain public order, is not a brief or temporary intervention directed to the handling of an extraordinary situation. The armed forces have been camping in some parts of the North-East for the past quarter century, to the extent of having become permanent fixtures of social life. About Punjab, the report says, 'the information collected points to widespread use of torture, fabrication of evidence, severe harassment of families of which male members are missing, absconding, mindless and arbitrary use of laws often either to settle personal scores or to teach a lesson to anyone who dares to voice any protest against anti-democratic laws and procedures'. In Jammu & Kashmir, the situation is worst. It is nothing but naked state terrorism against Kashmiri militants terrorism, and the common people are the worst sufferers.

The worst draconian law was the Terrorists and Disruptive Activities (Prevention) Act, 1984 (know as TADA) which was on the statue book till recently and which is likely to be re-enacted with great stringency at any time now. It was the flagrant violation of the various provisions of the international covenant on political and civil rights (1966) to which India is a signatory. The terrorist and disruptive activities were so loosely and broadly defined as to cover all normal criminal offences, added with specific intention or knowledge (means rea). Normal right to bail is taken away with the result that once a person is accused under TADA, he will remain in jail till the conclusion of the trial which will normally take a long time. Confessions before police officers are admitted as evidence and normal safeguards of procedural criminal law and though the Supreme Court observed that the act is a draconian law to be used only when the use of ordinary criminal law is totally ineffective, the act has been widely and extensively abused. Even though Gujarat was a non-terrorist state, largest number of TADA prisoners were in Gujarat with 17,546 as against terror affected Punjab with 14,457. Same was the case with POTA. Thousands of persons – suspected and innocent were arrested. It was the most astonishing fact that the state of Gujarat where there was no terrorism or terrorist activity stood first in the maximum number of persons arrested under TADA. It was used even for labour disputes between landlords and tenants. The success ratio of the use of TADA resulting in the conviction of the accused is less than 5 per cent (the Delhi PUDR Report). The real purpose of the Act is to put a person in jail for long without bail. In many cases, the death penalty is the mandatory punishment upon conviction. In Gujarat, administration of the act has been highly communalized mainly used against Muslims. It was shocking that the Supreme Court upheld its constitutional validity, in spite of its observations. 'It is true that on many occasions, we have come across cases wherein the prosecution unjustifiably invokes the provisions of the TADA which an oblique motive of depriving the accused persons form getting bail and in some occasions when the Courts are inclined to grant bail in cases under ordinary criminal laws, the investigating officers in order to circumvent the authority of the Courts invoke the provisions of the TADA. The kind of invocation of the powers of the TADA in cases, the facts of which do not warrant it, is nothing sheer misuse and abuse of the Act by the Police.' Generally it is true that the act will not be declared unconstitutional on the ground of possibility of abuse, but when its abuse has become widespread and inherent in its very provisions, the courts should declare the law unconstitutional and TADA was such a law. This was so obvious that the

National Human Rights Commission itself demanded its repeal and had decided to challenge it in the Supreme Court. The TADA is certainly a classic case of a lawless law and example of the state's lawlessness. One of the most disturbing recent event is that four convicted persons in Rajiv Gandhi murder case have been sentenced to death on the basis of a trail under TADA, though none of the accused was convicted of any offence under TADA. After the lapse of TADA, the old cases filed under the Act have continued, as if TADA continues to haunt, with the continuance of all stringent procedural provisions of the act. With the increasing terrorism, both national and international and the conversion of Pakistan – Indian regions into nuclear areas and the resulting militancy in Jammu & Kashmir, the insurgency in the North-East, the escalating activities of the Naxalites in Andhra Pradesh and other areas, there is a strong demand from many state governments and others who have become panicky for an effective anti-terrorist law like TADA. Many states are thinking of enacting their own laws like TADA. It appears that the preventive detention laws which provide for detention without trial and only on the basis of suspicion, and anti-terrorist laws which ensure detention of persons who are only accused of some offences, who are waiting for an indefinitely delayed trial and who are denied the normal provisions of bail have become the normal and permanent features of the Indian polity, leaving wide open for gross abuse of these powers and flagrant violation of basic human rights. Apart from these drastic and repressive laws which by themselves constitute gross violations of human rights, there are many other ordinary laws which are implemented and enforced by way of abuse of power denying or violating the basic rights. Though they seem to be common place and invisible, they are much more dangerous because they enable large number of state officials at the lower level to use or abuse them without real accountability. Let us examine briefly some of these laws.

Bail Provisions

Section 438 of the Code of Criminal Procedure, 1975 provides for anticipatory bail in cases of non-bailable offences to avoid arrest, if the accused apprehends his arrest. Section 439 provides for regular bail in cases of non-bailable offences after arrest by the police, with stringent requirements as to release on bail in cases of grave offences. While the former power is exercisable either by the Supreme Court or the High Court, the later power is exercisable by Magistrate upwards. The principles governing both kinds of bail are well-established and repeatedly enunciated by the Supreme Court. The court has emphasized the basic principle, namely 'bail, not jail' and personal liberty of a person as of paramount importance. As criminal trial takes a long time and the police power of arrest is extensively abused, this principle is of extreme importance. But, unfortunately, the lower courts pay only lip sympathy to the principle and uses the bail provision with a predetermination that the accused in many cases are not to be released. They say, 'They are accused of serious offences. Let them remain in jail, even before conviction'. Such pre-trial arrests are used as if they are punitive and for deterrence. It is largely the poor and disadvantaged who suffer most. In many cases, they are not released on bail. In many cases, they cannot afford lawyers and go to the court and where they can, they have no means or connection to offer sureties or securities. As a result, they remain in jails. The situation became so scandalous when pre-trial detenues remain in jail for periods longer than the period of jail they would get if convicted. The Supreme Court must have ordered the release of thousands of such poor victims. Yet the problem still persists. The government and the High Court have not evolved any mechanism to notice it or check it. The breakdown of the lower criminal justice system which finds it impossible to conclude criminal tribals for long has resulted in unduly long incarnation of the accused. If they are subsequently acquitted, what about their illegal deprivation of liberty for such a long period? In spite of the recent judgment of the Supreme Court for fixing the time table for keeping persons in jail during the pendency of trials, the evil system continues. Like detention laws, again the function of criminal law turns out to keep persons in jail for long without conclusion of trials and before conviction. On the other hand, the provisions of anticipatory bail has come to be effectively used by the rich, powerful and notorious to avoid arrest even in serious socio-economic offences. The poor normally cannot afford it.

Abuses and Excesses of Police Powers

The criminal law and the police are rightly perceived by the poor to be laws only for the poor and against them, and gross violations of their elemental rights are not even noticeable or worthy of human rights struggle. There are various kinds of such police abuses, excesses and illegalities.

False Criminal Cases

In innumerable cases, the police file false criminal cases, arrest of the persons and harass them, either for political purposes or for personal reasons or for extracting illegal money or at the instigation and instance of powerful forces. Such abuses are rampant in industrial disputes where the workers are harassed or arrested or tortured at the behest of the owners and management. The people's movement, filing of such false criminal cases against leaders or even common workers either to terrorize the agitators or to pre-empt their programme or to justify their own illegalities or excesses, poor tribals and others are also victims of such concocted or cooked-up cases, particularly of gambling or drinking, with the sole object of extracting money. I know hundreds of such cases in trade union struggles, landless labourers' demands for minimum wages, in struggle against Narmada dams and in forest areas.

Excess Use or Abuse of Police Powers

Extensive powers have been conferred upon the police officers under the Criminal Procedure Code, Bombay Police Act and other related minor criminal acts for prevention of offences and for dealing with law and order situations. These powers relate to restraining or prohibitory orders, power to arrest or detain, powers to prevent entry into certain places, prohibition or regulation of assembly or association activities, etc., one of the grossest abuses or excesses committed by the police during last 50 years is the excessive and unjustified use of police force to deal with rioting or unlawful assemblies or processions. Though the purpose of the use of force is admittedly preventive and for the minimization of mischief or disturbances, thousands of innocent men, women and children have been killed or maimed in police firing, Lathi charge, tear gas use, etc., even though the rioting mobs could have been controlled by intelligent and deft handling of the situation. Many reports, either administrative or judicial, have discussed the problem and have suggested graded measures for controlling riots, but they are rarely respected or even heeded to by the police. In the cases of vehement demanded by the people against police excesses, the government appoints judicial commission to inquire into, not to learn lessons from the past, but to pacify the people, to postpone taking of any action and ultimately to forget it after the commission submits report after a long period. Even High Court judgments are totally ignored and in many cases, the police department is not even aware of any such judgment. Though handcuffing and use of rope to bind the accused are strictly prohibited by various judgments of the Supreme Court under the threat of contempt of Court if the directions are ignored, there is no perceptible change in the attitudes and actions of the police. Killing of leaders or known criminals or terrorists by the police under the guise of 'deaths in encounter' – cases of clear murders by the police – are widespread throughout the country, particularly in Andhra Pradesh and other disturbed areas. Such cases of encounter deaths are increasing in a more advanced and well-administered state of Gujarat and no one believes the fake stories projected by the police to justify their actions. It is said that even a child would not believe it. Disappearance of people under suspicious circumstances is increasing and people are totally helpless, when they are told that the police, in spite of its efforts, has not been able to trace him. Approaching ordinary courts or many times even the High Courts in all such cases of police abuses is useless or ineffective for many reasons, such as want of reliable evidence, reluctance of witnesses to come forward to give evidence, false affidavits filed by the police confusing the whole issue, etc. Even the ambivalence of the courts is also responsible because they feel that to maintain law and order is not their function and therefore, their interference or enquiry would hamper effective measures by law and order machinery or might demoralize the police. Unwritten illegal practices by the police are legion, for example, calling a person to the police station for information or for questioning, forcing him to remain in police station for a day or two without any record or registration and then to record his arrest with subsequent date, if arrest is necessary. There is no record to prove that such a person was under police custody or in the police station for these days. Even when you are a complainant, you are harassed by police enquires so much that you feel you are the culprit, not the complainant. Complaints by poor people or resourceless people are not registered by the police who blatantly and shamelessly drive you away. Discriminatory treatment and measures against the minorities or Dalits or tribals are common. In communal riots, the police action is mainly targeted against the minority groups, killing and beating them, trespassing their houses, molesting or insulting or humiliating women, combing the entire area, seizing weapons from one side only then filing criminal cases against the members of that group to justify their excesses or illegalities. The police is also known for not going to their rescue, even when they are informed of such attacks or assaults by others.

Illegal Detention

The police has developed a new practice of illegal detention. After the 2002 riots, the police called Muslims for questioning, kept them in custody for days together, torture, them to find out more names, did not register the arrest. Even the family members went everyday to give food, but they were threatened that if they did anything, POTA will be invoked. In many cases when the court was approached, the police immediately registered the case and produce the detenues before the court and got remand. This abuse was resorted in large number of cases involving Muslims. The entire Muslim community was suffering from the fear of 'knocks at the door' at night.

Custodial Violence

Custodial violence is not only a widely accepted fact of life, but it is increasing everywhere in the country, in spite of many judgments of the higher judiciary condemning such atrocities by the police. The entire system of criminal law is so rotten that the police openly say that they cannot investigate and unearth the crimes and criminals except by third-degree methods. Whenever an offence is reported, the police will arrest, suspected or even innocent persons, take them into custody up to the maximum period of 24 hours and torture them by all means. The extremely cruel and inhuman methods adopted by the police to extract information from those arrested are beyond any sensitive person's imagination. When the arrested persons are produced before the magistrate, the magistrate, though duty-bound to enquire about their complaint, if any against police is not serious about it, does not bother to enquire and decide to release them on bail or remand them to custody. The arrested also do not dare to complain because they know that they have to go back to the police afterwards. The police torture in custody is so common that the order of remand by the magistrate is always considered equivalent to beating by the police in society. Cases of custodial death are increasing and ordinary cases of custodial injuries cannot be counted. Such police treatment is so dreading that either the persons arrested or his relatives and friends bribe the police to see that the police does not use third-degree methods or he will approach the High Court through an expensive lawyer only to create some fear in the minds of the police. In other words, Fundamental Right to physical security form the police violence (Article 21) has to be purchased. Magisterial enquiries are of no use; judicial remedies are normally futile. The phenomenon of custodial violence is known to everyone – higher police officials, the government, the judges themselves. On October 27, 1980, the Union Home Minister had the audacity to say as reported 'Though a shameful thing, third-degree methods has to be applied because there were hardened criminals who would otherwise not come out with the truth' (Amnesty International Report, 1980). Similarly, in spite of clear directions and guidelines about the time and manner of investigation of women, women are arrested at any time, even during late night, kept in custody and subjected to all kinds of sexual assaults including rape.

Encounter Deaths

Encounter deaths have increased during Modi's regime. Even when the police know that encounter deaths are outright murders, they follow the same method. The same story which even a child would not believe would be concocted. At least, they could have got training from the cinema story writers. Now there are encounter experts, who threaten the people even in the corridors of High Court that they would encounter them. These encounters are committed with specific directions even from the ministers. The encounter experts are made heroes and when they are arrested if at all, there are stage managed demonstrations. Encounter deaths do occur in other states of unwritten law. When such cases are ordered to be investigated, the ruling party publicly protests and considers it as encouraging terrorism and demoralizing the bold police officers and attack upon Gujarat.

Denial or Curbing of Ordinary Civil Liberties

Denial or curbing the ordinary civil liberties guaranteed by Article 19 of the Constitution in the name of security, public order, law and order, defamation, incitement to offence, decency or morality is an everyday affair, raising doubts whether these freedoms are to be justified or the restrictions. Freedom of press is sought to be controlled by various, indirect, if not direct, methods such as abusing the patronage power of giving or denying government advertisements which are an important source of income for the press. Right to know and freedom of information is seriously jeopardized by directing, unofficially, the press not to publish the news or views about many events or movements, by launching a massive misinformation campaign in support of government's policy or action or against people's movements hostile to its policy or ideology. False news are deliberately planted and newspaper space is purchased by the government to project its views as 'news'. Recently, the government directed all public or aided private schools to have compulsory singing of 'Vande Matram' which is not the national anthem. The government's monopoly over broadcasting (radio and television) and its abuse continue on a large-scale, though the Supreme Court has held that the air waves are not government's property, but public property and government is only a trustee, and broadcasting must be entrusted to independent public cooperation (AIR 1955 SC). Certain programmes organized under government auspices may be cancelled in cases of certain artists; selection of TV programmes on certain occasions may be purely biased and dishonest. In the name of decency or morality, some kind of pre-censorship is imposed upon artistic programmes, though the requirement of certificate from some government-appointed body and licence from the police Section 144 of the Criminal Procedure Code and provisions of the Bombay Police Act are frequently, almost regularly, used to prohibit public meetings, processions or protest programmes. It is the workers and the poor who are the targets and particularly any protesting groups of associations. In such temporary restrictions. The courts also would not like to intervene. Rights to free movement may be denied by declaring certain areas as 'prohibited areas' such as the Sardar Sarovar Project area under the Official Secrets Act. People's right to carry on trade, commerce and business is sought to be restricted by various dubious methods, e.g., closing down all public slaughter houses for 15 days during a religious festival of a particular community of the Hindu majority or removing thousands of small men and women earning their livelihood by selling goods on pavement of public places.

Denial of Access to Justice

Right to equal justice to all is a constitutional mandate. It is an inherent part of rule of law, equality before law and equal protection of the laws under Article 14. In general, the poor and resourceless have always suffered from the denial of effective and quick justice because of many institutional barriers and expensive lawyers. Even when they win, they may not be able to get the results of their victory. But of late, a very dangerous trend has developed. The authorities and certain sections of the civil society are systematically denying access to justice to certain communities. After the 2002 riots in Gujarat, the Muslims have been virtually excluded from effective justice. Their complaints are not registered or distorted, no real investigation is carried out by the police, witnesses are threatened or even eliminated, prosecutors are appointed by the government which has itself sponsored the riots and many of them are either from RSS or VHP or Bajrang Dal or BJP. They are not prosecutors but really defenders of the accused. The magistrates may or may not be openly biased, but coming from the society as it is, many of them have biases and prejudices against Muslims and have a fixed negative image. The chances of getting justice are dim. Even the High Court has also many times failed and the classic example of distorted and perverted approach is Justice Shethna's judgment in the Best Bakery case which was very severely criticized by the Supreme Court. The entire criminal justice system in a state-created communal atmosphere has totally collapsed, exposing the inherent weakness of the present criminal justice system which is controlled by the state government when the large-scale majoritarian riots take place and particularly when the government is a party. Today, in Gujarat,

Muslims are disenfranchized, right-less 'citizens' who live at the mercy of the government and Hindu fanatics. They cannot even think of approaching the courts as they are haunted by the police repression and either POTA or Criminal Act or encounters. Just consider to what extent the system has degenerated when SIT is investigating the Sohrabuddin encounter case under the orders of the Supreme Court and the net is spreading to the highest, the ruling party comes forward and stages demonstrations against CBI tortures and anti-Gujarat bias. The party's supporters put up banners and posters justifying the 'encounters' of dangerous criminals and condemning the attempt to demoralize the brave police officers. Modi's government is silent. The Muslims are outside the constitutional and legal system.

There are innumerable forms of state terrorism of state lawlessness practiced on a large-scale throughout the country. Even well-administered and advanced states of Gujarat and Maharashtra are no exceptions. It may be that the elites, the privileged and the conformists may not feel the pinch of it, but that is not the test of freedom enjoyed by the people. 'Who suffers' is the correct test. The history shows that the two classes of people are the victims. First, thousands of poor and disadvantaged people. Some may have committed normal crimes, many may be protesting against injustices or exploitation or may be fighting for work, minimum wages or a piece of land, or security of hut or drinking water. It is these people who are fighting for basic socio-economic rights, are denied or deprived of their basic civil and political rights. In the result, they lose both. Second group is those who lead the people's movement or who fight for the poor or who are protesting against injustices, both state and private or who are non-conformists. When we fight for all kinds of fundamental rights, we sometimes forget that people's elemental rights – Right to Physical Life, Safety and Minimum Personal Liberty – are widely denied – 'You have to protect people from the police', and therefore you have to purchase your Elemental Right – not to be illegally arrested, not to be beaten, not to be killed or raped – with many either directly given to the police or by expending money through court procedure. It is the state lawlessness which is a very serious threat to human rights – sometimes not drastic or draconian laws but ordinary day to day practices of the state machinery, slowly, not clearly visibly, most imperceptibly, incrementally corroding the rights and liberties of the people.

Private or Social Terrorism

The guarantee, security and enjoyment of human rights by all irrespective of race, caste, color, birth, sex, residence, etc., demands not only a democratization of the state requiring the state to protect and ensure such enjoyment of rights, and restraining the state from violating or denying such rights, but also a democratization of civil society which alone can guarantee day to day enjoyment of human rights by all members, and which can control and restrain the strong centres of private or social power from violating the rights of individuals, weak and poor. The Constitution of India guarantees fundamental rights to citizens and persons against the state to implement the socio-economic rights of Part IV, but that does not mean that these rights are to be ignored or bypassed in the social relationships among individuals and groups in the society. First, the state is bound to secure these rights by constitutionalizing the private laws – civil, criminal, taxation, corporate, business laws, etc., and suffusing them with the fundamental values. Second, the state must enact laws and policy to ensure these rights. Third, the state must enforce the compliance by all with these laws and must effectively intervene to present and punish gross violations of these laws.

Unfortunately, the denial, deprivation, destruction and suppression of the various civil-political and socio-economic rights of various classes of people by centres of private power and by socio-religious groups are so common, widespread and persistent that we may describe this as nothing but private or social terrorism, which strangulates and destroys all processes of democratization of the society. In this section, we examine various forms of such private or social terrorism very briefly, so as to focus on the issues and challenges involved therein.

Privatization of the State

The state in India is substantially privatized, either being defied, used or abused by private forces for their own purposes.

(a) The violation of laws, social or public and their large-scale evasion or avoidance has always been there in India, as in many other soft states, but the planned or organized evasion, avoidance, distortion, frustration, perversion and defiance of all public or social welfare laws by the powerful private interest landed, trade, business and industry, corporations, etc., is a new phenomenon, which is nothing but subversion of the legal system and rule of law. On the one hand, the Directive Principles of State Policy enjoin upon the state to implement them and the democratic political pressure from the electoral process have compelled the state to make large number of labour welfare, public interest poor-oriented beneficial laws and laws for distributive justice. On the other hand, the well-entrenched interests of the dominant sections of the ruling class, the weak, spineless, unwilling and manipulable administration, and large-scale corruption and powerful private interests, all have combined to evade, avoid, distort and frustrate all such laws, such as minimum wages laws, Factories Act, equal remuneration laws, other labour laws, land reforms laws, urban ceiling laws, etc. After conducting a detailed survey of the working and living conditions of thousands of workers in the textile processing units in Surat, the committee appointed by the Gujarat High Court found that 'it is not a case of isolated violations of individual laws, but a planned subversion of the entire legal system'. The public interest litigation for the enforcement of minimum wages for agricultural workers in Sabarkantha district in Gujarat had the only impact of raising the corruption rates of the minimum wages inspection. Laws themselves, being the result of compromises, are full of loopholes and can easily be evaded. They may not have sufficient teeth. The enforcement machinery may be absent or weak or unwilling. The subjects of legal regulations may bribe the officers, may effectively use the loopholes to avoid them, may openly defy the laws, knowing fully well that nothing was going to happen to them or even purchase the violations of laws by payment of fines, as punishment is cheaper than compliance. The beneficiaries may not be organized and assertive and the legal system will be very frustrative. Not only this, but if the beneficiaries attempt to enforce their demand, the owners or others may call in aid the local police to suppress them. Thus, state in India in the sphere of private laws acts in two ways. One, the state does not mind if its laws are openly flouted, thus becoming equal partners in the subversion of its own laws. On the other hand, if an attempt is made by workers or other beneficiaries to secure these rights, the state rushes to the rescue of the private interests to suppress such protests and agitations by the workers, justifying Marx's statements that 'state is nothing but an executive committee of the capitalists'. Thus, the state, willingly or unwillingly, plays a very dubious role in respect of its positive obligations under Part IV of the Constitution. While enacting welfare or socio-economic rights and laws, the state pretends to be implementing the Directive Principles of State Policy promising socio-economic rights. By allowing or permitting those bound by such laws to defy or violate them with impunity, the state escapes from its obligations, thereby raising its hands. 'I have done my duty'. If people do not obey laws, what can we do? It is as if the public power and private power have conspired to deny or deprive or negate the socio-economic rights of the people.

(b) *Criminalization of the state:* The increasing tendency towards criminalization of the state is a result of various factors. With the complexity of the society, urbanization and ghettoization, breaking up of traditional social bonds, importance of money, the normal criminal activities have multiplied. To these are added the modern crimes of smuggling, food adulteration, drug peddling, manning gambling and liquor houses, weapons trade and other economic offences involving large and organized network. With increasing affluence of the section, has arisen a 'serving section' to supply all needs, legal and illegal, of the former. The law and order machinery and the system of criminal law and justice are unable to deal with organized crimes, for various reasons, such as inefficiency, lack of resources, collusion, corruption, etc. The collapse of the system of administration of justice, both civil and criminal, has also rendered the ordinary people totally helpless in securing the enforcement of their ordinary civil rights because of undue delay, expensive litigation, corruption, etc. This has helped the rise of the private system of justice – engaging criminals and mafias to secure your right at a price. Both, the beneficiaries and the victims are at the mercy of these criminals. Thus debts can be recovered, bank guarantees can be enforced, houses can be vacated, matrimonial disputes can be settled through these 'private enforcers' of laws. As politics has become politics of resources and patronage, a new and vast field is opened up for looting. Criminals have now directly entered politics, instead of assisting politicians from outside. For completely opposite reasons, namely the failure of the political system to satisfy the demands of distributive justice, regional autonomy, community identity and the control of normal democratic processes by money and muscle power have generated number of political terrorists of all kinds. The political terrorism is met with state terrorism, with the result that common people in between the victims of violence by both. Their basic rights are violated. Of course, the political terrorism cannot be equated with other kind of criminalization, and calls for a different approach and treatment. But the sufferings of the sandwiched people are used to rationalize the state terrorism and to condemn the human rights groups who try to understand the nature of political terrorism.

One thing is certain, In all these cases discussed above, the basis of the rule of law is undermined. The state whose primary function is to make laws for the people, enforce them and administer justice failed in the discharge of its essential functions, enabling the strong private power centres to violate the basic rights of common people.

(c) *Communalization of the society:* The recognition and consolidation of two major communities in India, namely Hindus and Muslims for valid reasons and the resulting communalization of the politics finally led to the partition of India into India and Pakistan on religious basis, though both the countries even after partition continued to have substantial Hindu and Muslim minorities. Pakistan, solely claimed on the basis of Muslims as a distinct nation and 'Islam is in danger', declared itself an Islamic state based upon the fundamentals of Islam. Her subsequent history believed her leaders' expectations. Pakistan came to be divided in to West Pakistan and Bangladesh and the West Pakistan continued to suffer from internecine war between provinces and communities, and to oscillate between military dictatorship and limited or guided democracy. India met a different fate, though the Hindu–Muslim disunity and their mutual hatred continue to haunt India. India even after partition has today more than 100 million Muslims and a few millions of other religious minorities, mainly Christians and Sikhs. The trauma of partition, the communal holocaust accompanying it and forcible migration of lakhs of Hindus and Muslims both ways, burning problem of Jammu and Kashmir and continued communal tensions have left behind a dangerous legacy. The peculiar nature of India's independence movement, which united various castes and communities into a political struggle, but without any modern cultural revolution, the subsequent failures of the policy on various fronts, particularly in its task of a radical transformation of the socio-economic system, the failure of modernizing agencies such as science or technology, education and media to challenge people's superstitions, traditions and mind set and the dynamics of mass electoral polities have finally led to the political consolidation and militant strengthening of the Hindu majoritarianism committed to the Hindutva ideology and further marginalization and ghettoization of the Muslims leading to the frustration, bitterness and fundamentalism. While the latter emphasizes upon maintaining of separate Muslim identity, even if it is necessary to go back in history and to keep the community backward, the former emphasize upon the mythical Hindu identity, with the slogan of Hindi-Hindu-Hindustan and 'one people, one nation, one culture.' The emergence of the Sangh Parivar as a dominant political force, committed to the ideology and programme based upon 'India is Hindu: Hinduism is nationalism, unite all Hindus and make them masculine', looks upon Muslims as anti-national and their separate identity and fundamentalism as greatest obstacles in the path of India's unity, integrity and power. The coming into power of the BJP–VHP–RSS combine and the weakening of secular forces have created serious threats to human rights of various classes of people.

(i) Muslims are, by and large, socially, educationally and economically marginalized, leading to great inequality between the communities.

(ii) Though the Constitution guarantees freedom of religion including freedom to profess, practice and propagate (Article 25), and right to autonomy to denominations in regard to religious affairs and educational institutions, the Hindu majoritarianists by insisting upon absolute equality of freedom of religion are trying to deny real equality to minority religions and to subjugate them under Hindu majoritarianism. Any special concern for a religious minority or any sensitized approach to the minorities' fear and hopes is condemned as pseudo-secularism and as violation of equal treatment of all religions.

(iii) As secularism in India is understood more as equal respect for all religions than as separation of state from religion, the public life in India – all state institutions, state affairs, educational institutions, courts, public functions – are largely Hinduized suffused with Hindu rituals, practices and beliefs. The unfortunate part is that the members of the majority community are not even aware of the insidious and invidious violation of the basic rights of the members of the religious minorities. One will find subtle and sometimes crude denial of freedom of religion of large number of minorities.

(iv) In public and private affairs – in state matters and spheres of the civil society – the Muslims suffer all kinds of discrimination in respect of education, jobs, housing or other facilities.

(v) The government controlled by the Sangh Parivar is also known for their direct attack upon the minority's culture, rights and interests, e.g., attempt to impose total ban on all animal slaughter, compulsory closing of legally existing public slaughter houses for 20 days on account of the religious festival of a small sect of Hindus (Jains), attempt to change the name of Ahmedabad (Amdavad) to Karnavati, government direction of perform religious ceremonies on the day of the Hindu festival of Dusshera, compulsion to sing Vande Matram in all schools, communal use of repressive laws against Muslims, etc.

(vi) The Muslims continue to suffer gross violation of basic rights on account of widespread biases, prejudices, attitudes heavily weighted against the Muslims – e.g., no equal opportunity in the private sector, tendency towards polarization resulting in forced segregation, admission to schools, condemnation of Hindu – Muslim marriages, particularly when the boy is a Muslim and girl is a Hindu and resulting violence in Gujarat, discrimination in trade, business and industry, and professions and occupations.

(vii) Communal Riots: Politically inspired communal riots are a recurring phenomena. Though members of both communities suffer, it is mainly the minorities who suffer very heavily both in terms of losses to life and property. The communalized police, communalized administration and highly communal mass media, particularly local newspapers worsen the situation for the Muslims. Every major riot has meant a severe set-back to the Muslims in their economic advancement. Their business suffer heavy losses, they are targets of economic boycott, etc.

(viii) The communal atmosphere of hatred, intolerance and violence has led to two further dangerous consequences. One is the strong revivalist movement both among Hindus and Muslims bringing back the religious heads and priests, to the centre stage and harming social reform movements. The second is the fear of the Muslims from the attacks upon their religion, community and identity, which has made the task of reforming the Muslim law particularly towards gender equality extremely difficult. It is the women of both the communities who are the sufferers.

(ix) Article 28 of the Constitution guaranteeing autonomous rights to religious denominations in respect of their internal religious affairs has created a serious threat to individual autonomy and freedom, by considering the latter as a direct attack upon the religious autonomy of a group or sect or denomination.

(x) The Hindu majoritarianism in power is trying to conceal their rabid communalism and anti-minority hatred in the name of cultural nationalism in which all diversities will merge. 'Majoritarian nationalism means Hindu nationalism and Hindu nationalism means cultural nationalism' is their equation for all. Either Muslims or Christians have to be prepared for being condemned as of alien culture or anti-national.

(xi) The Hindu communalists have recently made the Christians the targets of their attack, both ideological and physical, particularly in the tribal areas in the name of forcible or fraudulent conversion of tribals to Christianity. This is a double attack. The tribals who are not Hindus are first treated as Hindus – an imposition of religion. The Christians are denied their freedom to convert. There have been large-scale assault, attack and damage to Christians, their religious places and their properties.

The communalization of the society in the name of religion and culture is increasingly trenching upon artistic freedom of writers, painters, dramatists, etc. On the one hand, the Muslim fundamentalists instigate common Muslims against any liberal or progressive writings or arts among Muslim artists, attacking them, demanding ban on the books. On the other hand, the Hindu orthodox groups and Hindu militants have let loose a kind of cultural or religious terrorism, e.g., burning books which they disapprove, attacking theatres and cinema halls showing films they condemn, preventing artists, etc., from shooting, filming, playing, issuing fatwas for imposing their own cultural norms, rewriting history of India, Hinduization of school textbooks, allowing Gujarat state employees to join and participate in the activities of a militant Hindu organization RSS on the pretext that the RSS is only the social service and cultural organization. Communalism also has a direct impact upon the right to equality of the minorities in the private economic sphere. As the majority community has the monopoly on trade, business, industry and profession, the doors to them are largely closed to Muslims, accept where requirement of specialization or expertise cannot avoid Muslims.

The second major challenge, mainly the private terrorism in its various forms, transcends the boundaries of state and enter into the spheres of the civil society, where we find interesting but dangerous interfaces between state machinery and private forces. Three types of situation are important:

1. Where state terrorism and private terrorism work hand in hand. The state assisting, colluding, conniving or conspiring with private repressive forces to oppress or terrorize the poor or the weak, or the state uses it powers to suppress the movements of the poor and weaker sections against the rich and strong.
2. When the oppressors in the society exploit, harass, torture, or intimidate the oppressed such as Dalits, tribals, minorities, women, etc. The state may remain a silent spectator for neutral or passive or may respond very late after the mischief is done.
3. Where the sate fails to take positive measures to free the weaker sections from the oppressive situation or classes, to take measures for empowering the poor or the oppressed, to create new institutions or laws enabling the poor or the weak to rise in protest and to fight.

Thus in the sphere of private terrorism, we have to face a dilemma. We want the state to act to control or contain the anti-poor activities of the strong classes or castes in the society and to protect the poor and the weak. At the same time, we also want the state to observe and respect human rights of all even while helping the poor and the weak, and the state not to indulge in state terrorism.

Economic and Development Terrorism

The development model which the ruling classes in India adopted to eliminate poverty and underdevelopment has certainly 'developed' India's resources, but at the cost of the large section of the people, mainly the poor and disadvantaged, and has succeeded in creating 'islands of prosperity' in the mid of the poverty of the masses. On the eve of independence, India had two models of development before it – the western model with emphasis upon rapid industrialization and the Gandhian model. While the former looked at the development of resources with emphasis upon economy, efficiency, rationality, productivity and growth, the latter looked upon the people to develop their resources with greater emphasis upon priority of basic needs of all, starting with the poorest and the lowest, equity, social justice, human values and humane society. The former will, it was hoped, benefit the common people by the process of 'trickle down' from the top to the bottom, the latter starts with empowerment of the people at the bottom and development from bottom, benefiting ultimately the whole society. The former labeled the common people as 'backward, inefficient, irrational, fatalists, incapable of independent development and requiring their modernization', while the latter consider the people as resourceful, innovative, willing to grow, with huge experience of life, and if given the opportunity, capable of moving up. The former is an imposed model which will fashion the people into its mould, the latter is a model to evolve from below by the people who will mould the model itself.

In the first phase, the Congress government adopted a model of planned economy under the impact of the soviet model and visualized a dominating role of the state in the national economy – a kind of mixed economy when the public sector will be at the commanding height. In the beginning, the then Prime Minister, Jawaharlal Nehru tried to involve people in the community development programme for overall development in each district, but it did not work, and ended with the skewed development and already developed and resourceful sections monopolizing the available resources. The public sector did developed industries and resources, in many key areas where private capital was not able or willing and created a strong top-and middle-level bureaucracy with extensive control over resources. Ultimately, the public sector became supportive of and subservient to the private sector. The private sector developed with the public or state money and facilities, and reached a stage where it could come into its own and could demand the dismantling of the state sector. Socialism turned out to be state capitalism or bureaucratic socialism, which was condemned as a Raj (government) of licences, permits and quotas.

From the point of view of human rights, a few developments are significant. In rural areas, the government's objective was to carry out comprehensive land reforms, so as to radically restructure the dominant agriculture sector. However, for various reasons, constitutional, legal and sociological, the programme stopped at what is called 'a middle-class revolution' with abolition of the zamindari system and providing ownership rights to the intermediate tenants. But, the redistribution of land-holdings, abolition of tenancy and share-cropping system and protection of landless labourers did not succeed. The caste-ridden, unjust, inegalitarian and oppressive, a moral society could not be broken. A new alliance of rich peasants, upper and intermediate castes, feudal mindset and capitalist ruthlessness, and control of all rural political, financial and cooperative societies, and religious militancy turned out to be a far more worse repressive socio-economic and politico-cultural system which prevented the fuller democratization of the rural society. The urban economy also developed almost in the same manner. The upper and middle classes and castes dominated the trade, business, industry and profession. Few workers were organized, the number could not be unionized. The spill over of the jobless and landless people from rural areas in the cities created an informal sector, working for the cities with cheap labour, living in slums under constant threat of demolition and having no place or voice in the urban affairs. The poor, marginalized and pauperized sections suffered from absence of permanent and secure work, homelessness, non-availability of drinking water, inadequate sanitation facilities, sub-standard schools and hospitals, degraded and polluted life, and the tyranny of the police and mafias. The public sector created almost anti-poor middle class and worked like the private sector, sometimes worse than that. Corruption, highhandedness and close affinity with the rich and powerful marked its working. The public sector, claiming to be a people's sector, was infact highly bureaucratic, top-down management, undemocratic and non-participatory. Its business principles and development goals were as bad and insensitive as those of the private sector. In its dealing with the low-class workers, it was ruthless, defying all constitutional obligations and in its dealings with the people, it was highly discriminatory and subservient to the private sector. The private sector, on the other hand, remained by and large highly exploitative, indifferent to constitutional values, purely commercial, moved by profit motive and insensitive and unresponsive to social needs or public interests. The workers are worst exploited and consumers are defrauded. It used the state and state machinery to further its commercial or business interests, without bothering about its social and constitutional responsibility. The increasing tendency towards privatization of state power, instrumentalities and resources by the private sector has created 'a private state' free from the constitutional limitations and obligations.

The overall impact of the old economic policy was:

(i) No socialism or socialistic pattern of society, no community ownership, management or control of nation's resources.

(ii) Growth of state capitalism, providing supportive, financial, infrastructure facilities for the private sector.

(iii) Control and license raj, the strong bureaucratic and administrative staff, large-scale corruption, private use of public power, big incentives to the big capital and detriment to initiative, creativity, resourcefulness, indigenous abilities of the common people, denial of right to development.

(iv) No rational allocation of resources, with the wastage, inefficiency, less productivity, diversion of resources.

(v) Preparing and paving way for private capitalism.

(vi) Strong-landed gentry in the villages, controlling rural economy.

(vii) State becoming medium of transferring resources from the common people to trade, business and industry.

(viii) Failure to eliminate poverty, inequality and destitution, absence of any real development of the people, new kind of poverty, known as destitution, unemployment, greater inequalities, less opportunities.

(ix) Neglect of basic needs – work, housing, drinking water, education, health, social security.

The Nehruvian model worked and contributed to significant developments in many key areas, but instead of becoming an instrument of radical, just and equitable restructuring and growth of India's economy, it fitted well in the normal model of economic growth, with greater role of the state. It failed to satisfy the elemental needs of the large majority of the people, created artificial islands of prosperity and affluence, increased inequalities, strengthened and pampered the private sector and created many bottlenecks. A new rich middle class was created, with increased demands for more durable consumer goods, the private sector came into its own, public sector and state planning came to be blamed for all the ills of the Indian economy, the rising middle class was fed up with the 'license, permit and quota raj'. South-East Asian economies were seen to have made fast and spectacular development and China was diluting its socialism and opening up its economy to private market forces. All these led to the gradual liberalization of Indian economy, dismantling of state overgrowth, delicensing and relaxation in the latter part of the 80s. Then, the foreign exchange crises suddenly showed its ugly face in the 90s, giving in to the pressures of the World Bank and IMF which insisted upon structural adjustment policy. Soon, the government embarked upon the new economic policy based upon liberalization, privatization, marketization and globalization. The old model of development proved to be too heavy, highly centralized, non-participatory, resource-oriented rather than people-oriented, more geared to efficiency and economy than to justice and equality. The common people suffered in two ways. On the one hand, whatever little resources they had to survive or subsist – land, forest, water – came to be acquired in the name of development, destroying their life-support system. On the other hand, they could not get the benefits expected or promised to flow from development. Thus, the development projects, such as large hydro-electric projects, afforestation plans, town planning and infrastructure projects such as roads, large industrial complexes, etc., finally paved the way for massive schemes for the wholesale transfer of resources from the poor to the rich. It created a huge army of uprooted people in search of livelihood who disappeared in urban ghettos or wandered as migrant workers. The state development policy came to be perceived by the victims of development as nothing but developmental terrorism, which terrorizes, pauperizes and dehumanizes the vast humanity, paradoxically in the name of their very development. The New Economic Policy will further worsen the situation leaving the vulnerable sections to the ruthless forces of 'free markets' controlled by the national and multinational corporations. The aggressive 'development' policy pursued by the private enterprise and guided by profits and market will render the people totally defenseless against their pauperization and marginalization, immune from any constitutional limitations. The policy of globalization will bring in the giant multinationals, acting for gratifying their greed for new markets and new profits, working under less stringent and more favourable conditions and free to exploit local resources and local people. The people's right to development – their access, control and use of their resources – is being undermined, in which their own state is a party. The creation of local affluent class living in and craving for the western lifestyle, and with high consumption pattern will further deprive the common people of resources necessary for their daily needs. The gap between the North and the South in the world will be replicated inside every developing country. The development of the western countries and of a small minority in the developing countries will be the very cause of underdevelopment of the vast sections of the people of the latter countries. The human rights movement in these countries will have to face new and far more serious challenges.

(i) The privatization of state activities and institutions, at present subject to constitutional limitations, will lead to a new process of deprivation and denial of fundamental rights under the Constitution, known as 'deconstitutionalization process'. The private institutions and enterprises will be free from Part III constitutional obligations, particularly Article 14, Article 19 and Article 21 and constitutional remedies under Article 32 and Article 226.

(ii) In the craze for rapid industrialization and modernization by the private enterprises, with the active encouragement and support of the state, the common people who are already condemned as 'inefficient, irrational, wasteful, outdated and backwards' will be forced to give up whatever resources they have, on the specious ground of more efficient, rational and productive use of these resources in 'the national interest'. The erstwhile process of deprivation by state-sponsored development will continue with greater

intensity under the new process of privatization and marketization snatching away people's resources though state's sovereign, proprietary and contractual power.

(iii) The new policy will also lead to greater degradation of natural resources such as land, water, forest, air under the false dichotomy of development v/s environment. In a country like India, this will directly affect the poor and the weak who have to use land, water, forests, for their very subsistence. A new class of 'environment refugees' will be created.

(iv) The NEP will also directly affect the worker's rights. The private enterprises have started demanding the reversing or reviewing of the judgment of the Supreme Court in Bangalore Water Supply case, regarding the interpretation of the term 'industry' for the purpose of the Industrial Disputes Act. They want a large area of economic and other related activities to be free from the demands of the industrial law. We also find increasing tendencies towards:

(a) Depriving of permanency rights of workers.
(b) Casualization of workers.
(c) Employment of labour by a process of contracting and sub-contracting.
(d) Loss of jobs through retrenchment and closures.
(e) Demand for so-called reform of labour laws so as to deny or curtail the rights of workers.
(f) Child labour.
(g) Exploitation of women workers.
(h) Deskilling of workers.
(i) Insistence upon giving up security of job, etc.

(v) With the weakening of the state to intervene effectively in core social areas such as education, health, public services, will be substantially reduced. Just as the withdrawal of the state from economic activities means entrusting these activities to market forces and their immunity from Part III of the constitution, the minimalization of the state will also mean its failure, unwillingness and refusal to provide, protect and ensure the socio-economic rights to work, to education, to health, to social security.

The 'development' model followed so far – both the old so-called socialist and the new 'free enterprise' – has resulted into a distorted development – jobless, ruthless, rootless, voiceless and futureless. Neither the old model led to empowerment of the people in the control and management of nation's economy, nor the present model will lead to and ensure democratization of the nation's economy. The vast majority of the poor and the weak remained mere objects of state policy, rather than its subjects and will now be outside the operation of market forces and remain the victims of market. Their socio-economic rights will be jeopardized, and their struggle for these rights against private sectors will be crushed by the supportive state. In this new atmosphere, the tendency to regard human rights as nuisance and obstacles in the path of rapid economic development is already visible in many quarters and will become stronger as the time passes. Now profits, efficiency, economy and productivity will be the main goals of the economic activities, and not human rights, socio-economic justice and concern for the weak and the disadvantaged. With the increasing withdrawal of the state from socio-economic spheres, shrinkage of human rights will be the direct consequences, and people will be more and more subject to the arbitrary, uncontrolled and life-and-death power of the national and multinational corporations. The citizens of India will be converted into mere factors of production and consumers of goods. The deconstitutionalization, commercialization and dehumanization will pose new threats to the basic human rights of the people.

As we have seen, the economic policy and development policy, and the development model has created the following major problems:

(i) Deconstitutionalization of economic organizations through denationalization or disinvestment.

(ii) Deindustrialization resulting in the exclusion of more and more economic or productive activities from the domain of industrial law by redefining the meaning of 'industry' for the purpose of industrial law.

(iii) Direct impact upon workers:

- (a) Retrenchment or closure or voluntary retirement scheme resulting in the loss of jobs.
- (b) Reduction in the number of permanent jobs and increasing casualization of workers, deprivation of benefits of regular employment.
- (c) Contractualization of workers – increasing cases of contracting and sub-contracting directly undermining the trade unionism, depriving workers of the status of belonging to the organization for which they are working, denial of rights and benefits of the regular employees of the organization.
- (d) Persistence and increase of the child labour in all kinds of industries, whether hazardous or not.
- (e) Adverse impact upon woman workers – less employment of women, reduction in their jobs, unequal remuneration, exploitation, etc.

(iv) Increasing demand by the industries and employers/investors for changes in the existing labour laws, with the object of giving more freedom to the employers.

(v) Increasing privatization in the core centre of social services, such as education, health services, provision of basic necessities, etc., housing facilities, transport, drinking water, entertainment, etc.

(vi) Environmental degradation, industrialization by the state at any cost, increasing air, water and soil pollution.

(vii) Consumerism making the consumers the apparent kings, but virtually victims and slaves of modern production.

(viii) Deprivation of people of their life-support system or economic base, i.e., land, water, forests, community, etc., as a result of large development project. The impact is particularly severest on the tribals.

(ix) Transfer of resources of people through market forces. This is the case of high level of industrialization which demands more and more agricultural lands of private owners, even by paying in a few cases, high prices.

(x) Depletion of community resources such as grazing land, government waste lands, forests, open community plots in the cities sold out for commercial purposes, conversion of riverbeds, small ponds, seashore into commercial enterprises.

(xi) Direct cut in the necessary subsides so far provided to the poor and other needy people, other than those subsidies which benefit the rich and resourceful.

(xii) Increasing proportion of cash crops meant for domestic sale or for export to earn foreign exchange, at the cost of coarse grains and particularly pulses which provide protein to the common people.

(xiii) Increasing import of luxury consumer goods from western countries.

(xiv) Increasing predominant role of giant corporations and multinationals controlling larger and larger economic fields in the country.

(xv) Increasing foreign investment which compromises with the economic sovereignty, and which renders the local economy completely dependent upon whim, caprices and profit calculation of foreign investors.

(xvi) Tendency towards national government and state governments becoming the obedient/implementing agencies of international economic order dominated by the developed countries and multinationals.

(xvii) The direct impact of (xvi) above upon the political authority, legitimacy and power of the national and state governments to provide effective democratic governance, directly undermining the possible people's control at least of the political power. The new economic order tends to weaken and subjugate the democratic system and democratic control of the people.

(xviii) The decreasing concern for social justice and role of social sector providing core social services. The diminishing percentage of budget allotment for this, such as education, health, etc.

(xix) Common people losing whatever control they have over local resources, shifting the decision-making centres away from villages to distant places.

(xx) Role of foreign and even imitating local media in changing the mind set and values and imposing the western lifestyle and modes of thinking, destroying the cultural diversity and imposing homogenization.

(xxi) The ruthless performance of market forces in the name of illusory economy, efficiency, rationality, leading to condemning indigenous system as inefficient, backward, wasteful and the poor people as obstacles to development and making them dispensable as sacrificial goats.

(xxii) Accentuating the existing great divide between two Indias, in fact, creation of these Indias – Super-rich, middle-rich and destitutes, iron curtain between the two classes – those who exploit and enjoy the fruits of the labour of others and those who toil and die – two having nothing in common, such as residencies, education, health, luxuries, entertainment, transport, drinking water, etc.

As these have appeared on the horizon of Gujarat and are part of the Gujarat's socio-economic life. How have the people resisted this economic, neo-colonial aggression? What are the challenges and our strategies? What can we learn?

(a) So far the economic struggle for securing workers' rights has been mainly fought by the trade unions and workers' groups. This was purely in the area of and within the confines of industrial relations. Notwithstanding the professions and preaching of the communists and Marxists, the trade unionism has remained economism and has not, except in very few cases, extended beyond it. Except recently, these workers' struggles were not projected as part of Human Rights movement. They remained highly political parties' – affiliated, fragmented, scattered and without any clear goal. Sometimes they start an agitation and resort to different forms of direct action, such as demonstration, picketing, go-slow, strike, etc., but such agitations cannot continue for long, remain confined to specific industrial units and either fizzle out or result in some kind of compromise or settlement. By and large, because of the peculiar legal framework of industrial relations legislation, namely, central positions of compulsory third-party adjudication, the trade unions have remained litigants or claimants in labour/industrial courts or tribunals. The workers' battle has largely remained legal or court-battle with all evils of the litigation process, namely, delay, arrears, technicalities, procedures, judge-oriented, series of appeals non-participatory so far as workers directly are concerned. Though the objective of labour law is to move towards collective bargaining, the goal is very far off. The effective struggles of the workers inside the courts or outside are confined to large organized industries where reasonably strong trade unions exist. Even then, the percentage of unionization is low, large number of industrial units are small, the workers are unorganized and it is still difficult and risky for workers to try to form unions. The trade unions of employees of public corporations are elite unions, so far enjoying security of job and good salaries. Now, under the New Economic Policy, they face serious problems such as threat of closure, retrenchment, voluntary retirement scheme. They have also lost the fighting capacity and have so far kept themselves away from poor workers' struggles. The increasing privatization poses greater challenges. In the absence of reasonable support from the state, the workers will find it extremely difficult to maintain their present standard of living. When under a so-called socialist-minded government, even statutorily fixed minimum wages were not implemented in most parts of Gujarat, what would happen now under NEP? The Communist or Marxist ideology has at least for the present, lost its ground. The union has become commercialized. The idealism has evaporated. In these circumstances, the Human Rights ideology with its emphasis upon the unity and universality of both civil/political and socio/economic rights can play a very important role. It provides to the workers' struggles the authority and the legitimacy from the Constitution's Human Rights and International Human Rights law. It can free the professional trade unionism from the bondage of pure economism. Human rights organizations have a special responsibility in working with the workers organizations and in building up a wider human rights movement with socio-economic content.

(b) In totally unorganized sectors, outside trade union have been inactive and ineffective. Sometimes public interest litigations by Human Rights organizations, raising issues of gross violations of socio-economic rights as part of Right to Life and Equality has provided some succor or help to the workers. For example, the PIL filed in 1986 by Lok Adhikar Sangh in the Gujarat High Court for and on behalf of 100,000 or more sugarcane harvesting workers, mostly migrant tribals, in South Gujarat has exposed the destitution of the workers, their almost bonded conditions in a concentration camp and has helped them in getting more. But in the absence of their own organization, we have been now stuck up. How can we get the maximum from this litigation? No pre-litigation organization nor post-litigation organization was working with the result that orders of payment of higher wages could not be completely enforced or implemented. Human rights approach helped us and put the workers, claims on somewhat a higher level. This is true of my other struggles in the unorganized sectors in Gujarat. The PIL can act like a catalytic agent, but cannot be a substitute for the workers' own organization or struggles.

(c) The struggles against the various manifestations of the New Economic Policy, such as a denationalization or privatization, closures or and loss of jobs have to be politicized and on a border level. As it involves vital policy questions flowing from economic ideology, litigation strategy cannot work, except in gross cases of totally irrational or malafide use of power. We challenged the decision of the government to disinvest in the case of Ahmedabad Electricity Company in favour of private enterprise, but the petitioners withdrew their petition. We have at present challenged the decision of the government of India to disinvest the Indian Pharmaceuticals Limited, Government of India undertaking on several grounds, particularly workers' interests, irrational decision-making process, creation of monopoly, etc., but we do not know how the high court will handle it. The policy of privatization or disinvestment itself is beyond judicial challenge. So litigation strategy cannot succeed. Workers' mobilization may be inadequate, unless larger movement is built up. In Gujarat, no prospects for such are in sight. The critical evaluation of any such policies in terms of people's rights can ensure public debate and greater legitimacy to the general movement.

(d) It is proving to be very difficult to halt the process of casualization of workers and contractualization. Workers are losing permanent jobs and are now replaced by ad hoc or contingent or project-wise or casual workers. Litigation in the labour Courts and Industrial Tribunals is meaningless and outside struggle is very difficult. Similarly, the contract-labour system has been condemned by the Supreme Court of India in a series of cases and there is litigation to regular and to abolish contract- labour system is expanding. Industrial processes are undergoing the processes of contracting and self-contracting both by national and multinational companies. The outside movement is not strong, while the legal process under the Contract labour Act of 1972 for abolition of the contract- labour system in an industrial establishment or in a given process is a lengthy and uncertain process, and is in the hands of the government which has to decide the question. Litigation strategy has not worked successfully.

Similarly, the evil of child labour is so widespread that it has become a substantial and inseparable part of the production process. The legislation prohibits it in hazardous industries and regulates it in other industries. The Constitution prohibits it. The Supreme Court of India has recently delivered a long judgment condemning the system and giving directions for its elimination. In Gujarat, child labour is everywhere just as you step out of your house and yet the government, after spending more than five million rupees on the survey, could find out only three to four thousand child workers. This has been severely criticized by the Gujarat High Court. Some organizations are working very bravely in this field, combining children education with campaign for removal of child labour. The state is neither serious nor keen to act decisively. It does not follow the constitutional directive of free and compulsory education for children up to 14 years and does not enforce the child labour act also. In its craze for cheap labour and for more exports, it indirectly encourages it. Children's basic rights are openly and shamelessly violated. No general movement exists, nor can litigation strategy work.

(e) In the craze for heavy industrialization, worth more than 100,000 crore rupees, large numbers of landholders, small and marginal, are losing their agricultural lands. Some lands are acquired by companies through sale, by using all types of pressures upon landholders – political, economic, Panchayat, castes, etc. The remaining lands are acquired by the government under the Land Acquisition Act, 1894 for the companies. The two conditions are:

(1) It must be for a public purpose.
(2) Market price must be paid towards compensation.

Outside agitation has not worked and the legal challenge to the compulsory acquisition rarely succeeds, as the Court does not generally challenge the government's claim of public purpose. But in one case of acquisition of fertile lands in Saurashtra for Ambuja Cement Company, resistance by a few landholders and litigation in the High Court could defer the acquisition for four to five years, resulting into more bargaining power for the farmers.

The government finds it more convenient and easier to hand over its own lands or public lands to the companies, without bothering about the adverse impact of such transfer of community resources upon the common people of the areas. There are agitations by local people organized by some Gandhian organizations and other NGOs. The struggle is very difficult because the people have to fight against both the government and the private industries. The latter uses all strategies to break the agitation, using private force, bribes and divide and rule policy, while the former is there to render all police assistance to the company. Though the Supreme Court of India has evolved the doctrine of community ownership distinct from state ownership and private ownership, the doctrine has not percolated to the lower echelons of the government.

Litigation strategy has not helped the people much because of the so-called policy issues involved and the domination of development ideology among the decision-making. The struggle has not been properly and effectively articulated in terms of socio-economic rights of the people.

(f) Though the sole justification for the Sardar Sarovar Dam Project on the Narmada River in Gujarat was to provide water to the drought-prone areas of Kutch, Saurashtra and North Gujarat, though constituting of 25 per cent of Gujarat's area, and subject to the worst drought, was given a meagre share of only two per cent of the Narmada waters. This would practically mean destruction of Kutch. In the beginning, the people of Kutch did not start agitation because they did not want to support, even indirectly the anti-Narmada movement. However, slowly they realized that gross injustice is being done to Kutch and if they do not get enough waters of Narmada that would mean total disaster. They started the agitation, but did not get sufficient response from the government. Finally, they have filed a public interest petition in the High Court of Gujarat on the ground that right to water is a part of Right to Equitable Distribution of Natural Resources and Right to Life, right to Equitable Distribution of Natural Resources and Right to Development. They are expecting some concrete result from the court case. On the one hand, the litigation strategy is the best possible method, given the local character of the struggle and the impossibility or difficulty of getting any result from domestic majoritarian politics. You at least get the best hearing of your case. But, on the other hand, the issue is so delicate, explosive and full of political implications that the country may not like to intervene positively, and may avoid it on the ground that it is a political problem to be sorted out outside or it involves policy issues, not fit for the court to decide. Many developmental issues are of this type. Because the issue affects a particular region or group of people, it cannot be the basis for state-wide movement. Politically and electorally you cannot be effective because you are in a minority. Court will not help you because it is a political or policy issue. What is to be done? This suggests the necessity of a larger movement against the developmental model or policy.

(g) Similarly, the tribals who have been dispossessed of their lands by outside forces, have been fighting for right to survival through cultivation of some forest lands. As forests are legally vested in the state, they demand regularization of the unauthorized cultivation of forest land. On the one hand, they are part and parcel of the forests, their relation is symbiotic. On the other hand, the forest resources are independently considered as economic resources to be used or exploited for the whole society or as part of ecology and must be preserved. The tribals cannot move outside and will not be permitted to live inside. The court did protect them from dispossession for many years by interim orders, but they cannot directly order regularization. Here, political mobilization of tribals did work and could secure a government measure permitting regularization if they have been cultivating forest lands before 1980, as post-1980 cultivation cannot be regularized by the state government without previous approval of the central government. However, the government resolution insisted upon the proof o the form of some forest offence case or fine receipt or some financial assistance under some projects. In an overwhelming majority of cases, the tribals would not succeed in the absence of either proof. The whole resolution is set at naught. We have approached the court on the ground that regularization is a part of their socio-economic empowerment which the supreme court of India has declared a fundamental right. The case is still pending. Thus, there is proprietary right of the state environmental demands of conservation and community, and survival claims of the tribals. How is it to be resolved? When the tribals of Dang District militantly fought for their right to survival and development, their movement was branded as a Naxalite movement and the people were ruthlessly suppressed by the combined forces of police and the forest officials. The court did intervene, secured the release of their leaders who were preventively detained under the National Security Act and allowed us to visit the area and submit the report. Thereafter, nothing substantial happened.

(h) In North Gujarat, the Gujarat Mineral Development Corporation, a Government of Gujarat undertaking decided to establish a copper industrial unit and to dig two

French Wells on the Sabarmati river to draw nine lakhs litre of water everyday. The project will drain off the available water, so as to deprive the people, mostly Adivasis, of 40 villages on the banks of the river of the water they were getting and using. They started a militant agitation. We also filed a PIL in the Gujarat High Court. The case remained pending for long. In the meanwhile, the people prevented the Corporation's officials from entering the area and working on the project. The agitation and pendency of the case for long finally succeeded in frustrating the design of the Corporation which had to face financial and other difficulties. At present, the project seems to have been dropped.

On the other hand, people's court cases against the establishment of the salt unit by Adani Chemicals in Mundra in Kutch and Cement factory by Sanghi Cement Industries in a dereserved Narayan Sarovar Sanctuary in Kutch could not succeed. In the former, the company used its clout with the then Chief Minister to break and split the agitation, while in the latter case, the Supreme Court of India permitted the industry with some conditions upon the industry. The court seems to be carried away by the areas' backwardness and need to develop, without bothering to enquire as to what type of development they would achieve.

(i) The cases of environment pollution provide some interesting lessons. In the city of Ahmedabad, big and middle-sized, mainly chemicals, engineering and pharmaceuticals, grew up in the most haphazard manner in the industrial estates and were causing excessive pollution, particularly water and air pollution. A PIL was filed on the basis of a news report. The Gujarat High Court took a very serious view of the industries' failure and the government/pollution boards' apathy, indifference and complicity. After investigation and the long discussion, the court ordered a closure of all the units and directed them to pay wages to the workers. The remedy proved to be too much. The government wanted to get out, the industries were caught up in a trap and the workers wanted work and wages. The court personnel changed. Attempts were made by individual units to escape from the closure order. Hundreds of applications came up before the High Court which could not deal with them. Slowly it was realized that the burden upon the court was too heavy. Other cases from other areas also came up before the court. The court was trapped and wanted to get out from the mess. In course of time, cases of pollution were disposed of on one or the other ground like satisfactory report of the Pollution Control Board. The lawyers earned crores of rupees by way of fees, the officials enriched them through bribes, the industries had to spend money, the workers in many cases lost their wages. All pollution cases were disposed off and pollution has continued. For some time it appeared that the people's movement would start and become powerful. But it did not happen, though people in many areas became conscious of the environment pollution. But the movement failed. The polycentric problems of environment and industrial pollution proved to be too difficult and complex for the court to solve. The government was crazy for industrialization and was worried about possible unemployment. The industries were shameless, adamant and defiant. The courts were confused for ideological conflicts arising from the false dilemma of development versus environment. The last remedy, i.e., the court also failed. Many of us felt that it would have been better, had the court not intervened at all. The environment movement was either too weak or premature. The movement suffered a terrible blow.

On the other hand, the NGOs' movement based upon proper study for preventing further pollution of the Narmada river by the new, coming up, industrial estate in Jhagadia in Bharuch district was well-planned. It raised people's awareness, fought on the land, continued to lobby before the authorities and prevailed upon them to construct a long pipeline to carry the treated water pollutant deep into the sea. A PIL was also filed. Ultimately, the court directed the authorities to evolve standards of the Amla creek and the river are to receive the affluent and not to allow new industries in the estate till this is done. At least, some positive result was secured.

(j) Under the NEP, the social sector is suffering, directly affecting the poor people. Take education. Take primary education upto 14 years that has been constitutionally enjoyed since the beginning and yet even the state of

Gujarat, otherwise claiming to be an advance state, has 30 to 40 per cent people illiterate and thousands of children out of the school system. The public school system is now meant for the poor people, while the other classes opt for private schools because the latter do not want their children to sit and study with the children of the poor. The former are totally neglected both in terms of quality of teachers and of resources. The children are simply promoted, but no real education takes place, Illiteracy or semi-illiteracy is transmitted. The dropout rate is more than 60 per cent. But there is no social movement for ensuring even this elementary right of the children. The craze is for privatization. Recently, the Ahmedabad Municipal Corporation decided to close down a municipal primary school with a reasonably good building and shift about 400 children to the nearby school building overcrowded and without even elementary facilities. The corporation wanted to hand over the building to a new trust for starting an international school, charging fees of more than ₹ 10,000 a year. The children of the poor people who were attending the old school were driven out. A strong agitation was started by the local children and leading citizens of the city. The issues were properly highlighted. A PIL was also filed in the Gujarat High Court raising the basic human rights issues. In the High Court, we lost not because we had no case, but simply because the court could not understand the socio-economic dimensions of the problem. The court simply considered that the alternative school building is offered and it was required to be renovated because of the court case. The underlying reason was the stumbling block – fascination for elite education and false notion of modern education. As it was the agitation by the poor and the marginalized class, it did not create enthusiasm and interest in the middle and upper class. The movement fizzled out once again showing the difficulties of isolated movement in the absence of wider movement with broader and clear perspective.

After NEP, the state government is withdrawing from the field of education in the name of education and better facilities by private institutions. The Supreme Court opened the gate for commercialization and privatization of educational institutions, particularly higher professional educational institutions in T.M. Pai's case in 2002. Now mushroom growth of 'education selling shops' has cropped up in Gujarat, charging exorbitant fees both for admission and for tuition. The sub-standard medical colleges are exploiting the aspiring middle class by charging heavy fees for producing doctors to serve 'poor' people. Ordinary persons – even middle class families – find the doors closed, in all institutions. Education is necessary for the elites, only a luxury for the plebeians. Gujarat has now become a commercial centre for education. Whenever my driver or helper or clerk asks me about his children's admission, I am confused. I do not know what to say. Should I advice him to send his children for education and spoil them in fashion shops or advise him to remain where they are? Really I have no answer. Even the constitution has no answer. What a great deception is going on in the name of education and placement! The American island like IIM in Ahmedabad or Scandinavian island like NID are constantly making at lacs of helpless students coming out of schools. What about primary education – a fundamental right? Why was it introduced as a fundamental right at a time when good education is left only to market forces of profit? Why was the need for joke? I see all around in the slums, in chawlis, on the pavements, in forests, in villages illiterate – mark not ignorant or unskilled – people everywhere. Markets do not need their knowledge, common sense, skill, they want their degrees or credits or certificates and the slaves to serve. What would happen to these so-called unemployable poor people? What about their next generations doomed to their fate? The society will have to find out some way to deal with them. Similarly, in respect of public health services, the supreme court of India has recognized the Right to Health as Right to Life and given various directions to the government in respect of facilities and amenities in state-owned or aided hospitals. But in view of the private character of medical services, subject to market forces and the deteriorating quality of public health services, the ordinary poor people are really deprived of qualitative health services. There are some NGOs in the field of people's health, but not very effective. The direct impact of the NEP is to leave even people's health to the market forces. The people outside the market forces have to go without good health services. As the poor cannot influence the market forces and their numerical strength does not jointly affect the political forces, there is no sufficient pressure for improvement of health services. Sometimes in cases of epidemics due to the neglect of the public authorities, we approached the High Court. Some improvement takes place, but the court cannot continue to supervise the administration and the cases are disposed off, with some directions. The administration relapses into its original inaction and nothing changes.

Unlike other capitalist countries, our state is also silently withdrawing from the health sector. Public hospitals are under equipped, under-staffed, under-financed. Health is now privatized. Private thriving specialists – have gone affordable family doctors – five-star hotel like hospitals, most updated health instruments, extraordinarily attractive, more American than American facilities for tourists are cropping up. We do not know about what to do with ordinary common diseases. 'If you have the status of having a dignified disease, come, we will be at your service.' People die of diseases, old and new, traditional and the products of the affluent society, but they cannot avail of modern treatment. Only those who can afford can come. Unlike Bible's sermon, only the rich will enter. The common Gujarati have become unfortunate, unwanted resident Gujarati, while those who left Gujarat not for Gujarat but for their development are the few fortunate non-resident Gujaratis who are welcome for the criminal deserters! But in the modern amoral globalized world, there can be no criminals, they are the entrepreneurs, financiers, speculators, builders, go-getters, middle men, darbars intellectually, subservient MBAs, lawyers at their call service – they are the saviour of the world. The poor have no diseases, they themselves are diseased. Their diseases are not to be treated, they themselves have to be dealt with. This is the 21st century Gujarat where people are educated only if they have money. Modi does not even allow Desi dam to the people who want to forget their miseries and pain. The heavenly nectar is only for the tourists, foreigners, for the five-star hotels, who try to submerge their shallow and hollow life.

(k) The urban slums and the related problem of homelessness are another issue of basic human right to shelter. In Ahmedabad, the biggest city in Gujarat and virtually the capital, about 40 per cent of the people are living in slums. The people are very poor and have come to the city in search of livelihood. They occupy the space, public or private, available. Their occupation is illegal, their huts or hotels are unauthorized and they survive from one demolition to other. We have filed a number of PIL in the High Court of Gujarat, on the basis of their Right to Life including livelihood and shelter. The Supreme Court of India, for the first time, in Olga Tellis case (AIR 1986 SC 180) said that the slum-dwellers including pavement dwellers are spill over from the decadent and stagnant rural areas and generally are forced to come to the cities in search of livelihood, that they constitute what is now known as informal sector of economy contributing to the development and prosperity of the city, but have no space of their own. Their Right to Life includes Right to Livelihood and as they have to stay near the place of work, their Right to Shelter is also a part of Right to Life, and they cannot be deprived of their right to life without a fair, just and reasonable procedure, they must be given reasonable notice and heard. Thus, their right not to be evicted without notice was recognized. In subsequent cases, the court went further and recognized Right to Shelter as a Fundamental Right, after referring to the International Covenants and imposed constitutional obligations upon all public authorities to provide facilities and amenities for realizing this right. At the same time, the court said that they have no right to encroach upon roads or pavements or places reserved for public purposes. What does this mean? The forcible evictions continue in all places on various grounds. The recognition of their right did not make any difference, except right to notice. Even this was not given on the shameless ground that if notice was to be given, they could go the court and obtain injunction or stay order. In spite of thousands slum dwellers, there is no powerful organized movement for fighting against forcible eviction and for positive right to shelter. Approach to courts may or may not help, depending upon the judge's concerned. This is one area where direct approach to the SC of India in

Olga Tellis case proved to be a double-edged sword. Though the court talked of human rights, it, in the same breadth, permitted eviction, and subsequently diluted the requirement of notice and hearing. Many activists believe that previous to this judgment in 1986, many HC and other lower courts used to protect slum dwellers from eviction and restraining orders continued for long. After the supreme court judgment, large number of stay orders were vacated. Today, it is a big gamble. No notices are given, commando-like demolition campaign is launched, bulldozers are used and police are there to crush any resistance. Only recently in one of our cases, the High Court recognized that the forcible demolition without notice is illegal and violation of human rights. The problem of homeless is intimately connected with the question of land ownership and management, and urban planning in which this informal sector is still not recognized as having a voice and share.

Similarly, the street vendors and hawkers in thousands of number have to meet the same fate, though street-hawking was recognized by the SC as a fundamental right to carry in trade, business occupation. Though they supply goods and services to the people, they have no place or voice in the city. In some cases, the local authorities were asked to reserve hawking zones for these people, but the selection of the site is always highly controversial and almost deterrent or forbidding.

(l) Similar is the sad story of drinking water. Even after 50 years of planning, the society has not been able to secure pure drinking water to all people. Take the case of Gujarat. It is the second state in India after Maharashtra, which has the largest number of major and medium irrigation projects damming all rivers, including the controversial, but still incomplete Sardar Sarovar dam on the Narmada river. The poor people in the cities are struggling for adequate and regular supply of pure drinking water, while the common people in the large rural portions of the state are fighting for drinking water. The state has considered the problem from the point of view of supply side, but has failed to understand that the question is essentially one of rational and purposive management and control of the total water resources of the state. The development has meant for the common people unequal distribution and access to essentials of life, including water. They spent more time in procuring fodder, fuel, drinking water and the direct sufferers are the women. The people in the drought-prone areas are angry and agitated, leading to a number of police – people clashes. On the other hand, drinking water has become a marketable commodity to be monopolized by those who can pay. Some NGOs have done creditable work in local areas, but the overall impact is not substantial. Drinking water is of first priority and is recognized as part of fundamental or human rights. How to secure it? That is a big challenge. No readymade answer is forthcoming.

(m) Modi's Model and Style: Shri Narendra Modi – a Sangh Pracharak – is a modern 'Emperor', with his lifestyle, attractive dresses, pens, specks, make-up. He is a man of extravaganza, trying to make his name in history of 'Vikas Purush' by Roman circuses, summits, festivals and inaugurations. His super corporate office of five – CM supreme, Ambani Adani, Nirma, ESR and Tata – rule Gujarat. How fortunate is Gujarat to have such rulers. He wants to build Taj Mahals, of course not in the memory of near and dear one, but in permanent remembrance of one 'man' who lived in Gandhinagar. Kankaria lake – 500-years-old Moughal lake – has been beautifully fortified, denied access without fee to the common people of Ahmedabad for whom Kankaria was for many years only public place of amusement. These people typically lower middle class people after daylong work used to come to Kankaria and sit there relaxing and getting pure air. Now they have to pay. What globalization and glamorization means is pathetically exhibited by what a sweeper lady told the activists agitating against the project. She said, 'before this, I would come for sweeping with my five children who would play, now I, being the service provider – can come, but my children cannot come'. They cannot have even the glimpse of what Ahmedabad was for centuries, proud of a beautiful national heritage. Modi even does not know – or does not bother to know that people's Right to Life with dignity includes his rich heritage, his history, as the Supreme Court held in 1989 because for Modi, Gujarat's history starts from 2002. Moreover, his development is interesting. It has become a 'state of ghosts'. First, around 1967–69, the Hitendra Desai Congress (O) Government raised the ghost of Naxalites and arrested a few persons, but ultimately they were acquitted. Again in 1980 when the tribals of Valia Taluka of Bharuch District were fighting for minimum wages in agriculture against Patel, Rajputs, Muslim landlords, a bogey of 'Chambal-na daku' was raised, strong SRP was sent, poor tribals were beaten, tortured, arrested, ladies were harassed. For three full months a reign of terror was let loose. It was not a law and order problem, only a socio-economic problem, as was clearly pointed out by the then DIG Joseph's report.

Again during Narmada Bachao Andolan, the time of Pher Kua rally in Dec 1990, the chiman bhai's Government unleashed the campaign of lies, warning people of 'armed attack by MP tribals'. Around 1992, when the tribals of Dang were fighting against harassment by forest officials, the government accused their leaders of Naxalite activities and suppressed them. From 1985 till today, the Muslim terrorism is the excuse for types of oppressive measures.

Now, slowly and imperceptibly, peoples resistance against the so-called development projects is growing in villages and cities also. On the other hand, Modi boasts that in Gujarat, land acquisition for projects is smooth and without any resistance from farmers. But this is not true. In Kutch, fishermen and others are protesting against Adani's projects in Mundra. In Mahua, BJP's own MLA is leading a powerful farmers, movement against the Nirma Cement project which will destroy the water body and agricultural lands. In Alang and Surat, the large number of outside labourers are suffering from the worst type of oppression and exploitation, and some movement has started.

To suppress this, the government has once again branded their leaders as Naxalites and arrested them. The government's target is their leaders who must be suppressed and also human rights activists who are considered by the government as supporters of Naxalite. The sole aim of Modi government is to nip in the bud any people's movement. Remove the leaders, silence the human rights activists and the way to vibrant Gujarat is smooth, thus in Gujarat we do not have globalization in human face, but globalization with Modi's fist.

What Shall We Do?

We have seen that India is still a democracy with fairly free elections at regular intervals. Though many distortions and perversions have entered, the parliamentary institutions do work. The people do reject also not inclusive. One of the reasons projected for t fying Kankaria is to exclude the anti-social elements the area. What they actually mean, poor Muslims whc in the neighbourhood and would come to Kankar night.

Similarly, Modi's another grand project is Sabarmati project on the Sabarmati river in Ahmedabad. It always remained people's river – holy for the religi place of Gujri – held for the last several centuries on e Sunday. Now, these plebeians do not deserve this p Rivers are meant for kings and queens, rich and powerful and for those who can enjoy. People's river been converted into Moughal garden and Times Squar New York. 'Come, forget your miseries, enjoy, spend, l live for a movement in a fictitious world of your drea and then go back to your dirty homes and filthy plac Everything is marketable. If you want to sell your bo your sex, your beauty, come, you will get some open This is Modi's Shanghar of Vibrant Gujarat. Shri M does not even spare Gandhi. He and his party h hijacked Gandhi without his truth, non-violen simplicity, service, compassion. He has now b Mahatma Mandir at the cost of more than 100 crores an will be the centre of 2012 vibrant commercial corporate consumerist Gujarat. Poor dhoti-clad Gandh not commercialized. Of course, Modi has a different id He is constantly haunted by Gandhiji in Gandhinagar on Sabarmati. He wants to forget him. This is the best w After the German philosophy, make a thing so pure t you cannot even touch it, because if you touch it, becomes impure. Let us raise Gandhi so high that he cea to be a human being whom we can follow. Modi has ma him a God to be worshipped from distance but not to followed. How many times will poor Gandhi be killed? C only response can be a simple writing 'Gandhi was nev born here – nay – there was never any person as Gandl Modi follows his arch-rival – fanatic Saudi Arabia King build mosques and big palaces and mesmerize t populace.

(n) Recently, Modi government once again has raised a bog of Naxalites and has arrested a few persons for alleg Naxalite activities. Here, the history of Gujarat the governments of the day and install another government. The 'mainstream' of India do enjoy basic human rights and fundamental freedoms, but it is the emergence and consolidation of the peculiar 'mainstream' Hindu – Hindu-upper/middle class – higher castes and powerful landed, industrial, professional groups – which have disturbed, deviated and distorted the nation, making process and socio-economic – cultural path. It is from this that the various serious threats to basic human rights in India have arisen. If these threats are not properly understood and boldly met, India will have to face various scenarios, none of which will be palatable to us. The centripetal forces representing the national mainstream may grow stronger and ruthless and crush all dissenting or protesting forces and movements and in the process may develop a more authoritarian – repressive state, undermining, if not openly subverting, the very democratic basis of our constitution it may be that the centrifugal forces may become very powerful and may threaten the very unity and integrity of the country and may even balkanize the nation. What will be the fate of democracy and human rights in each of the region is extremely doubtful, as regional, parochial, religious, cultural forces might, in the process of fighting, become more fanatical, fundamentalist and intolerant. The clash between the two may also lead to a greater disorder, conflicts, insecurity, uncertainty and chaos – a state of internal wars – which would not be congenial for human rights. Many contradictory processes are also at work. The ideology of the new economic policy would demand dismantling of the state apparatus to substantial extent compelling it to withdraw from the economic sphere. On the other hand, the role of the state as a mediator of socio-economic forces, and as an apparatus to maintain and preserve the free economy would demand a reasonably a strong state. Can an Indian state which has always been a soft state though claming a commanding position be sufficiently strong so as to control and contain the ruthless market forces and to come to the rescue of the common people who will suffer in many respects from the free economy? Would it be able to deal with the problems of poverty, inequality, illiteracy, ill-health, unemployment, exploitation and sufferings of the people, which are going to be with us for a long time? It is possible that we might go back to the early period of ruthless expand in capitalism with no concern for laws, equity, justice, human welfare, environment, as it is clearly seen in Surat city and surrounding areas of South Gujarat. Similarly, in a conflict between the 'mainstream' and the various minority groups, the individual members of these groups would continue to suffer, just as the open conflict between the insurgent or secessionist or the terrorism groups and the Indian state, the ordinary citizens would be the victims of atrocities at the hands of the both. In addition, the social forces trying to enter the political arena and to assert their power are getting recognized and realignment of such forces is not stabilized, so far UP and Bihar are the classic examples.

In the mid of all these contradictory, conflicting and confused forces, the most important question is – how to preserve and protect democracy, rule of law and basic human rights? This is particularly a challenge, not to the elites – the rich and the powerful, but to the masses the poor and the weak. Without democracy and human rights, they have no future. Along with loss of freedom, they will also lose their battle for food, social justice and dignified life. It is a challenge to all those who have faith in and commitment to the basic values of democracy, rule of law and human rights, wherever they are. A fearless battle will have to be waged by all these people in all spheres of the society.

To protect human rights is not the function of the courts only. All other institutions are bound by the constitution and must respect, follow, and enforce the basic constitutional values. The general impression among many is that the other institutions such as the parliament or state legislatures or government or election commission may do their work without bothering much about the constitutional provisions because courts are their to check them and keep them within the limits. But this is very dangerous. The parliament or the state legislatures, while making laws or passing resolutions or exercising powers, must themselves see that they do not cross the constitutional limitations and they also respect, follow and promote the basic values. The focus will then move from the courts exclusively to the constitution and the other institutions. It is true that the other institutions have failed, but event then it is the functions of the human rights movement outside and inside institutions to ensure their proper functioning and their compliance with constitutional provisions both in letter and in spirit. The human rights activists and organizations must establish a special cell to examine closely all the legislative measures and governmental actions particularly from the point of observance of human rights so that a campaign can be started right from the beginning against any attempt to encroach upon the fundamental Rights of the people without waiting for any judicial intervention. Vigilance committees can also be set up both outside and inside for overseeing the work of other institutions.

The various threats to the human rights people can finally be countered only by a board, effective, powerful, broad-based people's movements for human rights. The movement will have to be built up on the basis of clear understanding of the modern threats to the human rights and clear perspective about the concept of democracy, the struggle for food and freedom, pluralistic society, development and progress. Right to Life and Right to Development can provide a very stable and effective foundation for such a movement because it is these two basic rights which are sought to be denied, deprived of and destroyed by the different ideologies and programmes. It will then not remain a remote fight for the abstract Rights or freedoms, but a fight for control over the resources around them and control over their own life. The tribals struggling for lands and forests, and against major 'development' projects, the slum-dwellers in the cities fighting to save their slum-houses and for having some land in the city, the Dalits striving for equality of opportunities in all spheres – in resources, in jobs, in education, in power, the workers, both organized and unorganized, struggling for control over work – relations in places of work, the scientists and intellectuals striving for autonomy both for individuals and for institutions, women fighting for control over their body, over their home, over the resources of family and over their voice in the society, the minorities struggling for participation in the socio-economic and political-cultural life of the nation – all can be comprehended and embraced within its broad national movement. It is these struggles which will strengthen the basic rights through day to day assertion, which will achieve greater and greater democratic participation in the decision-making process, which will bring about emotional integration and provide a basis for a rich diversified and cooperative life. It is these struggles which will determine the process of evolution and development, delineate the very concept of development and the broad features of the various institutions of the society. In other words, it will be a genuine movement for democracy and development from below, not from above, and human rights will be realized in the very process of struggle, not at the end of the struggle. Then, no power can dare to destroy the human rights because it will have to destroy the people themselves, and no people will tolerate their own extinction.

Index

Backward Classes and Social Justice